Welcome to Abaco! Great Abaco Island and its cays form one of the largest bodies of semi-protected waters in the Bahamas/Caribbean area. It is a perfect cruising ground for small boats—power or sail—from 14 to over 50 feet. Harbours or sheltered areas are always close by, and because the water is shallow, it is almost always possible to anchor. Miles of secluded beaches can be found, and settlements or towns, just a few miles apart, offer excellent restaurants, marinas, and other services. The people of Abaco are friendly and helpful; they are gracious and generous hosts who will generally do their best to make your visit a pleasant one. Enjoy the beautiful waters, beaches, and people of Abaco, but please remember to respect the privacy of the Abaconians as well as the fragile physical environment in order to save both for future generations.

This is the fourteenth annual edition of this cruising guide; it covers from Walker's Cay in the north to Hole-in-the-Wall in the south. We have continued the process of updating and improving our charts. Most of our work in 2002 was related to calibration of the charts using WAAS DGPS. Our goal is to achieve accuracy within about 25 feet.

Chelsea, our hydrographic research boat, is equipped with an on-board computer system linked to Garmin GPS units (a 125 which is connected to a Northstar differential beacon receiver and a new 76 WAAS unit). We use Maptech's digital version of our charts on their Bahamas CD with Maptech's Offshore Navigator software and Nobeltec's digital version with their Visual Navigation Suite. We also use our own proprietary hydrographic data system.

We strive to produce very accurate charts and believe our charts are the best available for Abaco. We have also worked hard to make this cruising guide as easy to use as possible. We hope its system of organization helps you to pilot your way through Abaco with ease, and that you will be able to locate needed information quickly. Our system of waypoints and courselines is matched by none, making cruising the Abacos easier than ever before. The charts and waypoints are all based on WGS84 map datum, and users should be certain their receivers are set accordingly. The termination of selective availability by the United States government and the advent of WAAS (Wide Area Augmentation System) has made GPS more accurate and more reliable, but all navigators should remember to trust their eyes and not over-rely on any single source of information or aide to navigation.

We are gradually adding services for cruisers to our website, www.wspress.com, with the goal of providing full service for those who cruise to Abaco. The site now includes information on all of our publications as well as a secure server for ordering online. During Spring, 2000, we initiated a message board restricted to information about cruising in Abaco. The response has been good, and we will continue this service. Hotlinks to several weather sites which provide valuable information for those contemplating crossing the Gulf Stream or making other extended passages have been established (see page 8 for further information). Also, we expect to have all the waypoints in this guide available for a nominal charge in most popular formats for downloading to GPS units by 1 January 2003. Our site is at **www.wspress.com**.

We have had a lot of help in collecting information for this edition of *The Cruising Guide to Abaco, Bahamas*. We thank all those who have made suggestions for improvements as well as those who have pointed out our mistakes. Finally, we again express special appreciation to the Lands and Surveys Department of the Government of The Bahamas, and the National Oceanic and Atmospheric Administration of the United States Government.

Important Note Regarding Charts

Despite the fact that we have been diligent and used the latest available technology to make our charts accurate, our survey was not uniform—some areas received more attention than others. Therefore, the accuracy of the charts varies somewhat. This, combined with shifting sand bars, and possible errors made in transcribing the data, make it necessary for us to remind all users that the prudent navigator will never rely solely on only one source of information. The author and publisher disclaim all liability for any errors or omissions. The author and publisher disclaim all warranties, expressed or implied, as to the quality, merchantability or fitness of this book and its charts for any particular purpose. There is no substitute for a sharp lookout on any boat to avoid possible hazards and dangers. All depths are given in feet at Mean Low Water (MLW). Because Mean Low Water is the average low tide, all should be aware that the water will be more shallow on spring low tides (full moon and new moon) than the charts indicate. Tide times and heights calculated by the United States National Ocean Survey can be found in the tide tables on pages 153-156. All course headings are given in magnetic, but true north is up on all charts.

Moraine Cay. 11 July 2002. Photo by Steve Dodge.

Contents

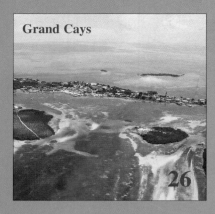

Grand Cays 26

Allens-Pensacola Cay 38

Green Turtle Cay 46

Snorkeling/SCUBA Charts 121

Abaco Chart Directory	inside front cover
Preface / Note Re: Charts	1
Abaco Portfolio	4-7
Weather and Weather Reports / Navigation in Abaco	8-9
Anchoring, Anchor Lights, and Power Cables/Observations Re: Passages Between the Sea of Abaco and the Atlantic Ocean	10
VHF Radio Tips and Courtesy/Fishing and Diving Regulations	11
Approaches to Abaco	12-13
Grand Bahama Section	17-20
Indian Cay Channel and West End	18
Dover Sound, Grand Lucayan Waterway and Bell Channel	20
Walker's Cay to Carters Cays	22
Walker's Cay	24
Grand Cays	26
Double Breasted Cays	28
Strangers Cay Channel and Anchorage	29
Carters Cays	31
Carters Cays to Moraine Cay	32
Fish Cays (North)	34
Hawksbill Cays and Fox Town	35
Moraine Cay	36
Moraine Cay to Spanish Cay	37
Allans-Pensacola Cay	38
Spanish Cay	40
Spanish Cay to Green Turtle Cay	42
Cooperstown and Powell Cay	43
Manjack and Crab Cays	44
Green Turtle Cay	46
Green Turtle Cay to Marsh Harbour	52
Marsh Harbour to Little Harbour	53
Whale Cay Channel	56
Treasure Cay	58
Great Guana Cay	62
Man-O-War Cay and its Approaches, Man-O-War Cay Harbour	68-69
Hub of Abaco	74
Marsh Harbour	76
Boat Harbour	94
Elbow Cay and its Approaches/Hope Town, Hope Town Harbour	98
White Sound	106
Lubber's Bank, Lubber's Channel, and Tilloo Cut	110
Tavern Cay to Lynyard Cay, including North Bar Channel	114
Snake Cay, Tilloo Pond and Bank, North Bar Channel	115
Approaches to Little Harbour, and Little Harbour	116-117
Lynyard Cay to Hole-in-the-Wall	119
Little Harbour to Cherokee Sound	120
Snorkeling/SCUBA Guide Abaco	121-127
Guide to Whales and Dolphins of Abaco	129
Fishing in Abaco	133
Abaco: The Year in Review - 2002	137
Abaco Road Map / Exploring by Land	138
Brief History of Abaco	141
Medical Tips for Tropical Waters	144
Business Directories	148-153
Tide Tables - 2003 (and December 2002)	153-156
Indexes - Abaco Place Names , Advertisers	157
Ferry Route Map and Schedules	158-159

Additional copies of this cruising guide may be ordered from White Sound Press, 379 Wild Orange Drive, New Smyrna Beach, Florida 32168 USA. Please enclose $19.95 plus 5.00 for postage and handling ($11.00 foreign). Phone: 386 423-7880 Fax: 386 423-7557. All our publications may be ordered on the web at www.wspress.com. E-Mail: orders@wspress.com.

Front Cover: Sand Cay anchorage at Double Breasted Cays, June 2002. Photo by Steve Dodge.

Abaco Portfolio

Atlantic Ocean beach northeast Great Guana Cay.

photo by Steve Dodge

Well Lane, Hope Town, with Marcus Bethel.

photo by Steve Dodge

Keeping cool in Coopers Town, July, 2002.

photo by Steve Dodge

photos by Steve Dodge

Schefflera Tree, commonly called Umbrella Tree in The
Bahamas, at M and M Restaurant in Coopers Town, Abaco.

e coral and Sea Fans.

photo © Mike Adair, Sports Photography, 2001

photo by Steve Dodge

e Only One D, a freight boat which makes periodic trips between the
t of Palm Beach and Green Turtle Cay, Abaco.

out the photographers

e Dupont is a retired IBM instructor whose favorite pursuit is under-
er photography. She particularly enjoys photographing invertebrates.
e and her husband spend most of their time cruising and diving the
amas on their 36' Grand Banks trawler *Carpe Diem*. When in Green
tle Cay, they love to dive with Brendal Stevens of Brendal's Dive Cen-

e and Ann Adair of Merritt Island, Florida sail their Morgan Out Island
Snorky, to Abaco every summer. They are accomplished sailboarders
divers and they operate a business called Sports Photography.

ve Dodge is the author of this cruising guide.

e Sound Press actively seeks submissions of photographs, transpar-
s or high resolution digital files for publication in the Abaco Portfolio.
pay on publication. Items submitted will be returned if accompanied by
amped, self-addressed envelope. Submit to White Sound Press, 379
Orange Drive, New Smyrna Beach, FL 32168 USA.

Captain Skeet LaChance, Anne Adair and tame Grouper. photo © Mike Adair, Sports Photography, 2001

Flamingo Tongue on Gorgoniean. photo © Mike Adair, Sports Photography, 2001

photo by Anne DuPont

Orange Cup Coral (*Tubastraea coccinea*) found off Green Turtle Cay in about 25 feet of water.
Anne Dupont found it while diving with Brendal Stevens, who showed it to her. Each polyp is less
than ½ inch long.

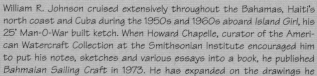

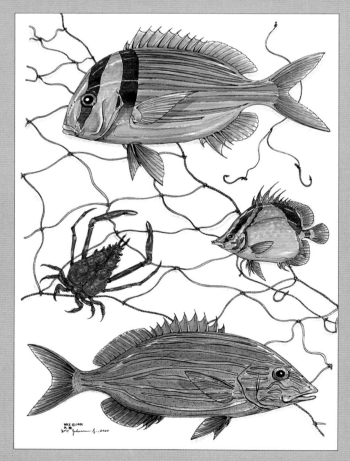

William R. Johnson cruised extensively throughout the Bahamas, Haiti's north coast and Cuba during the 1950s and 1960s aboard *Island Girl*, his 25' Man-0-War built ketch. When Howard Chapelle, curator of the American Watercraft Collection at the Smithsonian Institute encouraged him to put his notes, sketches and various essays into a book, he published *Bahmaian Sailing Craft* in 1973. He has expanded on the drawings he made for the book and is well known for his illustrated hand coloured maps of the Bahamas. He lives on Lubbers Quarters in Abaco. His artwork is most available at Sea Spray Marina and Resort at White Sound on Elbow Cay, Abaco, where he picks up his messages and mail. *Bahamian Sailing Craft* was been re-published by White Sound Press in 2000 (see page 128).

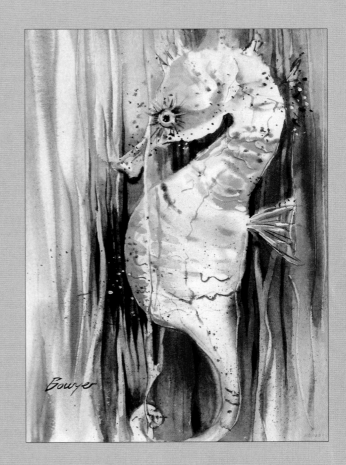

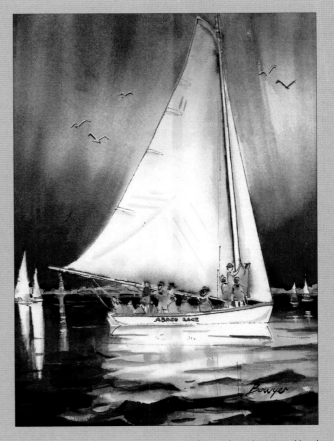

Brigitte Boyer Carey grew up in Hamburg, Germany, where she graduated from the "Kunstschule am Alsterdam," Europe's foremost graphics arts school. She moved to South Carolina where she lived, painted and continued her study of watercolour, and later moved to Abaco, Bahamas. She has won over 70 awards, and has perfected her wet-on-wet watercolours of Bahamian scenes. She lives on Tilloo Cay. Original work as well as high quality prints and cards can be purchased in several local establishments in Abaco as well as directly from the artists's studio (by appointment). New, are t-shirts which are printed locally. Brigitte Boyer Carey can be contacted via email (hunkaloo@aol.com) or by telephone (242-366-3150).

WEATHER & WEATHER REPORTS

Abaco is within the trade wind belt, so most of its weather is the result of the prevailing easterly winds. In the winter they tend to be easterly or northeasterly, and in the summer easterly or southeasterly. Winter winds are usually a few knots stronger than the summer winds, which average 5-10 knots.

This easterly pattern is disturbed in the winter by occasional outbreaks of cool continental air from the United States. These cold fronts are preceded by wind from the southwest. When the front passes, the wind shifts to the west or northwest and often blows hard (20-25 knots is common). Most cool fronts are dry, and the temperature dips to about 58 degrees. The wind eventually clocks to the northeast after the frontal passage; this process sometimes takes a couple of hours—more often a couple of days.

In the summer the usual 5-10 knot southeast breeze is sometimes disturbed by afternoon thunderstorms which build over the land mass of Great Abaco Island during the day. These storms sometimes meander against the prevailing southeast breeze and move from Abaco out to the cays. They have plenty of lightning and thunder, and lots of water, but the high winds are usually short-lived. The summer weather pattern may also be disturbed by a low pressure trough in the prevailing easterlies. These bring higher winds, overcast skies, and showers. If the winds in a trough (sometimes also called a wave) begin circular movement and reach 33 knots, the trough becomes a tropical storm. If the winds reach 64 knots, it becomes a hurricane. Hurricane season throughout the tropics extends from 1 June to 1 December.

There are a number of excellent weather forecasts available in the Abacos. The NOAA Wx forecasts can sometimes be heard on VHF Wx channels 1, 2, or 3 if a good antenna is available. These are continuous and give Florida coastal reports and prognoses. The cruiser's net on channel 68 at 0815 features a weather report and prediction based on data collected from several sources which is very comprehensive. Those planning Gulf Stream crossings can request special reports at about 0730 on channel 73; call *Blue Dolphin.* Silbert Mills of Radio Abaco (FM 93.5) gives a complete report at 0700 and again between 1800 and 1830 during the evening news.The satellite system he utilizes for data enables him to provide a very detailed report which often includes different predictions for northern and southern Abaco. In addition, Bahamian AM radio weather reports can be heard on ZNS Nassau (1540 kHz) at 0735 and 0755 (summary) and ZNS Freeport (810 kHz). Also, some cruisers regularly share their information and knowledge regarding the weather; listen on VHF 16 for announcements regarding the working channel which will be used.

Weather information is available almost 24 hours a day for those with short wave radios. The Waterway Radio and Cruising Club gives a report each day at 0745 on 7.268 MHz. This includes the Bahamas, SW North Atlantic, the Florida coast, and the Gulf of Mexico. All are welcome to listen, and hams with general class licenses or higher may join in if they have their Bahamas reciprocal licenses. For more frequent reports listen to NMN, WLO, or WOM; schedules are as follows:

NMN - Coast Guard, Portsmouth, Virginia

Time (UTC)*	4426	6501	8764	13089	17314
0400, 0530, 1000	x	x	x		
1130, 1600		x	x	x	
1730			x	x	x
2200, 2330		x	x	x	

WLO - Mobile, Alabama

Eastern Time	4369	8806	13152	17362	22804
0100, 0700, 1300, and 1900	x	x	x	x	x

*UTC is Coordinated Universal Time. Eastern Standard Time is 5 hours behind UTC and Eastern Daylight Time is 4 hours behind UTC.

WEATHER SITES ON THE WEB AND CROSSING THE GULF STREAM
by Harry Weldon

When planning a crossing of the Gulf Stream in a small boat, the wind speed and direction are probably the most important factors in deciding when to cross. I look for 10-15 or less and no northerly component in the wind. The Web can be an excellent source of information; the following are a few of the sites I use for gathering information useful in planning a crossing:

http://www.hpc.ncep.noaa.gov/ (Hydrometeorological Prediction Center) This is a good site for a broad overview of weather patterns showing fronts and spacing of isobars. What you really want to find is a nice fat high-pressure dome sitting right on top of the Northern Bahamas and Florida with isobars spaced wide apart. This is fairly common in the summer months. With all of the prediction models, I look for consistency in the prediction as it moves from the three or four day to the 24-hour prediction. This doesn't happen all that often but when it does you can sometimes find a window in an otherwise lousy bit of weather.

http://adds.aviationweather.noaa.gov/projects/adds/winds/ I look at this site several times a day even when I'm not crossing. Here you will find current surface wind conditions and predictions to about 48 hours out. The 0 to 12-hour forecast are updated every three hours, the rest are updated twice a day at 0 and 1200 UTC.

http://maps.fsl.noaa.gov/disp.cgi?/w3/rapb/rt_plots_40km20km/./+sa2_surf_wind+se Check this site out. It takes a little while to load, but provides an excellent view of surface winds.

http://www.ndbc.noaa.gov/station_page.phtml?$station=lkwf1 Reports conditions at Lake Worth, Florida.

http://www.ndbc.noaa.gov/station_page.phtml?station=SPGF1 Reports conditions at Settlement Point, Grand Bahamas

http://www.ndbc.noaa.gov/data/Forecasts/FZUS52.KMFL.html The NOAA text forecast. While not always the most reliable, this is a good check of the others.

http://www.srh.noaa.gov/radar/loop/DS.p20-r/si.kamx.shtml Radar which shows precipitation out to the East side of Great Abaco Island.

Safe crossing.

* Hotlinks to these sites are available on the White Sound Press website (www.wspress.com).

NAVIGATION IN ABACO

The Global Positioning System (GPS) is clearly the most significant improvement in navigation made during the twentieth century. It is truly amazing that a handheld electronic device costing $100.-$200. can tell you where you are, where you wish to go, and how long it will take you to get there. No one should go to the Bahamas without a GPS receiver. The advent of differential GPS a few years ago made it more accurate for those who purchased differential beacon receivers. The end of selective availability (the intentional de-grading of the signal by the United States Department of Defense) in May 2000 has made GPS more accurate for all users. The new Wide Area Augmentation System (WAAS) receivers, which became available in 2001 at very reasonable prices, regularly provide accuracy within 10-20'.

This cruising guide maximizes the advantages of GPS and the benefits it can provide. We offer a system of waypoints rather than random waypoints outside each harbour. We have refined the system during the past 7-8 years; we hope you find it practical and enjoyable. Except where noted, the continuous courselines connecting the waypoints are at least 6' deep at Mean Low Water (MLW) and free of obstructions (please note that discontinuous courselines are for small boats and generally carry only about 3' MLW).

While GPS is a wonderful navigational aide, the prudent mariner will not over-rely on it or any other single aide to navigation. Eyeball navigation and the use of the magnetic compass can confirm the information provided by GPS and vice versa. Cruisers visiting the Bahamas will quickly learn to know the approximate depth of the water on the basis of water color—which ranges from dark blue for deep ocean water, to medium blues, teals and greens in 10-25' over sand, to pale blues and greens in shallow water over sand (4'-10') and white in 1'-3'. Coral heads are brown, as are rocky

bars—both should be avoided. It is important to learn how to determine water depth based on colour because there is no better navigational device than your eyes, but some persons have greater color sensitivity than others and read the depth better than others. No one can do it going into the sun, in the middle of a rain squall, or at dusk, or at night. All mariners should try to maximize the advantages of all available aides to navigation.

To best utilize our GPS system set your GPS datum to WGS 1984, utilize routes rather than "go to," pay close attention to cross track error by utililizing the appropriate screen (or "page") on your receiver, and use your eyes and your compass to confirm or question what your GPS tells you. If you are unsure of where you are, stop and figure it out before proceeding.

The depth of the water can be determined by colour. This generally requires good sunlight. Photo taken at Tahiti Beach, Elbow Cay, summer 2001.

LEGAL ENTRY - CUSTOMS AND IMMIGRATION

Boats entering the Bahamas are required to clear customs and immigration as soon as it is practical by going to a Port of Entry. If the first landfall is not a Port of Entry, going ashore is not allowed, and the vessel should proceed to a Port of Entry. The yellow quarantine flag (a yellow rectangle) should be flown to indicate that the boat has not yet cleared. Convenient Ports of Entry for boats travelling from the United States to Abaco include: West End and Port Lucaya on Grand Bahama, Bimini, Nassau, and Walker's Cay, Spanish Cay, Green Turtle Cay, Treasure Cay and Marsh Harbour in Abaco. Clearance must be first priority—before re-fueling, lunch or shopping. Only the captain is allowed to leave the boat until the paperwork is completed. Required documents include the boat's registration certificate and identification for all persons on board (passport or a certified birth certificate with photo identifcation such as a driver's license for United States citizens). Citizens of other countries may need to apply for a visa in advance of entry and should check with an appropriate Bahamian embassy before departure for the Bahamas. Import permits are required for pets; they are available for $10. (call to verify current amount) from the Director of Agriculture, P. O. N-3704, Nassau, Bahamas (242 325-7502). Firearms must be accompanied by a valid permit, and must be kept under lock and key while in the Bahamas. The fee schedule was revised beginning 1 July 1999 and is now a flat $100 (cash only) for a twelve-month cruising permit, fishing permit and departure taxes (paid in advance) for up to four persons (at $15 each). Transportation charges for officials are no longer levied. Several forms must be completed; the officials are usually pleased to be helpful in this regard. After clearing, foreign boats should fly the Bahamian courtesy flag (ensign) from the starboard spreader or nearest equivilent.

Sometimes one anchor is enough, and sometimes it is best to use two. One is almost always adequate for daytime anchoring, or for anchoring in protected areas in settled weather. If the passage of a cool front is expected before morning, It is usually best to set a second anchor off to the west or northwest about 90° from the first (the wind often blows SW before a frontal passage). When anchoring in an area of strong tidal flows, the boat will lie to the current rather than the wind, and the current will reverse direction 180° about every six hours. This reversal could result in pulling the anchor out backwards, and it may not reset easily. In this situation a Bahamian Moor is desirable. Two anchors are set—one "upstream" and one "downstream"—with the boat inbetween. Both anchors are secured at the bow, allowing the boat to swing to current and wind.

ANCHORING, ANCHOR LIGHTS, AND POWER CABLES

The Bahamas functions under International Rules of the Road (rather than the U. S. Inland Rules), and under these rules there is no such thing as a "designated anchorage." All boats are therefore required by law to show a 32-point anchor light visible for 2 miles from sundown to sunup. However, even the most casual observer will soon notice that there are many boats moored or anchored on a long-term storage basis in many of Abaco's harbours which show no anchor light, so it has become common practice to anchor in harbours without showing a light. It is very important that this practice, which is still illegal, not be extended to areas outside harbours. No one should conclude that because there is an anchor in a certain place on a chart, that the spot is a designated anchorage. Remember, there are no designated anchorages in the Bahamas. All boats anchoring outside of harbours must show an anchor light. To do otherwise is to foolishly risk damage and injury to one's own boat and crew, to endanger the property and lives of others, and to break the law.

Also, when anchoring outside of harbours try to avoid the most direct access routes to those harbours as well as the high voltage electrical cables. Check the large scale harbour charts for approximate locations.

If you should accidentally snag a power line with your anchor, you will probably not be able to raise the anchor, and therefore you will not be certain of what you have snagged. But if it is in or near the power cable area, assume you have snagged a cable, and do not try to free it. The power cables carry 13,200 volts. Attempts to raise the anchor may well result in a disastrous electrical shock or in severing the power cable which supplies electricity to hundreds of people, or in both. The best thing to do is to buoy the rode, leave it there, and call Bahamas Electricity Corporation at 367-2740. They will arrange for the return of your anchor to you.

OBSERVATIONS RE: PASSAGES BETWEEN THE SEA OF ABACO AND THE ATLANTIC OCEAN

All passages between the Sea of Abaco and the Atlantic Ocean are at times impassable due to breaking seas. This condition is locally known as a "rage sea." These are not always the result of high winds; they may also be caused by ocean swells generated by far-away Atlantic storms. Some passages may be better than others in certain wind conditions. For example, Jane and Newell Garfield reported that North Bar Channel, which is used by the mailboat and generally considered to be one of the best and safest passages, was not passable during several days. A rage sea was the result of a strong northeaster. But the passage at Little Harbour, just four miles to the south, was viable because of some protection provided by a protruding reef. The best passage on any particular day depends on wind direction and strength, and on the orientation of the passage. One should note that Little Harbour, North Bar Channel, and Tilloo Cut generally face east, whereas all passages north of Tilloo Cut generally face northeast.

Also, everyone should be aware that there is another way of getting from Eleuthera or Exuma or Nassau into Abaco Sound. Tom and Sue Dickes were holed up at Eleuthera waiting to get to Abaco with a strong northeaster which they knew would make entering the Sea of Abaco treacherous. Instead of waiting, they sailed around the west side of Abaco, around Little Abaco Island, and around Crab Cay. It added some miles, but the sailing was good and they avoided negotiating a breaking or near breaking inlet. They arrived at Green Turtle Cay while some boats were still waiting for a break in the weather to leave Spanish Wells.

VHF RADIO TIPS AND COURTESY

Channel 16 is a calling channel only; switch to a working channel after establishing contact. Wait for a quiet space before trying to establish contact. Channel 68 is now also used as a calling channel in Abaco.

Do not give the USA call—it is time consuming and unnecessary. Simply give the call name of the party you wish to contact, repeat it, then give your call name. Example: Falusi, Falusi, Sand Dollar.

Wait a second after pressing the microphone button before speaking so your first word(s) will not be cut off; give the electrons a chance. Some VHF radios require that the "SELECT" button be pressed before the radio can be switched to another channel.

Please avoid using the following channels for non-emergency conversations; they are reserved for the following specified purposes:

06- local taxis
16- Emergencies/local businesses/calling channel
20- BASRA
22A- Coast Guard working channel
65- Dolphin research
66- Port operations
68- Cruising boat calling channel
70- Digital selective calling - distress and safety
72- Hope Town Fire Brigade
78- Abaco Regatta (4-12 July only)
80- Trauma One & Marsh Harbour Fire Dept.

If you are confronted by an emergency which threatens you or your vessel with grave and immediate danger, call Mayday on channel 16. Do not use Mayday unless you or your vessel are threatened with grave and immediate danger, and you wish to request immediate assistance. Call Mayday 3 times, give the name of your vessel and its position as accurately as possible, state the problem and the number of people on board, and describe the boat. Then repeat the entire message, and then allow time for a response. If none, say over again. Transfer to channel 22A only when told to do so. If you hear a Mayday call, listen. Write the information. Do not broadcast unless it is determined that you are in the best position to render assistance. If you are unable to provide assistance and no one else has acknowledged the Mayday, you may relay the Mayday by announcing Mayday Relay 3 times and repeating the information.

FISHING AND DIVING REGULATIONS

1. Scuba divers may take photos only; no spearing or shelling of any kind may be done while in scuba gear.

2. Spear guns of any type are illegal in the Bahamas. Pole spears and Hawaiian slings used while free diving are permitted.

3. It is illegal to spear within 200 yards of any island or cay.

4. Fowl Cay Reef and Pelican Cays Land and Sea National Park (Sandy Cay Reef) have been set aside for your enjoyment. Take photos only please. No spearing, fishing or shelling of any kind is permitted within the boundaries of either of these Bahamas National Trust Parks.

5. Foreign vessels must obtain a sportfishing permit. These can be obtained from Customs Officers at Ports-of-Entry. The cost is $20. per permit (this is now included in the $100. entry fee).

6. Crawfish season is open from August 1 - March 31. Their tails must be at least 6 inches, and no females with eggs may be taken.

7. The bag limit for kingfish, dolphin, and wahoo is a maximum combined total of 6 fish per person on the vessel, comprising any combination of these species. Vessel bag limits for other species are: 20 lbs. of scalefish, 10 conch and 6 crawfish. The possession of turtle is prohibited.

8. It is illegal to take any member of the grouper family weighing under 3 pounds.

9. It is illegal to take any live sea fans, corals or starfish anywhere in the Bahamas. Several local gift shops sell the preserved items which are suitable for packing and importing into the US.

10. Legal size conch must have a well-formed, flared lip. Never kill a conch just for the shell as they are much too scarce to waste.

Note: All cruisers should be aware that the Government of The Bahamas is very serious about enforcing its fishing and diving regulations, and that stiff penalties may be imposed for simple possession of out-of-season, undersized, or prohibited items, even if they were purchased from Bahamian fishermen. Visitors may legally purchase fish from Bahamians, but should have documented receipts and invoices to clarify the origin of any fish above their bag limit.

APPROACHES TO ABACO

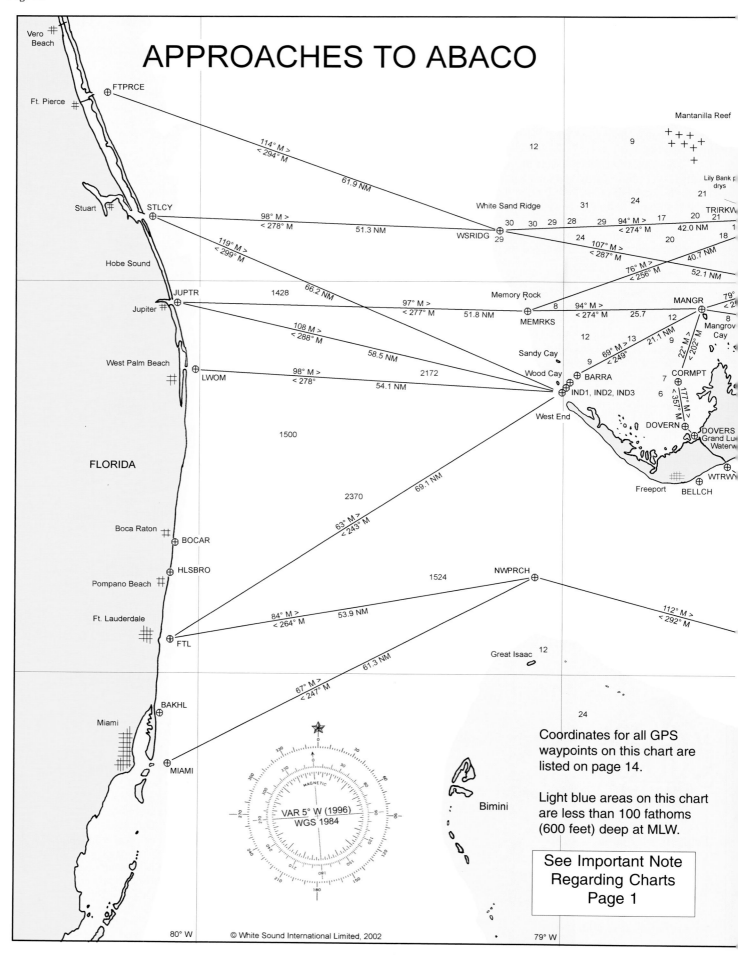

Coordinates for all GPS waypoints on this chart are listed on page 14.

Light blue areas on this chart are less than 100 fathoms (600 feet) deep at MLW.

See Important Note Regarding Charts Page 1

© White Sound International Limited, 2002

542

*uthern extremity of shifting sand
es of Lily Bank was N 27° 11.932'
78° 28.788' during summer 2000.*

Walkers Cay
Grand Cays
Double Breasted Cays
WALKER
TRIRKS

Strangers Cay
Carters Cays

LTLSAL
12   SALRCK
97°M>
121° M >
< 301° M
24.8 NM   6
13
12   Great
Sale
Cay
CRTBSW
116° M >
< 296° M
Allens-Pensacola Cay
Spanish Cay
HKBLL
104° M >
< 284° M
VETRK
84° M >
96° M >
< 276° M
CTWRK
CRABCY
Powell Cay
M >
° M   9
22.2 NM
9   86° M >
< 266° M
9 -
18.6 NM
Manjack Cay
13
GTSALE

Green Turtle Cay
Whale Cay

LITTLE ABACO
ISLAND

GREAT
ABACO
ISLAND

Great Guana Cay

Man-O-War Cay
OFFMOW
176° M >
< 356° M
3.62 NM
OFFELBOW
Elbow Cay

Treasure
Cay

Tilloo Cay

GRAND BAHAMA ISLAND

21

The
Marls

Marsh
Harbour

Lynyard Cay

Mores Island

6

Cherokee
Sound

Little Harbour
OFFOCP
172° M >
< 352° M

129° M >
< 309° M

81 NM

62.7 NM

101 NM

Gorda Cay
aka Castaway Cay

Sandy Point

169° M >
< 349° M

28 NM

183° M >
< 3° M

46.7 NM

26° N

25° M >
< 205° M

47.8 NM

South West
Point
SWPNT
81° M >
< 261° M
7.49 NM
HOLEWL
Hole-in-the-Wall

153° M >
< 333° M

131° M >
< 311° M   28 NM

BRIDGN

< 201° M
381° M >

22.7 NM

OFFMAN

EGGREF   Royal Is.
Egg Is.
Harbour Island

Berry Islands

45.8 NM

v to NASSAU

Eleuthera
Island

78° W

77° W

VAR 7° W (1996)
WGS 1984

MAGNETIC

27° N

APPROACHES TO ABACO

The route from West Palm Beach to Abaco via Indian Cay Channel is all over 6' except for Indian Cay Channel itself, which carries about 5' MLW. See the large scale chart on page 18. Boats drawing more need tide help. Planning the passage through Indian Cay Channel for 1-2 hours before high tide

GPS Waypoints for route from West Palm Beach to Green Turtle Cay on *Approaches to Abaco* (pp. 12-13):

WPT	Description of Position	Latitude	Longitude	Cum Dist	Brng Nxt Wpt	Rge Nxt Wpt
LWOMK	Lake Worth Outer Mark	N 26° 46.340'	W 80° 00.490'	0.0 NM	98° M	54.1 NM
IND1	50' N 1st pile Indian Cay Ch.	N 26° 43.180'	W 79° 00.210'	54.1 NM	37° M	0.71 NM
IND2	50' N 2nd pile Indian Cay Ch.	N 26° 43.770'	W 78° 59.800'	54.8 NM	37° M	1.12 NM
IND3	50' N 3rd pile Indian Cay Ch.	N 26° 44.720'	W 78° 59.140'	55.92 NM	46° M	1.41 NM
BARRA	½ NM SE Barracuda Sh. mkr.	N 26° 45.790'	W 78° 58.110'	57.33 NM	68° M	21.1 NM
MANGR	½ NM N Mangrove Cay mkr.	N 26° 55.710'	W 78° 37.260'	78.43 NM	104° M	22.2 NM
GTSALE	4 NM S Great Sale Cay	N 26° 52.520'	W 78° 12.710'	100.63 NM	85° M	18.6 NM
VETRK	½ NM S Veteran's Rock	N 26° 55.950'	W 77° 52.290'	119.23 NM	83° M	4.21 NM
HKBLL	¼ NM N Hawksbill Cay	N 26° 56.890'	W 77° 47.690'	123.44 NM	104° M	5.43 NM
CTWRK	½ NM S Center World Rock	N 26° 56.190'	W 77° 41.660'	128.87 NM	95° M	4.16 NM
CRABCY	½ NM N of Crab Cay	N 26° 56.271'	W 77° 37.000'	133.04 NM	110° M	1.97 NM
AFISH	¾ NM NE Angelfish Point	N 26° 55.810'	W 77° 34.860'	135.01 NM	129° M	4.92 NM
COOPER	1 NM NE Coopers Town	N 26° 53.200'	W 77° 30.200'	139.53 NM	139° M	11.6 NM
GTC	1 NM W New Plymouth, GTC	N 26° 45.350'	W 77° 20.700'	151.53 NM		

will provide 6½-7' on neap tides and 7½-8' on springs. Another alternative is to go north of Sandy Cay or either side of Memory Rock. White Sand Ridge is another deep water route, and is especially useful for boats departing from St. Lucie Inlet or Ft. Pierce and going to Walker's Cay. Note that we now show a route to Walker's Cay from a new waypoint TRIRKW; the route is north of Triangle Rocks and south of Lily Bank.

The routes north and south of Great Sale Cay both carry well over 6'; the northern route, which comes closer to visible landmarks, is 1.59 nautical miles longer. The Grand Lucayan Waterway carries 6-7' MLW, but the channel approaching it through Dover Sound at its northern end carries only about 3' MLW. See the large scale chart on page 20.

Boats entering the Sea of Abaco through North Man-O-War Channel or South Man-O-War Channel should go offshore to OFFMOW (and OFFELBOW if approaching from the south) before heading for the openings. From either OFFMOW or OFFELBOW one may go to the waypoints located "east, east" of the channels (SMOWEE and NMOWEE) and then approach the "east" waypoints for the channels (SMOWE and NMOWE). These courses will keep boats off the many dangerous reefs in the area. All boats should use them unless very familiar with the area. It is very important to stay east of Elbow Reef, which extends eastward from Hope Town. **More boats ground on this reef than any other in Abaco—please be wary of this reef and go to OFFELBOW when passing Elbow Cay and Reef.** For more detail and for waypoints and coordinates not on this small scale chart, please see the charts on pages 68 and 74. Boats leaving Abaco via these channels and heading south should use these same waypoints.

The best entrances to the Sea of Abaco for those coming from Eleuthera are North Bar Channel (see page115) and North Man-O-War Channel (see page 68 and paragraph above). The

waypoints at the Eleuthera end of the suggested courses provide access to Spanish Wells and Harbour Island. For details see the fifth edition of *The Bahamas Chartkit* published by Maptech. The waypoint BRIDGN is at the north end of the Bridge Point opening in Devil's Backbone Reef. Local knowledge and good visibility are required for this passage the first time.

Other GPS Waypoints on Approaches to Abaco (pp. 12-13):

WPT	Description of Position	Latitude	Longitude
SEBAST	E Sebastian Inlet (not shown)	N 27° 51.674'	W 80° 26.450'
FTPRCE	E Ft. Pierce inlet	N 27° 28.680'	W 80° 15.180'
STLCY	Outer mark St. Lucy inlet	N 27° 10.000'	W 80° 08.000'
JUPTR	1 NM E Jupiter inlet	N 26° 56.605'	W 80° 03.877'
BOCAR	E Boca Raton inlet	N 26° 20.061'	W 80° 10.940'
HLSBRO	SE Hillsboro Inlet	N 26° 15.116'	W 80° 04.420'
FTL	FtL outer mark	N 26° 05.400'	W 80° 04.700'
BAKHL	E Baker's Haulover inlet	N 25° 54.111'	W 80° 06.625'
MIAMI	S Govt. Cut Outer Mark	N 25° 45.950'	W 80° 05.000'
LTLSAL	½ NM NW Little Sale Cay	N 27° 03.274'	W 78° 10.809'
SALRCK	¾ NM N Sale Cay Rocks	N 27° 03.229'	W 78° 06.552'
CRTBSW	¾ NM SW of Carters Bank	N 27° 00.994'	W 78° 01.049'
WSRIDG	33 NM NNW West End	N 27° 08.000'	W 79° 10.500'
MEMRKS	2 NM S Memory Rock	N 26° 55.000'	W 79° 06.000'
GTSANC*	Great Sale Cay anchorage	N 26° 58.581'	W 78° 13.149'
TRIRKS	SE Triangle Rocks	N 27° 09.750'	W 78° 23.500'
TRIRKW	4 NM W Triangle Rocks	N 27° 10.638'	W 78° 30.045'
WALKER	S of Walker's Cay Markers	N 27° 14.077'	W 78° 24.145'
SWPNT*	3 NM WSW South West Point	N 25° 48.000'	W 77° 17.000'
OFFOCP	1 NM ESE Ocean Point	N 26° 17.079'	W 76° 59.349'
HOLEWL*	2 NM SE Hole-in-the-Wall	N 25° 50.000'	W 77° 09.000'
OFFMOW	5 NM NE MOW Cay	N 26° 37.820'	W 76° 55.000'
OFFELBOW	E of Elbow Reef	N 26° 34.270'	W 76° 54.250'
NWPRCH	West end NW Prov. Channel	N 26° 50.000'	W 79° 05.000'

Grand Bahama Island:

WPT	Description	Latitude	Longitude
CORMPT	Pole 2.5 NM NW Cormorant Pt.	N 26° 44.540'	W 78° 40.800'
DOVERN	Pole north end Dover Sound	N 26° 38.280'	W 78° 39.650'
DOVERS	south end Dover Sound	N 26° 36.800'	W 78° 38.470'
WTRWYS	Buoy S. end Grd. Luc. Wtrwy.	N 26° 31.670'	W 78° 33.270'
BELLCH	200' S buoy off Bell Channel	N 26° 29.826'	W 78° 37.791'

Eleuthera:

WPT	Description	Latitude	Longitude
BRIDGN**	N end Bridge Pt. reef opening	N 25° 34.298'	W 76° 43.344'
EGGREF	.8 NM west of Egg Reef	N 25° 31.102'	W 76° 55.031'
OFFMAN	2 NM NE Man Island	N 25° 33.500'	W 76° 36.500'

Nassau:

WPT	Description	Latitude	Longitude
NASSAU	north Nassau Hbr. entrance	N 25° 05.447'	W 77° 21.340'

* Waypoints designated by an asterisk were acquired from reliable sources but have not been personally checked on-site by the author.

**This waypoint is at the north end of the Bridge Point opening in Devil's Backbone Reef. Local knowledge and good visibility are required for this passage the first time.

Sailboat anchored at Mangrove Cay, which provides good protection from either easterly or westerly winds.

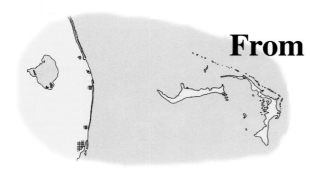

From Florida to Abaco --
Crossing the Gulf Stream

by Marcel Albury and Steve Dodge

The crossing from Florida to Abaco is about 135 nautical miles—55 miles across the Florida Straits from West Palm Beach to West End, Grand Bahama Island, and then 80 miles across Little Bahama Bank from West End to Crab Cay, where one enters into Abaco Sound, sometimes called the Sea of Abaco. It is another 15 nautical miles to Green Turtle Cay, and then another 20 to Marsh Harbour. A planing powerboat can make the trip in one day; a sailboat generally requires 3 to 5 or more days. There are good overnight anchorages or dockage at West End (Old Bahama Bay Marina), Great Sale Cay, Fox Town, Spanish Cay (Spanish Cay Marina), Powell Cay/Cooperstown, and, of course, Green Turtle Cay.

The most challenging part of the trip is crossing the Florida Straits. The Gulf Stream flows northward through the Straits at a speed of about 3 knots. It is about 20-25 miles wide, and is usually located in the center of the Straits. If the wind blows hard (15 or more knots) from the north—against the current—the equivalent of a tide rip 25 miles wide is created, with short, steep, treacherous waves. This condition often exists during the winter months after the passage of cold fronts, and makes the Gulf Stream almost impassable for small boats. Add to this the navigation problem created by the current sweeping one's vessel to the north when the destination is east and, of course, the usual challenges of any 50-mile open ocean crossing, and it should be clear that the trip across the Florida Straits must be taken seriously. But it is not difficult, and most anyone with some open water experience can do it successfully if they follow the general rules of good seamanship, and pay attention to certain special aspects of this crossing.

The single most important factor affecting the comfort and safety of crossing the Gulf Stream is the weather. One should make certain that there will be adequate time to cross before any bad weather moves in. Marcel Albury, who has crossed the Gulf Stream well over 100 times, drives over to the beach to look at the ocean before leaving. He does this even if the weather report is good: "If you see elephants out there on the horizon, forget it. It should look nice and flat. I realize that what you can see is not all that you are going to run into, but it gives you a pretty good idea. The weather report, along with what I can see— the two of these things together—is what makes me decide. And then I leave within about 2 hours. It takes about 6 hours to cross, and I know the weather will be good for that long, so I leave right away."

The boat and the boat's equipment should be in good condition with all standard Coast Guard equipment including life jackets, flares, etc. Fuel should be ample, which like an airplane, should be about 50% more than what you need for the trip. It may be necessary to reduce speed because of sea conditions, making the boat less efficient and the extra fuel essential. The most important extra piece of equipment is a VHF radio, which should be in good operating condition. Some boats carry a portable or a spare. The safety of the crossing can be greatly enhanced by travelling with another boat. Then if problems develop, help is close at hand. Crossing alone in a small open boat—a runabout—is not recommended. Larger boats may cross alone, but Marcel Albury does not recommend single-handed crossings, unless it is an emergency: "I have done it, but you get different as you get older. There are just too many things that can go wrong with me, or it, or that, or them, or what have you. I want somebody else; I just like company. I might twist my ankle and not be able to get up. When one thing happens, it causes something else to happen; it always seems to snowball. It's not in the best interest of anyone to cross the Gulf Stream single-handed."

Notify someone that you are making the crossing and arrange to call them after arrival. The Coast Guard can serve in this way, but it is probably better to call a relative or friend who will be more immediately concerned if you do not telephone on schedule indicating your arrival.

Do not depart from any point north of Ft. Pierce, because you will be fighting the current of the Gulf Stream. Embarkation from West Palm Beach puts the current on the beam, and departure from Fort Lauderdale gives the boat a boost getting to the north with the current helping. The Gulf Stream flows at about 3 knots, but you are not in it all the time as you are crossing. I figure 2 knots drift and usually that works out about right. So, if you figure the crossing to West End will take 6 hours, set your course for a spot 12 nautical miles south of West End. You should be able to see the condominiums at West Palm Beach for 20-30 miles, and you will pick up West End when still about 8 miles west of it, so you will only be out of sight of land for about 25 miles.

The landfall is an easy one—before you see the land you should be able to see the water tower at West End from about 8 miles out. If you make a little too much to the north, then you would probably see Sandy Cay, which lies about 6 miles north of West End and has a very high clump of casuarinas (Florida or Australian Pines) visible for about ten miles. So you've got two good landfalls. You can hardly be so far one way or the other that you're not going to pick up either Sandy Cay or the water tower at West End. You can see the tower if you are 6-8 miles south, and you can see Sandy Cay if you are 6-8 miles north, so you have a broad area there. Its not like going back to the states, when you can't miss it, but if you get within this 18-20 mile area, you will see one or the other landfall. If you go too far south, you will realize it because you are not in the shallow water of the bank, so if you turn and head north you will find Grand Bahama Island and Freeport. So, you probably are not going to miss land.

Memory Rock, which is about 8 miles north of Sandy Cay, is a fairly small rock and is therefore difficult to distinguish from a distance. You can enter on to Little Bahama Bank on either side of it. It is almost on a straight-line course to Sale Cay from West Palm Beach, but most small boats will need to re-fuel—they will not be able to make the additional 100 miles to Green Turtle Cay without re-fueling at West End. Other possible re-fueling stops are at Fox Town, Spanish Cay, and Cooperstown.

Finally, all boats entering The Bahamas are required to clear Customs and Immigration at a Port of Entry as soon as possible after arriving in Bahamian waters. This can be done at West End, Freeport, Walker's Cay, Spanish Cay, Green Turtle Cay, or Marsh Harbour.

Grand Bahama Section*

(pages 17-20)

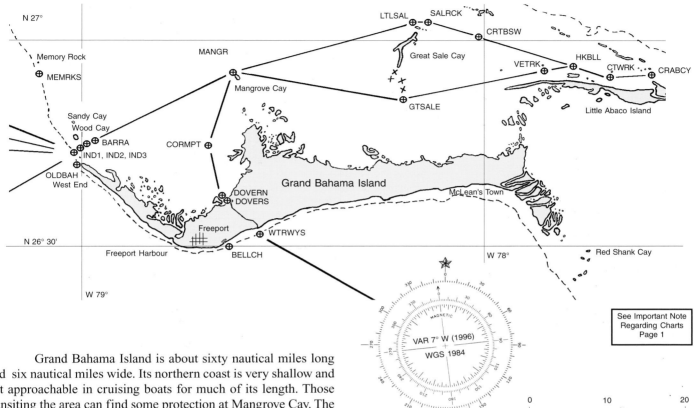

© Copyright White Sound International Limited 1998

Grand Bahama Island is about sixty nautical miles long and six nautical miles wide. Its northern coast is very shallow and not approachable in cruising boats for much of its length. Those transiting the area can find some protection at Mangrove Cay. The only other accessible anchorages are at Great Sale Cay (see p. 22). The Grand Lucayan Waterway bisects the island about 20 nautical miles east of West End (see the chart in this section on page 20).

The southern coast is close to the edge of Little Bahama Bank. A barrier reef parallels the coast for much of its length a short distance offshore, and just beyond that there is a steep drop-off to deep ocean water at the edge of the bank. Freeport, the Bahamas' second largest city, is located close to the southern coast, but Freeport harbour is primarily commercial and does not cater to cruising boats. There are several harbours with marinas east of Freeport Harbour. Closest is the Xanadu Beach Marina and Resort. Just beyond that is the Running Mon Marina, then the Ocean Reef Yacht Club, and then Bell Channel, site of the Lucayan Marina and Port Lucaya. See the chart on page 20 of this section for more information.

There is a land and sea park at Peterson Cay, 1¼ miles east of the southern entrance to the Grand Lucayan Waterway. Further east is McLean's Town. Refer to DMA chart #26320.

The redevelopment of West End will be of interest to many cruising in or transiting this area. The old Jack Tar Marina is now Old Bahama Bay Marina (see the chart on page 18 for the new entrance channel). Reconfiguration and reconstruction of the marina includes new docks and a new customs, immigration, and restaurant building located at the northeast corner of the main basin. A "beachfront cottage hotel" as well as residential lots are included in the redevelopment. The new docks are completed, and a bar and restaurant were operational during summer, 2002. Bicycles are available to marina guests, the beach is a very short walk away, and several snorkeling trails have been marked near the West End area.

GPS Waypoints for Grand Bahama Section (generally from west to east):

WPT	Description	Latitude	Longitude
MEMRKS	2 NM S Memory Rock	N 26° 55.000'	W 79° 06.000'
IND1	50' N 1st pile Indian Cay Ch.	N 26° 43.180'	W 79° 00.210'
IND2	50' N 2nd pile Indian Cay Ch.	N 26° 43.770'	W 78° 59.800'
IND3	50' N 3rd pile Indian Cay Ch.	N 26° 44.720'	W 78° 59.140'
BARRA	½ NM SE Barracuda Sh. mkr.	N 26° 45.790'	W 78° 58.110'
OLDBAH	500' W ent. Old Bah Bay Mar.	N 26° 42.256'	W 78° 59.818'
MANGR	1/2 NM N Mangrove Cay mkr.	N 26° 55.710'	W 78° 37.260'
CORMPT	pole 2½ NM NW Cormorant Pt.	N 26° 44.540'	W 78° 40.800'
DOVERN	pole north end Dover Sound	N 26° 38.280'	W 78° 39.650'
DOVERS	south end Dover Sound	N 26° 36.800'	W 78° 38.470'
WTRWYS	buoy S. end Grd. Luc. Wtrwy.	N 26° 31.670'	W 78° 33.270'
BELLCH	200' S buoy off Bell Channel	N 26° 29.826'	W 78° 37.791'
GTSALE	4 NM S Great Sale Cay	N 26° 52.520'	W 78° 12.710'
LTLSAL	1/2 NM NW Little Sale Cay	N 27° 03.274'	W 78° 10.809'
SALRCK	3/4 NM N Sale Cay Rocks	N 27° 03.229'	W 78° 06.552'
CRTBSW	3/4 NM SW of Carters Bank	N 27° 00.994'	W 78° 01.049'
VETRK	1/2 NM S Veteran's Rock	N 26° 55.950'	W 77° 52.290'
HKBLL	1/4 NM N Hawksbill Cay	N 26° 56.890'	W 77° 47.690'
CTWRK	1/2 NM S Center World Rock	N 26° 56.190'	W 77° 41.660'
CRABCY	½ NM N of Crab Cay	N 26° 56.271'	W 77° 37.000'

* Grand Bahama Island is on the way to Abaco from Florida. For several years *The Cruising Guide to Abaco, Bahamas* has included some information regarding Grand Bahama Island, because many visitors to Abaco stop at Grand Bahama on their way across or on the trip back. This special section of *The Cruising Guide to Abaco* recognizes that more complete information would serve the needs of these persons. It is our intention to further develop this section of *The Cruising Guide to Abaco, Bahamas*, during the next few years.

Indian Cay Channel and West End, Grand Bahama Island

The water tower at West End and the tall stand of casuarinas on Sandy Cay six miles to the north can be seen for about 8 miles. These are the first landmarks one will see when approaching West End. The entire area between Sandy Cay and West End is fairly shallow and strewn with rocky bars and reefs, but Indian Cay Channel, which carries about 5' MLW (7-8' at high tide), is a viable route through the area. Boats drawing more than 5' will need tide help or should go about 4 NM north of Sandy Cay. Indian Cay Channel is marked with three pilings. There is also a light on a small steel tower on Indian Cay Rock. **The light is not a marker for the deepest water; the pilings are**. Leave all three pilings to the south. Small arrows attached to each piling point to the north. The third piling has been missing for several years; the second piling may be lit at night. The Barracuda Shoal marker, located northeast of Indian Cay Channel, is mounted on the shoal itself and should be given about a ¼ NM berth; go SE of it. Entrance to Old Bahama Bay Marina is from the west. The channel is wide and deep (15-17'). Entry is straightforward except for a breakwater extending across the channel after you are inside. Leave it to port. Proceed eastward around the breakwater, and when you cannot go further east, turn to starboard to enter the main marina basin. The new docks were completed in 1999, and work on the new customs building and restaurant as well as resort accomodations was almost finished in summer 2002. See page 17 for waypoint coordinates.

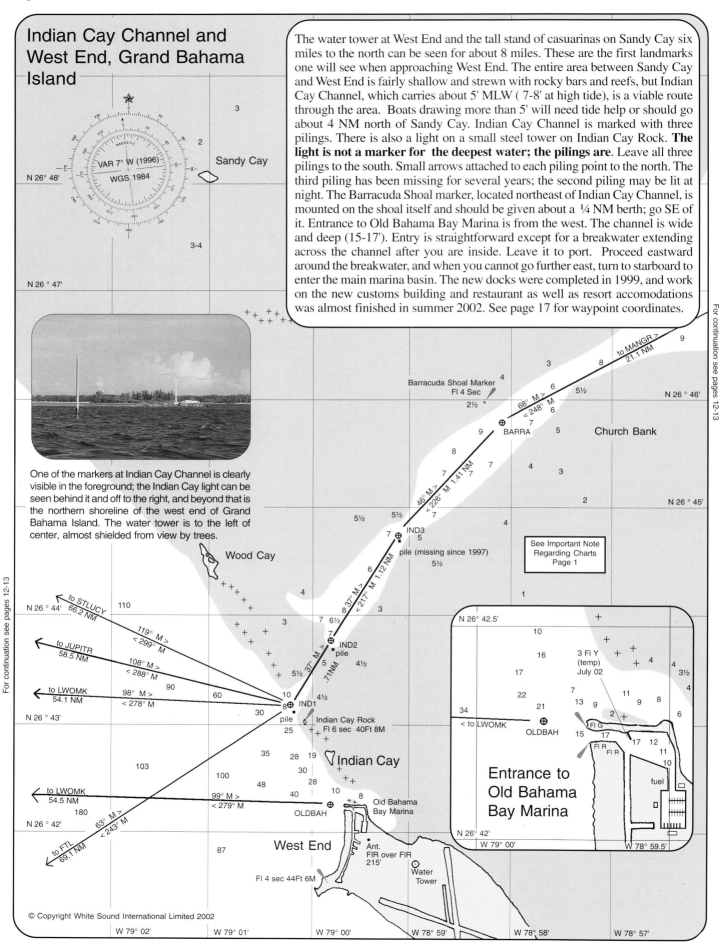

One of the markers at Indian Cay Channel is clearly visible in the foreground; the Indian Cay light can be seen behind it and off to the right, and beyond that is the northern shoreline of the west end of Grand Bahama Island. The water tower is to the left of center, almost shielded from view by trees.

VAR 7° W (1996)
WGS 1984

Sandy Cay

N 26° 48'
N 26 ° 47'

For continuation see pages 12-13

3
2
3-4

to MANGR 21.1 NM
9
3
8
N 26 ° 46'
Barracuda Shoal Marker
Fl 4 Sec
2½
4
6
5½
68° M
< 248° M
6
7
9
BARRA
5
Church Bank
8
46° M >
< 226° M 1.41 NM
7
7
4
3
N 26 ° 45'
5½
5½
4
2
IND3
7
5
pile (missing since 1997)
5½

See Important Note Regarding Charts Page 1

Wood Cay

6
3
1
4
37° M >
< 217° M 1.12 NM

N 26° 42.5'
10
16
3 Fl Y (temp) July 02
17
22
7
11
9
4
13 9
9
4
34
21
< to LWOMK
OLDBAH
Fl G
2
15
Fl R
17
12
Fl R
11
10

Entrance to Old Bahama Bay Marina

fuel

N 26° 42'
W 79° 00'
W 78° 59.5'

For continuation see pages 12-13

to STLUCY 66.2 NM
N 26 ° 44'
110
119° M >
< 299° M
to JUPITR 58.5 NM
108° M >
< 288° M
90
98° M >
< 278° M
to LWOMK 54.1 NM
N 26 ° 43'
60
30
10
8
IND1
pile
7 6½
7
5
IND2
pile
4½
5½ 37° M
.77NM
.77NM
4½
4
3

Indian Cay Rock
Fl 6 sec 40Ft 8M
25
35
28 19
Indian Cay
30
30
28
48
40
10
8
OLDBAH
Old Bahama Bay Marina

103
100

to LWOMK 54.5 NM
N 26 ° 42'
180
99° M >
< 279° M
63° M >
< 243° M
to FTL 69.1 NM

87

West End
Ant. FIR over FIR 215'
Fl 4 sec 44Ft 6M
Water Tower

W 79° 02'
W 79° 01'
W 79° 00'
W 78° 59'
W 78° 58'
W 78° 57'

Entrance to Old Bahama Bay

Approach from the west. After entering between the breakwaters, move to the starboard side to avoid the spur breakwater , which is presently marked by three flashing yellow lights. After passing it and the branch canal which goes to the south, turn to starboard and enter the marina basin. The fuel dock is on on the starboard side as you enter.

Fish muds are common on Little Bahama Bank in the area north of Grand Bahama Island. This one was photographed from the air in July, 2002. When approaching them in a boat they often appear, at first, to be a shoal area, but homogenous colour and sometimes fuzzy edges give them away as fish muds rather than shoals. There are several theories regarding their cause; the most common being schools of bottom feeding fish.

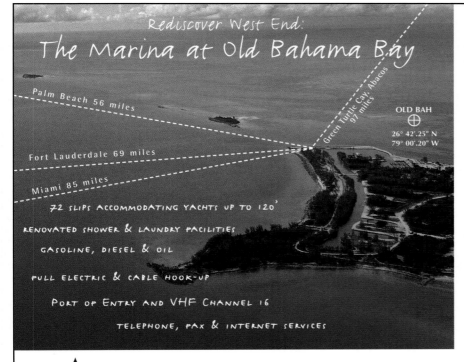

For continuation see pages 12-13

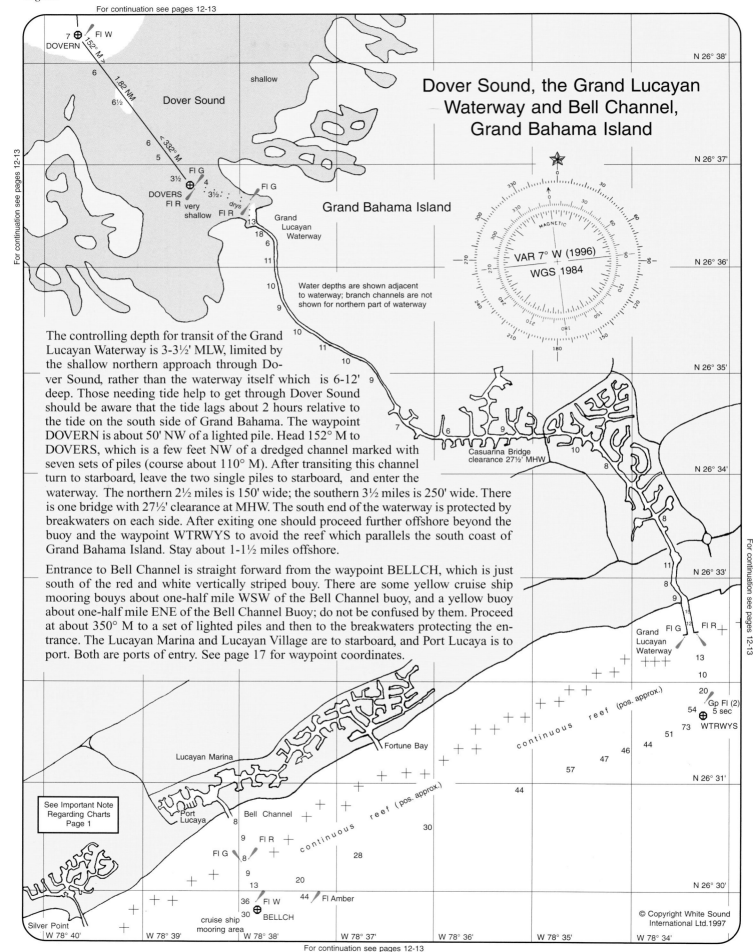

Dover Sound, the Grand Lucayan Waterway and Bell Channel, Grand Bahama Island

Dover Sound

shallow

Grand Bahama Island

DOVERN

DOVERS
Fl R

very shallow

Fl G

Fl R

drys

Grand Lucayan Waterway

Water depths are shown adjacent to waterway; branch channels are not shown for northern part of waterway

VAR 7° W (1996)

WGS 1984

The controlling depth for transit of the Grand Lucayan Waterway is 3-3½' MLW, limited by the shallow northern approach through Dover Sound, rather than the waterway itself which is 6-12' deep. Those needing tide help to get through Dover Sound should be aware that the tide lags about 2 hours relative to the tide on the south side of Grand Bahama. The waypoint DOVERN is about 50' NW of a lighted pile. Head 152° M to DOVERS, which is a few feet NW of a dredged channel marked with seven sets of piles (course about 110° M). After transiting this channel turn to starboard, leave the two single piles to starboard, and enter the waterway. The northern 2½ miles is 150' wide; the southern 3½ miles is 250' wide. There is one bridge with 27½' clearance at MHW. The south end of the waterway is protected by breakwaters on each side. After exiting one should proceed further offshore beyond the buoy and the waypoint WTRWYS to avoid the reef which parallels the south coast of Grand Bahama Island. Stay about 1-1½ miles offshore.

Entrance to Bell Channel is straight forward from the waypoint BELLCH, which is just south of the red and white vertically striped bouy. There are some yellow cruise ship mooring bouys about one-half mile WSW of the Bell Channel buoy, and a yellow buoy about one-half mile ENE of the Bell Channel Buoy; do not be confused by them. Proceed at about 350° M to a set of lighted piles and then to the breakwaters protecting the entrance. The Lucayan Marina and Lucayan Village are to starboard, and Port Lucaya is to port. Both are ports of entry. See page 17 for waypoint coordinates.

Casuarina Bridge clearance 27½' MHW

Grand Lucayan Waterway

Fl G

Fl R

continuous reef (pos. approx.)

Gp Fl (2) 5 sec
WTRWYS

Lucayan Marina

Fortune Bay

continuous reef (pos. approx.)

See Important Note Regarding Charts Page 1

Port Lucaya

Bell Channel

Fl R

Fl G

continuous reef (pos. approx.)

Fl W
BELLCH

Fl Amber

cruise ship mooring area

Silver Point

For continuation see pages 12-13

NOW, THE #1 MILITARY GRADE NAVIGATIONAL SYSTEM™ FOR AMERICAN SPORT FISHING & PLEASURE CRAFT OWNERS

NavigatorPC has set new standards for marine computer systems. All NavigatorPC's computers, displays and accessories start in the engineering department and are designed for the tough marine environment; *Not just a home PC fitted for a boat.* **NavigatorPC produces the fastest marine computers and brightest marine displays on the market today.**

Pedestal Mount

Flush Mount

Experience the combination of NavigatorPC's 800MHz powerhouse with Maptech's Contour Professional and Offshore Navigator and the ocean belongs to you! Features include a blazing high-speed Intel PIII 800 MHz packed with 256 megabytes of RAM and a whopping 20-gigabyte hard drive.

NavigatorPC combined with Maptech's digital 2001 Chartkit and Contour Professional makes navigation safe and easy as never before. Being able to see your vessel on a digital chart and a three-dimensional bathymetric view of the ocean's bottom contour, while looking dead ahead for one mile. **It can't get any safer than that.**

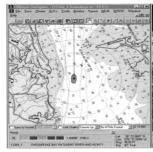
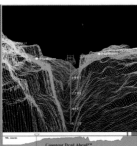

Sunlight Viewable Waterproof Screen

www.NavigatorPC.com
Email: info@NavigatorPC.com
1-888-307-3265

MAPTECH®

© 2001 NAVIGATORPC™

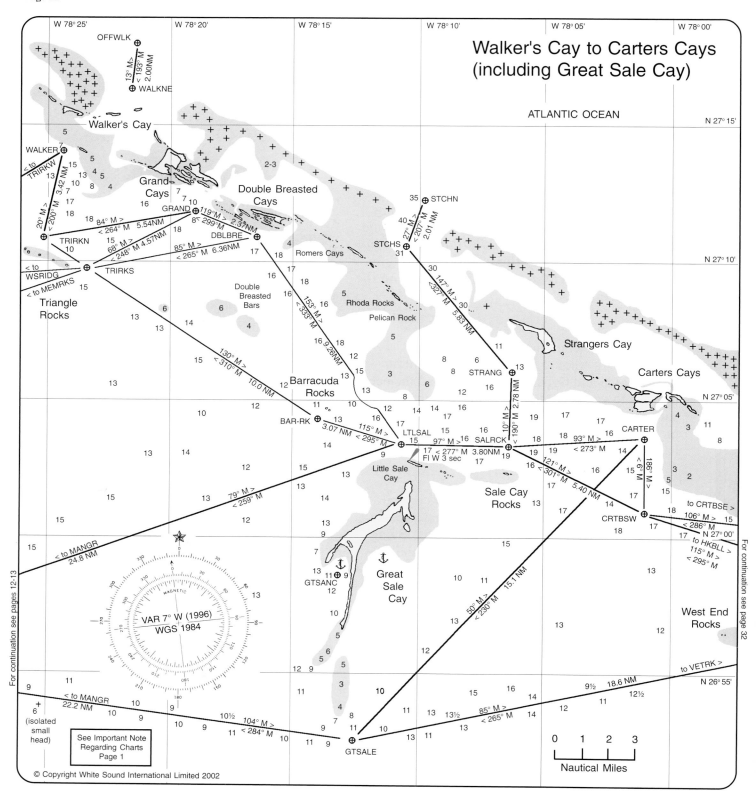

Walker's Cay to Carters Cays
(including Great Sale Cay)

ATLANTIC OCEAN

© Copyright White Sound International Limited 2002

GPS Waypoints for *Walker's Cay to Carters Cays* (generally from north to south):

WPT	Description of Position	Latitude	Longitude	WPT	Description of Position	Latitude	Longitude
OFFWLK	3.8 NM NE Walker's Cay	N 27° 18.000'	W 78° 21.350'	CRTBSW	Southwest of Carter Bank	N 27° 00.994'	W 78° 01.049'
WALKNE	2.0 NM ENE Walker's Cay	N 27° 16.289'	W 78° 21.598'	GRAND	South of Grand Cays	N 27° 11.884'	W 78° 18.970'
WALKER	South of Walker's Cay markers	N 27° 14.077'	W 78° 24.145'	DBLBRE	South of Double Breasted Cays	N 27° 11.000'	W 78° 16.500'
TRIRKN	Northeast of Triangle Rocks	N 27° 10.766'	W 78° 25.056'	STCHN	N end Stranger Cay Channel	N 27° 12.400'	W 78° 09.770'
TRIRKW	4 NM W Triangle Rocks	N 27° 10.638'	W 78° 30.045'	STCHS	S end Stranger Cay Channel	N 27° 10.500'	W 78° 10.500'
TRIRKS	Southeast of Triangle Rocks	N 27° 09.750'	W 78° 23.500'	STRANG	1¾ NM S of W tip Stranger Cay	N 27° 06.000'	W 78° 06.350'
BAR-RK	Southwest of Barracuda Rocks	N 27° 04.258'	W 78° 14.071'	CARTER	Southwest of Carter Cays	N 27° 03.528'	W 78° 01.087'
LTLSAL	Northwest of Little Sale Cay	N 27° 03.274'	W 78° 10.809'	GTSALE	4 NM south of Great Sale Cay	N 26° 52.520'	W 78° 12.710'
SALRCK	North of Sale Cay Rocks	N 27° 03.229'	W 78° 06.552'	GTSANC*	Great Sale Cay anchorage	N 26° 58.581'	W 78° 13.149'

WALKER'S CAY TO CARTERS CAYS
(including Great Sale Cay)

Boats drawing 4' or more and transiting the area from Walker's Cay to Carters Cays must take care to avoid the shoal between Walker's and Grand Cays, the Double Breasted Bars which are about 5 NM S of Double Breasted Cays, and the large shoal extending from the Rhoda Rocks and Pelican Rock. GPS waypoints are shown on the chart for this route. It extends generally S from Walker's Cay to Triangle Rocks, then SE to Barracuda Rocks, ESE to Little Sale Cay, and then E to Carters Cays. This route is not the shortest distance between Walker's and Carters, but it is clear of obstacles and carries over 6' MLW (except for the final approach to Walker's over the bank there, which carries about 5-5½' MLW). Waypoints for this route are listed below the chart.

Possible overnight anchorages along the way (within about 5 NM) include Grand Cays, Double Breasted Cays, Strangers Cay and Great Sale Cay. Grand Cays is the next anchorage to the SE. Grand Cays has a settlement with restaurants and stores, and fuel service is available. Beaches on the east side of the cays are beautiful, and bone-fishing is good in the entire area. See the chart on page 26 for more detail.

Double Breasted Cays is a beautiful collection of small cays and rocks. An anchorage offering protection from the west, north, and east is available near the NW end of the archipelago. See the chart on page 28 for more detail.

Strangers Cay has a settled weather anchorage near its NW tip. See the chart on page 29 for more detail.

Great Sale Cay has a bight on its west side which offers good protection from west, north, and east winds, but is open to the south. It is a favorite overnight stop for boats making the Abaco-Florida passage. The approach to it is straightforward—the only obstacle is a shoal extending westward from Great Sale Cay. Give it a wide berth. Another possible anchorage is just east of the cay—but this offers protection only from the west and north, being exposed to the east and south.

Note that the old Elephant Rock route between Walker's Cay and Grand Cays silted in as a result of hurricane Floyd (it is now about 2-3' MLW). A new route carries about 5'. See the Grand Cays chart on page 26.

Double Breasted Cays can be approached directly from the waypoint GRAND or from the SW tip of Big Grand Cay on the Atlantic side. See pages 26-28 for larger scale charts and a detailed description.

From the waypoint DBLBRE note that a straight courseline to LTLSAL, the waypoint north of Little Sale Cay, passes near the edge of the bank extending south from the Rhoda Rocks and Pelican Rock. Watch cross track error carefully here, or just alter course to the west to make certain that you avoid the edge of the bank.

There is a deep and wide channel from the Sea of Abaco to the Atlantic Ocean NW of Strangers Cay. See page 29 for more details.

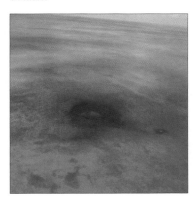

This blue hole is located on the shoal extending from the southern tip of Great Sale Cay. Blue holes are located in the shallow waters (or on the land areas) of the Bahama Banks. They are connected to deep ocean waters through a tunnel or tunnels cut through the limestone base of the banks by rainwater during the ice ages when sea level was several hundred feet lower than it is today.

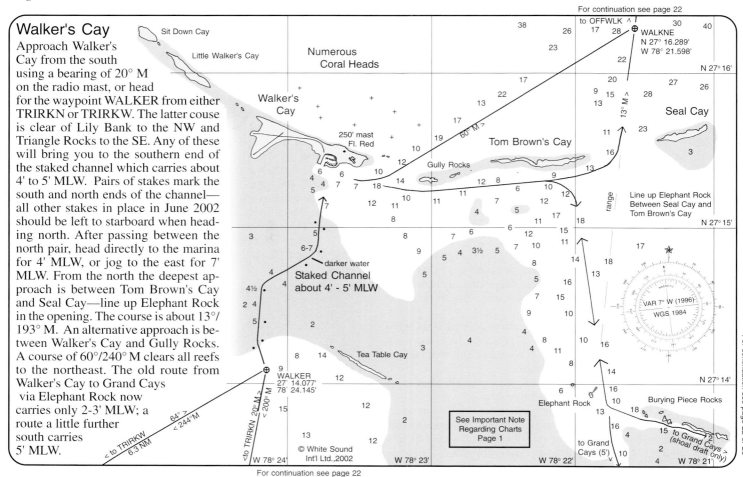

Walker's Cay

Approach Walker's Cay from the south using a bearing of 20° M on the radio mast, or head for the waypoint WALKER from either TRIRKN or TRIRKW. The latter couse is clear of Lily Bank to the NW and Triangle Rocks to the SE. Any of these will bring you to the southern end of the staked channel which carries about 4' to 5' MLW. Pairs of stakes mark the south and north ends of the channel—all other stakes in place in June 2002 should be left to starboard when heading north. After passing between the north pair, head directly to the marina for 4' MLW, or jog to the east for 7' MLW. From the north the deepest approach is between Tom Brown's Cay and Seal Cay—line up Elephant Rock in the opening. The course is about 13°/193° M. An alternative approach is between Walker's Cay and Gully Rocks. A course of 60°/240° M clears all reefs to the northeast. The old route from Walker's Cay to Grand Cays via Elephant Rock now carries only 2-3' MLW; a route a little further south carries 5' MLW.

Sit Down Cay
Little Walker's Cay
Numerous Coral Heads
Walker's Cay
250' mast Fl. Red
Tom Brown's Cay
Gully Rocks
Seal Cay
Line up Elephant Rock Between Seal Cay and Tom Brown's Cay
darker water
Staked Channel about 4' - 5' MLW
Tea Table Cay
WALKER
27' 14.077'
78' 24.145'
Elephant Rock
Burying Piece Rocks
VAR 7° W (1996)
WGS 1984
See Important Note Regarding Charts Page 1
to Grand Cays (5')
to Grand Cays (shoal draft only)
© White Sound Int'l Ltd.,2002

WALKNE
N 27° 16.289'
W 78° 21.598'

to OFFWLK

For continuation see page 22

For continuation see page 22 or 26

For continuation see page 22

WALKER'S CAY

Walker's Cay has a fine marina with full services and is one of the premier sportfishing centers of the Bahamas. There is a hotel, a dive shop, a grocery store, and an airport with regular flights to Florida.

Walker's is a port of entry and a convenient place to clear, especially for boats coming from St. Lucie Inlet or Ft. Pierce. The route for the crossing is almost a straight line from St. Lucie Inlet (STLCY) to White Sand Ridge (WSRIDG) to Triangle Rocks (TRIRKW) to WALKER (see the chart on pages 12-13). It is usually possible to tie up at the fuel dock, clear, and then refuel.

Diving is excellent on the numerous coral heads and reefs north of Walkers Cay. A full-service dive shop at the marina offers trips every day, and the shark dives are well known throughout the islands. For a diving/snorkeling chart of the Walker's Cay area, see page 124.

Chelsea, the author's hydrographic research boat, at Walker's Cay in June 2000.

darker water

Walker's Cay

Walkers Cay Marina from the south. Note that recent dredging, filling and bulkhead work have changed the shape of the opening of the marina. This photo was taken on 11 July 2002.

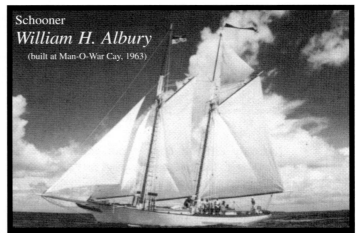

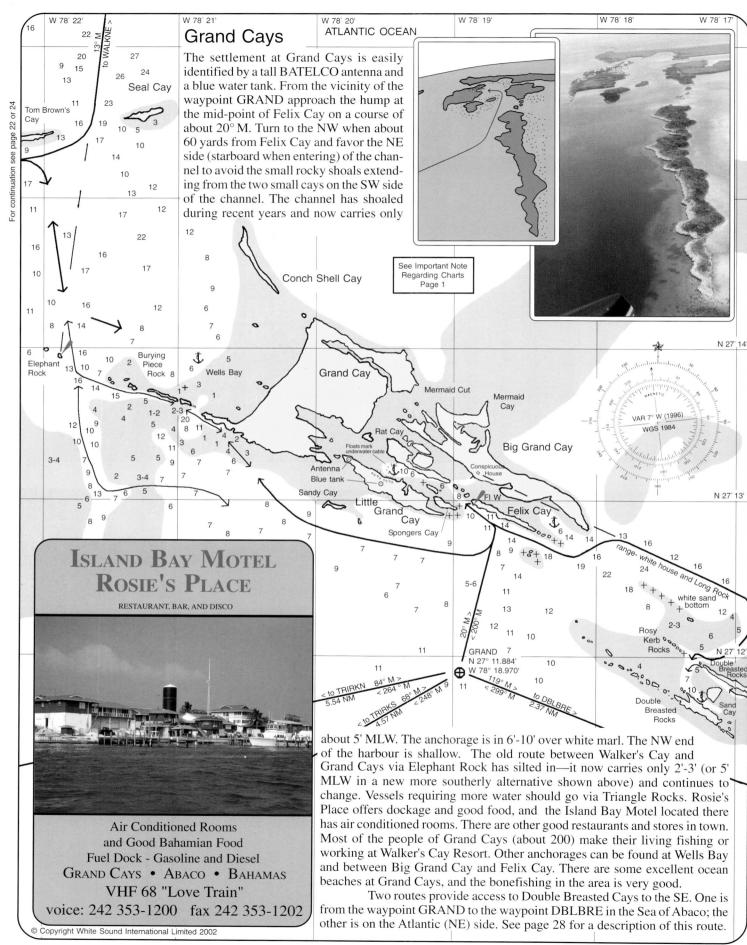

Grand Cays

The settlement at Grand Cays is easily identified by a tall BATELCO antenna and a blue water tank. From the vicinity of the waypoint GRAND approach the hump at the mid-point of Felix Cay on a course of about 20° M. Turn to the NW when about 60 yards from Felix Cay and favor the NE side (starboard when entering) of the channel to avoid the small rocky shoals extending from the two small cays on the SW side of the channel. The channel has shoaled during recent years and now carries only

See Important Note Regarding Charts Page 1

ATLANTIC OCEAN

VAR 7° W (1996)
WGS 1984

GRAND
N 27° 11.884'
W 78° 18.970'

< to TRIRKN 84° M >
5.54 NM   < 264° M
< to TRIRKS 68° M >
4.57 NM   < 248° M 9
       < 299° M >   to DBLBRE >
119° M   2.37 NM

ISLAND BAY MOTEL
ROSIE'S PLACE

RESTAURANT, BAR, AND DISCO

Air Conditioned Rooms
and Good Bahamian Food
Fuel Dock - Gasoline and Diesel
GRAND CAYS • ABACO • BAHAMAS
VHF 68 "Love Train"
voice: 242 353-1200   fax 242 353-1202

© Copyright White Sound International Limited 2002

about 5' MLW. The anchorage is in 6'-10' over white marl. The NW end of the harbour is shallow. The old route between Walker's Cay and Grand Cays via Elephant Rock has silted in—it now carries only 2'-3' (or 5' MLW in a new more southerly alternative shown above) and continues to change. Vessels requiring more water should go via Triangle Rocks. Rosie's Place offers dockage and good food, and the Island Bay Motel located there has air conditioned rooms. There are other good restaurants and stores in town. Most of the people of Grand Cays (about 200) make their living fishing or working at Walker's Cay Resort. Other anchorages can be found at Wells Bay and between Big Grand Cay and Felix Cay. There are some excellent ocean beaches at Grand Cays, and the bonefishing in the area is very good.

Two routes provide access to Double Breasted Cays to the SE. One is from the waypoint GRAND to the waypoint DBLBRE in the Sea of Abaco; the other is on the Atlantic (NE) side. See page 28 for a description of this route.

For continuation see page 22

Entrance to Grand Cays Harbour

Approach the hump at the mid-point of Felix Cay on a course of about 20° M.

Turn to the NW. Leave the rock with the Fl W light to starboard.

Favor the NE (starboard side when entering) to avoid small rocky shoals extending from the two small cays on the SW side of the channel.

Turn to port a little and enter the anchorage. Rosie's Place is just to the right of the blue water tower in this photo.

Grand Cays harbour from the west. Note the radiotelephone antenna (extreme left) and the large blue water tank (extreme right); these are the first landmarks seen when approaching Grand Cays.

Double Breasted Cays

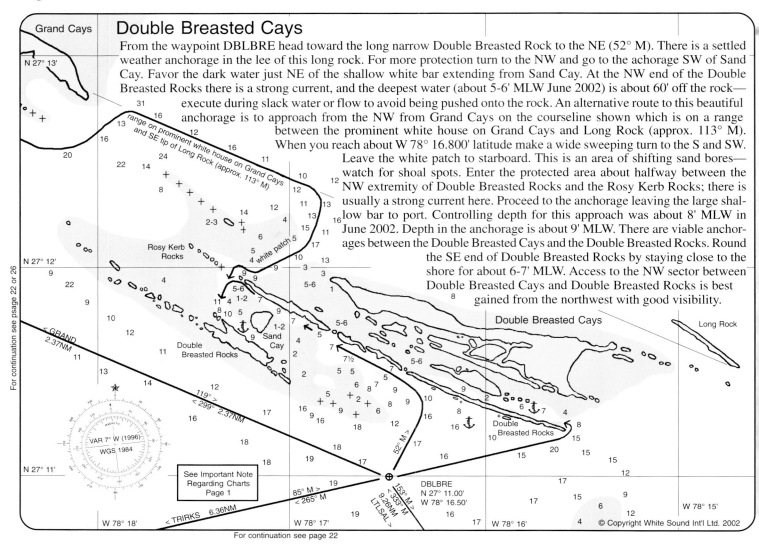

From the waypoint DBLBRE head toward the long narrow Double Breasted Rock to the NE (52° M). There is a settled weather anchorage in the lee of this long rock. For more protection turn to the NW and go to the achorage SW of Sand Cay. Favor the dark water just NE of the shallow white bar extending from Sand Cay. At the NW end of the Double Breasted Rocks there is a strong current, and the deepest water (about 5-6' MLW June 2002) is about 60' off the rock— execute during slack water or flow to avoid being pushed onto the rock. An alternative route to this beautiful anchorage is to approach from the NW from Grand Cays on the courseline shown which is on a range between the prominent white house on Grand Cays and Long Rock (approx. 113° M). When you reach about W 78° 16.800' latitude make a wide sweeping turn to the S and SW. Leave the white patch to starboard. This is an area of shifting sand bores— watch for shoal spots. Enter the protected area about halfway between the NW extremity of Double Breasted Rocks and the Rosy Kerb Rocks; there is usually a strong current here. Proceed to the anchorage leaving the large shallow bar to port. Controlling depth for this approach was about 8' MLW in June 2002. Depth in the anchorage is about 9' MLW. There are viable anchorages between the Double Breasted Cays and the Double Breasted Rocks. Round the SE end of Double Breasted Rocks by staying close to the shore for about 6-7' MLW. Access to the NW sector between Double Breasted Cays and Double Breasted Rocks is best gained from the northwest with good visibility.

For continuation see page 22

Artist Phil Capen's painting of Double Breasted Cays. The scraggily growth on small rock islets is typical of the area.

Four sailboats in the anchorage northeast of Double Breasted Rocks at Double Breasted Cays.

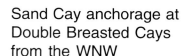

Sand Cay anchorage at Double Breasted Cays from the WNW

Strangers Cay Channel and Anchorage

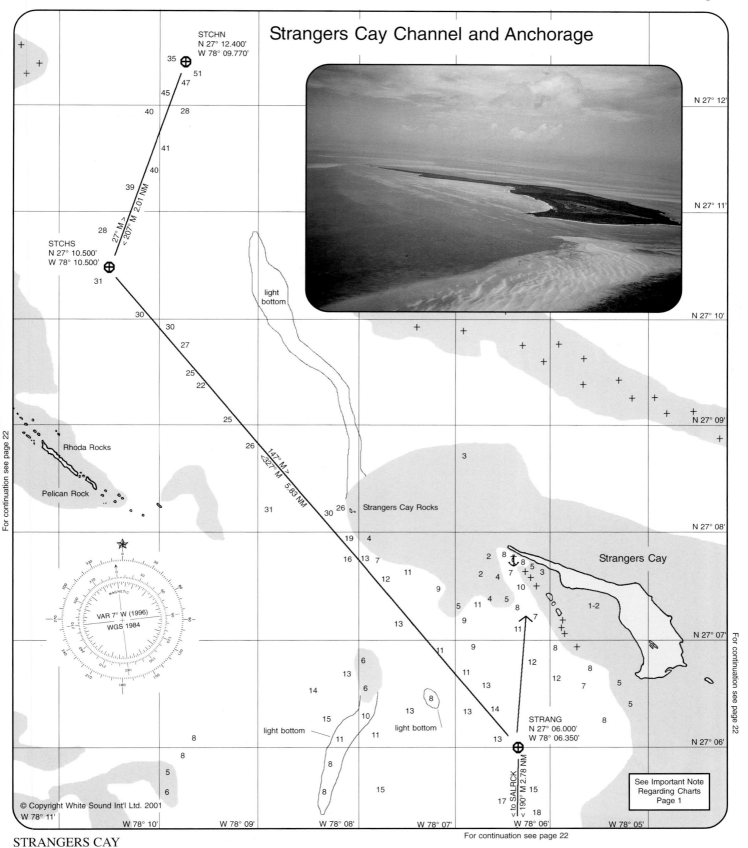

STCHN
N 27° 12.400'
W 78° 09.770'

STCHS
N 27° 10.500'
W 78° 10.500'

light bottom

Rhoda Rocks

Pelican Rock

VAR 7° W (1996)
WGS 1984

Strangers Cay Rocks

Strangers Cay

light bottom

light bottom

STRANG
N 27° 06.000'
W 78° 06.350'

See Important Note
Regarding Charts
Page 1

For continuation see page 22

STRANGERS CAY

Strangers Channel is a deep and wide route between the Sea of Abaco and the Atlantic Ocean. It is not frequently used because Strangers Cay has no development and only a marginal anchorage. The channel is remote from Bahamian communities, secure anchorages and marinas. The waypoints and routes should keep one in deep water, but please remember to keep a sharp lookout for stray coral heads (we looked, but found none close to the routes).

The anchorage at Strangers can be approached from the waypoint STRANG. The shoal water on both sides should be clearly visible. The anchorage is in 8' MLW, but it is small and completely exposed to winds from SSE to NW. Use it as a daytime anchorage, or stay overnight in settled weather. There are some nice beaches on the NE side of the cay, but the anchorage presents only a rocky shoreline.

Carters Cays

Proceed from the waypoint CARTER toward Gully Cay using the marker range (bottles tied to stakes) on a course of 39° M. Depth of the approach was 4-5' when last surveyed with one 3½' bump (marked on chart). When about 50' off Gully Cay turn to port and head roughly NW until clear of the end of Gully Cay. Anchor between Gully Cay and Big Carters Cay to avoid the swift current which runs in the main part of Carters Cay Harbour. The anchorage area is not large, and shoals rapidly as you go east. An alternative entrance across the bar on the SW side of the "harbour" carries only about 3' MLW. Big Carters Cay has some temporary houses on the SW point which are inhabited during the crawfishing season, and it has the remnants of a US missile tracking station. A small hurricane hole called Hogstye Harbour is located between Old Yankee Cay and Top Cay. The entrance carries 3' MLW; there is 13' inside.

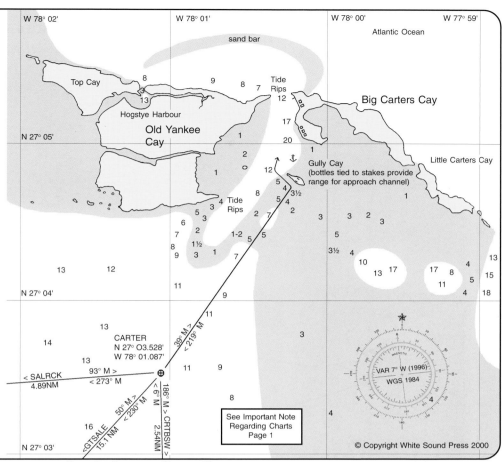

See Important Note
Regarding Charts
Page 1

VAR 7° W (1996)
WGS 1984

© Copyright White Sound Press 2000

For continuation see page 22 or page 32

Three boats rafted up on a quiet summer day on the small sand bank extending westward from Old Yankee Cay in the vicinity of Top Cay and Jacks Cay.

Boats in the anchorage at Carters Cays. Gully Cay is in the foreground, Big Carters Cay on the right, the east tip of Old Yankee Cay on the left, and the Atlantic Ocean in the back. By anchoring on the extreme east side of the cut, the boats have avoided the strongest current in the center.

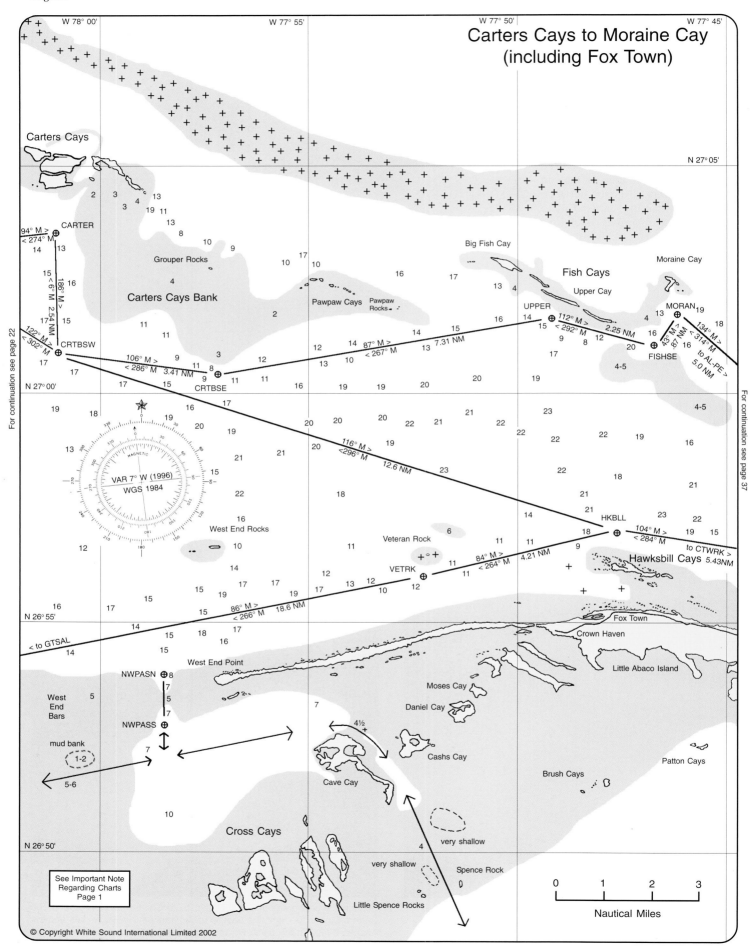

Carters Cays to Moraine Cay
(including Fox Town)

W 78° 00'   W 77° 55'   W 77° 50'   W 77° 45'

N 27° 05'

Carters Cays

CARTER

94° M >
< 274° M
14   13

15   186° M >
<.6° M   2.54 NM
16

17°M
122° M >
< 302° M   CRTBSW
17

Carters Cays Bank

Grouper Rocks

Big Fish Cay

Fish Cays
Moraine Cay

Upper Cay

UPPER   112° M >
< 292° M   2.25 NM

MORAN 19
134° M >
< 314° M   to AL-PE
5.0 NM
FISHSE

Pawpaw Cays   Pawpaw Rocks

106° M >
< 286° M   3.41 NM
CRTBSE

87° M >
< 267° M   7.31 NM

N 27° 00'

VAR 7° W (1996)
WGS 1984

West End Rocks

116° M >
<296° M   12.6 NM

HKBLL

104° M >
< 284° M
to CTWRK >
Hawksbill Cays   5.43NM

Veteran Rock

VETRK   84° M >
< 264° M   4.21 NM

86° M >
< 266° M   18.6 NM

N 26° 55'

< to GTSAL

West End Point

NWPASN   8
7
5
West
End
Bars   5

NWPASS

mud bank
1-2

5-6

10

Cross Cays

4½

Moses Cay

Daniel Cay

Cashs Cay

Cave Cay

Fox Town

Crown Haven

Little Abaco Island

Patton Cays

Brush Cays

very shallow

very shallow   Spence Rock

Little Spence Rocks

N 26° 50'

0   1   2   3

Nautical Miles

For continuation see page 22

For continuation see page 37

CARTERS CAYS TO MORAINE CAY (including Fox Town)

Boats transiting this area from Carters Cays to Moraine Cay or beyond must avoid the Carters Cays Bank and also the shoals stretching southeast from the Fish Cays. Waypoints for a suggested route are shown on the chart, and coordinates are printed below.

The preferred route from the Carters Cays to the Fish Cays requires a detour to the south around the Carters Cay Bank, which extends about 7 nautical miles ESE from the Carters Cays. There are several islets and rocks along its northern edge—the Pawpaw Rocks, the Pawpaw Cays, and Grouper Rocks. It is possible to go on the Atlantic side of the bank, but access to Carters Cays is more difficult from this side, so the Sea of Abaco route is generally better. Anchorages can be found at the Fish Cays (for more detail see p. 34) and Moraine Cay (see page 36).

Boats transiting the southern portion of the chart are also provided with GPS waypoints. The suggested route passes south of Veteran Rock and West End Rocks, and north of the Hawksbill Cays. West End Rocks are generally plainly seen, but Veteran Rock is low-lying and difficult to see—we passed it several times going back and forth from Abaco to Florida before we saw it. Pay close attention and keep a sharp lookout when near it.

Along this route the only reasonable stop is Fox Town, which is on Little Abaco Island south of the Hawksbill Cays. See the large scale chart on page 35. Go west around the outermost rocks extending from Hawksbill Cays and proceed SE toward Fox Town. Avoid taking the western "short cut" when approaching or leaving Fox Town from the west because of several submerged rocks and heads in this area. Fuel, lodging, restaurants, and groceries were all available here, but Fox Town was badly damaged by hurricane Floyd. Fox Town Shell rebuilt and was fully operational during summer 2001. It is also possible to anchor just south of the Hawksbill Cays and dinghy over to Fox Town.

Note that approximate course lines are provided for the Cave Cay/Spence Rock route to the Bright of Abaco. Give West End Point a 4.5 mile berth (off chart to west) to round West End Bars, then head for the northern tip of Cave Cay. Keep a sharp lookout and negotiate on a rising tide if you draw more than 4½'; controlling depth for this part of the route is about 5-6' MLW. A shorter route from the north to the south side of Little Abaco Island was recently found a little less than one nautical mile west of West End Point. Called the NW Pass, it carries 5' MLW over a hard rock and coral bottom. The course is true north and south (7°M/187°M). Waypoints are provided for it; attention should be given to cross track error. The route around the east side of Cave Cay and south to Spence Rock and the deeper waters of the Bight of Abaco will carry only about 4' MLW.

GPS waypoints for *Carters Cays to Moraine Cay*:

WPT	Description of Position	Latitude	Longitude
Northern route, west to east:			
CARTER	1 NM SSW Carters Cays	N 27° 03.528'	W 78° 01.087'
CRTBSW	½ NM SW Carters Bank	N 27° 00.994'	W 78° 01.049'
CRTBSE	SE corner of Carters Bank	N 27° 00.440'	W 77° 57.277'
UPPER	¼ NM S Upper Cay	N 27° 01.683'	W 77° 49.210'
FISHSE	1 NM SE Fish Cays	N 27° 01.085'	W 77° 46.779'
MORAN	½ NM S Moraine Cay	N 27° 01.781'	W 77° 46.201'

Southern route, west to east (This is a portion of route from Florida to Abaco; for the entire route see page 14):

VETRK	½ NM S Veteran Rock	N 26° 55.950'	W 77° 52.290'
HKBLL	½ NM N Hawksbill Cays	N 26° 56.890'	W 77° 47.690'

NW Pass waypoints:

NWPASN	N end NW Pass	N 26° 53.900'	W 77° 58.150'
NWPASS	S end NW Pass	N 26° 52.830'	W 77° 58.150'

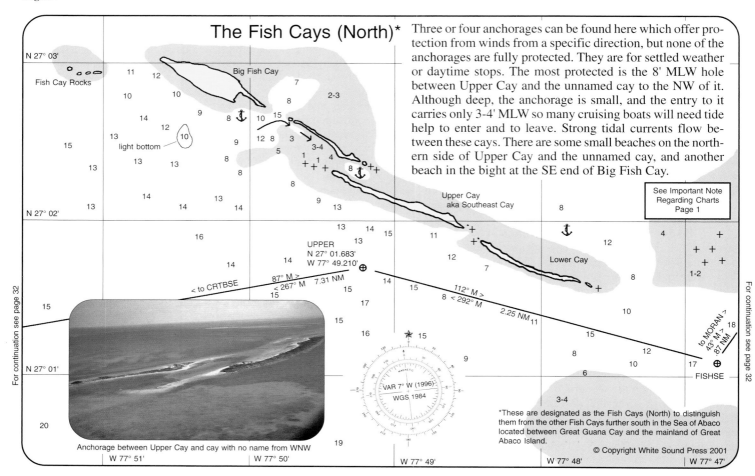

The Fish Cays (North)*

Three or four anchorages can be found here which offer protection from winds from a specific direction, but none of the anchorages are fully protected. They are for settled weather or daytime stops. The most protected is the 8' MLW hole between Upper Cay and the unnamed cay to the NW of it. Although deep, the anchorage is small, and the entry to it carries only 3-4' MLW so many cruising boats will need tide help to enter and to leave. Strong tidal currents flow between these cays. There are some small beaches on the northern side of Upper Cay and the unnamed cay, and another beach in the bight at the SE end of Big Fish Cay.

See Important Note Regarding Charts Page 1

N 27° 03'
Fish Cay Rocks
Big Fish Cay
light bottom
For continuation see page 32
For continuation see page 32
N 27° 02'
N 27° 01'
UPPER
N 27° 01.683'
W 77° 49.210'
< to CRTBSE
87° M >
< 267° M   7.31 NM
Upper Cay
aka Southeast Cay
Lower Cay
112° M >
< 292° M
2.25 NM
to MORAN >
43° M >
87 NM
FISHSE

VAR 7° W (1996)
WGS 1984

Anchorage between Upper Cay and cay with no name from WNW

*These are designated as the Fish Cays (North) to distinguish them from the other Fish Cays further south in the Sea of Abaco located between Great Guana Cay and the mainland of Great Abaco Island.

© Copyright White Sound Press 2001

W 77° 51'   W 77° 50'   W 77° 49'   W 77° 48'   W 77° 47'

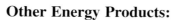

Hawksbill Cays and Fox Town

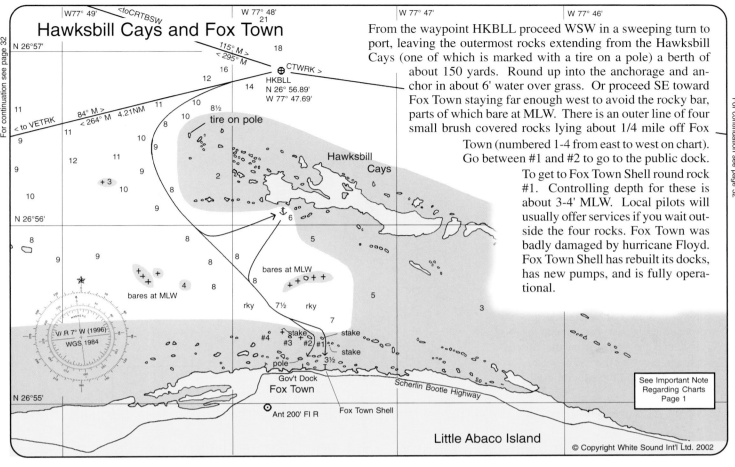

For continuation see page 32

For continuation see page 32

From the waypoint HKBLL proceed WSW in a sweeping turn to port, leaving the outermost rocks extending from the Hawksbill Cays (one of which is marked with a tire on a pole) a berth of about 150 yards. Round up into the anchorage and anchor in about 6' water over grass. Or proceed SE toward Fox Town staying far enough west to avoid the rocky bar, parts of which bare at MLW. There is an outer line of four small brush covered rocks lying about 1/4 mile off Fox Town (numbered 1-4 from east to west on chart). Go between #1 and #2 to go to the public dock.

To get to Fox Town Shell round rock #1. Controlling depth for these is about 3-4' MLW. Local pilots will usually offer services if you wait outside the four rocks. Fox Town was badly damaged by hurricane Floyd. Fox Town Shell has rebuilt its docks, has new pumps, and is fully operational.

See Important Note Regarding Charts Page 1

© Copyright White Sound Int'l Ltd. 2002

Fox Town

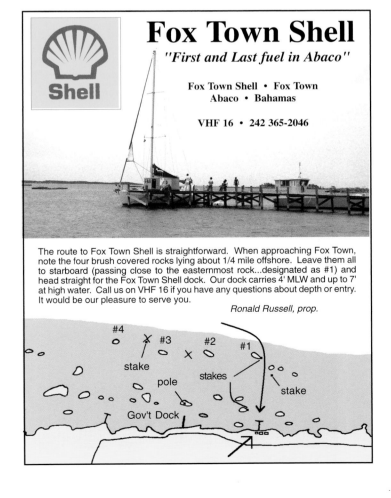

Moraine Cay

Proceed directly toward the midpoint of the beach on Moraine Cay from the waypoint MORAN and enter the anchorage in about 7-8' MLW. Anchor in about 6-7' MLW over grass. This reef protected anchorage offers protection from west, north, and east winds, but is fully exposed to the south. Moraine Cay is a delightful daytime or (good weather) overnight stop. The beach is just a few feet from the anchorage, and the reef to the east is pristine and beautiful. There are paths crisscrossing the cay which make exploration easier. The reef, which breaks in almost all weather, offers protection but does not impede the view, and the vistas from this anchorage give one the feeling of being anchored on the edge of civilization.

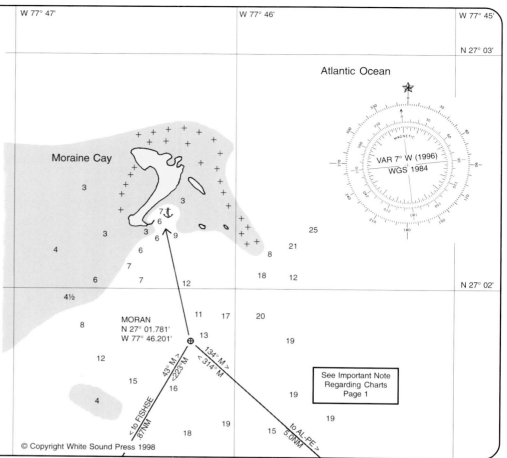

© Copyright White Sound Press 1998

For continuation see page 32 or page 37

A sailboat approaching the anchorage at Moraine Cay.

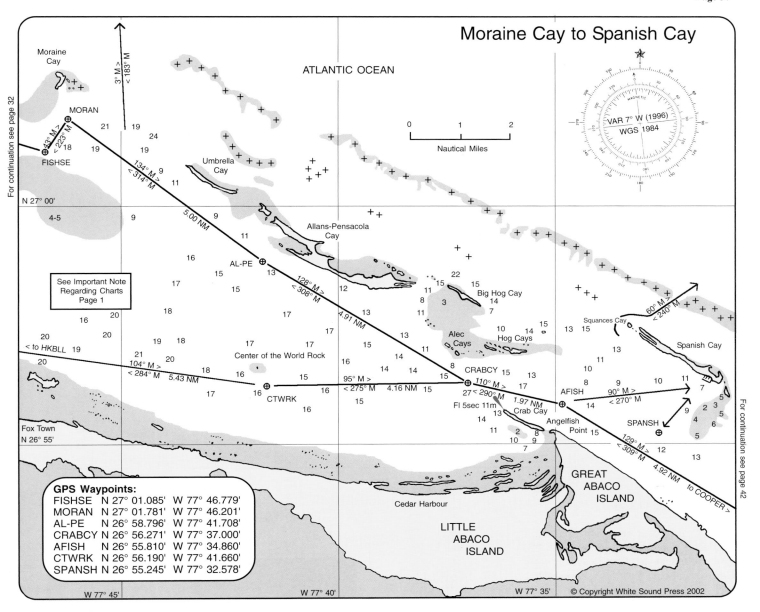

MORAINE CAY TO SPANISH CAY

Boats transiting this area need to avoid three shoal areas: the first is a very large area which extends southeastward from the area of the Fish Cays, which are off the chart west of Moraine Cay, and stretches to the south of Moraine Cay, the second surrounds the Hog Cays, and the third lies south of the southeast point of Spanish Cay. Also, the north coastline of Little Abaco Island is shoal and sprinkled with small, low islets. One should stay a mile or two off shore. Fox Town is the only settlement on Little Abaco Island which has an anchorage for boats drawing over 1-2'. Center of the World Rock, lying about two miles north of Little Abaco Island, is about halfway between Crab Cay and Foxtown. It is marked with a white post.

Moraine Cay is a beautiful reef anchorage exposed from the southeast to southwest, but offering good protection in other winds. It has a beautiful beach and the reef offers excellent snorkeling. See the chart on page 36.

Allans-Pensacola has an abandoned missile tracking station, some nice beaches, and a good harbour at its northwest end. See the chart on page 38.

The Hog Cays are a group of small cays and rocks on a shallow bank, but there is deep water and a reasonable anchorage off

the southwest corner of the southeasternmost cay. The very small harbour on the north side of this same cay has shoaled in recent years and is no longer useable by boats larger than outboards.

There is an anchorage protected from the east and south located west of Crab Cay. Round the northern end of the cay and go either side of a shoal area (2-5' MLW) running roughly parallel to Crab Cay. Anchor in 8' MLW just SW of the SE end of Crab Cay. There are no beaches and no development in this area, but plenty of small islets and shallow water for dinghy exploration.

Spanish Cay Marina was completely rebuilt after Floyd and is now fully operational. A new restaurant and marina store are expected to open in early 2003. See page 40 for more detailed information about Spanish Cay.

Support the Bahamas Air-Sea Rescue Association.

You are not required to take an active part in BASRA.

Send $25.00 for one year's membership dues to:
BASRA ABACO, Hope Town, Abaco, Bahamas

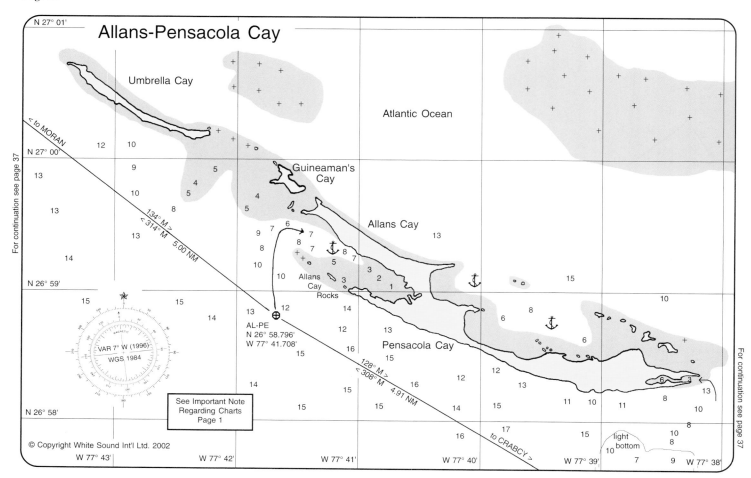

Allans-Pensacola Cay

Umbrella Cay

Atlantic Ocean

< to MORAN

134° M >
< 314° M   5.00 NM

Guineaman's Cay

Allans Cay

Allans Cay Rocks

VAR 7° W (1996)
WGS 1984

AL-PE
N 26° 58.796'
W 77° 41.708'

⊕

128° M >
< 308° M   4.91 NM

Pensacola Cay

to CRABCY >

light bottom

See Important Note
Regarding Charts
Page 1

© Copyright White Sound Int'l Ltd. 2002

N 27° 01'
N 27° 00'
N 26° 59'
N 26° 58'

W 77° 43'   W 77° 42'   W 77° 41'   W 77° 40'   W 77° 39'   W 77° 38'

For continuation see page 37

For continuation see page 37

Allans-Pensacola Cay

To enter the principal anchorage at Allans-Pensacola Cay proceed to the north from waypoint AL-PE toward Guineaman's Cay. Leave the northwesternmost Allans Cay Rock about 75 yards to starboard to avoid the submerged rocks and bar extending from it, and then turn to starboard into the harbour favouring the northeast side. Anchor in 7-8' over grass and sand which is over marl. The holding ground is not the best. Allans-Pensacola's popularity is based on the easy access and good protection in all winds except W and NW. For winds in this sector, shelter can be found on the Atlantic Ocean side of the cay (see anchorages indicated on chart), but these will be exposed and unsafe if or when the NW wind clocks to the N and NE as it usually does during the winter months.

Within the past few decades Allans Cay and Pensacola Cay were two separate cays. They were joined as the result of a hurricane, and now seem to be permanently a single cay—Allans-Pensacola. The ruins of a United States missile tracking station can be found on the isthmus at the head of the harbour, which is also the site of the best beach on the island. There is a "signing tree" on the ocean beach northeast of the anchorage, where cruisers have left signed momentos of their visit here.

There is complete protection in the very small mangrove-lined hurricane hole at the east end of the cay. Controlling depth in the small creek is about 3' MLW in several places (favour the south side)—there is 6' MLW inside.

Allans-Pensacola Cay

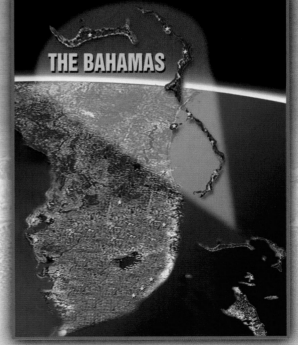

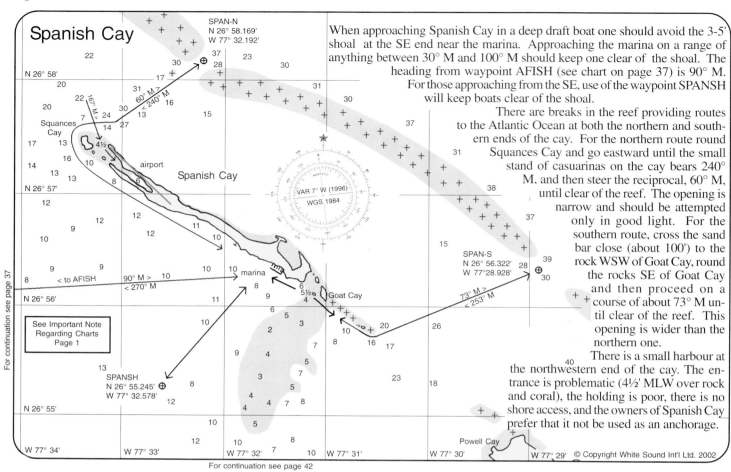

When approaching Spanish Cay in a deep draft boat one should avoid the 3-5' shoal at the SE end near the marina. Approaching the marina on a range of anything between 30° M and 100° M should keep one clear of the shoal. The heading from waypoint AFISH (see chart on page 37) is 90° M. For those approaching from the SE, use of the waypoint SPANSH will keep boats clear of the shoal.

There are breaks in the reef providing routes to the Atlantic Ocean at both the northern and southern ends of the cay. For the northern route round Squances Cay and go eastward until the small stand of casuarinas on the cay bears 240° M, and then steer the reciprocal, 60° M, until clear of the reef. The opening is narrow and should be attempted only in good light. For the southern route, cross the sand bar close (about 100') to the rock WSW of Goat Cay, round the rocks SE of Goat Cay and then proceed on a course of about 73° M until clear of the reef. This opening is wider than the northern one.

There is a small harbour at the northwestern end of the cay. The entrance is problematic (4½' MLW over rock and coral), the holding is poor, there is no shore access, and the owners of Spanish Cay prefer that it not be used as an anchorage.

For continuation see page 42

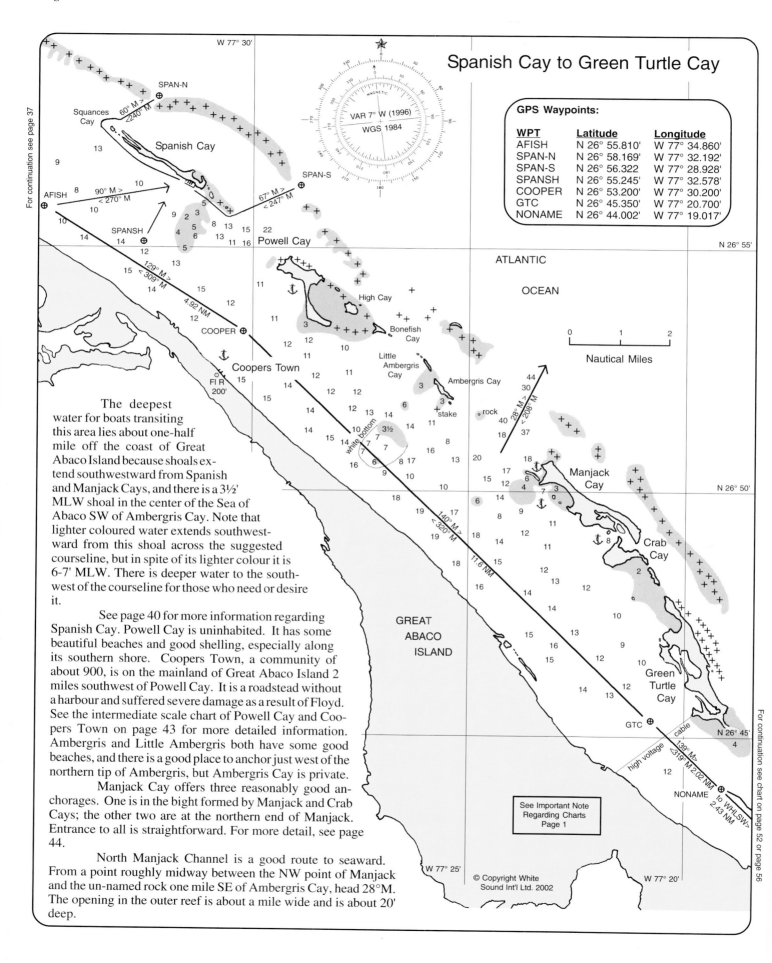

For continuation see page 37

Spanish Cay to Green Turtle Cay

W 77° 30'

SPAN-N

Squances Cay

Spanish Cay

60° M >
< 240° M

13

9

AFISH

8   90° M >
      < 270° M   10

10

SPANSH

14   14

12

SPAN-S

67° M >
< 247° M

9   2   3
5
4   8   13   15   22
13   11   16

Powell Cay

5

13
15
14

High Cay

11

11

Bonefish Cay

Little
Ambergris
Cay

Ambergris Cay

rock

stake

VAR 7° W (1996)

WGS 1984

GPS Waypoints:

WPT	Latitude	Longitude
AFISH	N 26° 55.810'	W 77° 34.860'
SPAN-N	N 26° 58.169'	W 77° 32.192'
SPAN-S	N 26° 56.322'	W 77° 28.928'
SPANSH	N 26° 55.245'	W 77° 32.578'
COOPER	N 26° 53.200'	W 77° 30.200'
GTC	N 26° 45.350'	W 77° 20.700'
NONAME	N 26° 44.002'	W 77° 19.017'

N 26° 55'

ATLANTIC

OCEAN

0   1   2

Nautical Miles

129° M >
< 309° M

4.92 NM

COOPER

Coopers Town

15

14

15

12

12

12

11

12
14

14   15

15

14   16

13   14

10
14   7   3½

7   7
16   6   9
8   17

44
30

40

18   37

28 M >
< 208 M

Manjack
Cay

8

11

13

20

18
17   6
15   12

10

6   14   7   3

9

11

12

Crab
Cay

8

2

Green
Turtle
Cay

4

N 26° 50'

FI R
200'

White bottom

15

19   17
19

18

15

16

14

15

12

12

11

10

13

12

10

14

13

12

9

140° M >
< 320° M

11.6 NM

18

The deepest water for boats transiting this area lies about one-half mile off the coast of Great Abaco Island because shoals extend southwestward from Spanish and Manjack Cays, and there is a 3½' MLW shoal in the center of the Sea of Abaco SW of Ambergris Cay. Note that lighter coloured water extends southwestward from this shoal across the suggested courseline, but in spite of its lighter colour it is 6-7' MLW. There is deeper water to the southwest of the courseline for those who need or desire it.

See page 40 for more information regarding Spanish Cay. Powell Cay is uninhabited. It has some beautiful beaches and good shelling, especially along its southern shore. Coopers Town, a community of about 900, is on the mainland of Great Abaco Island 2 miles southwest of Powell Cay. It is a roadstead without a harbour and suffered severe damage as a result of Floyd. See the intermediate scale chart of Powell Cay and Coopers Town on page 43 for more detailed information. Ambergris and Little Ambergris both have some good beaches, and there is a good place to anchor just west of the northern tip of Ambergris, but Ambergris Cay is private.

Manjack Cay offers three reasonably good anchorages. One is in the bight formed by Manjack and Crab Cays; the other two are at the northern end of Manjack. Entrance to all is straightforward. For more detail, see page 44.

North Manjack Channel is a good route to seaward. From a point roughly midway between the NW point of Manjack and the un-named rock one mile SE of Ambergris Cay, head 28°M. The opening in the outer reef is about a mile wide and is about 20' deep.

GREAT
ABACO
ISLAND

GTC

high voltage

cable

139° M >
< 319° M   2.02 NM

to WHLSW
2.43 NM

NONAME

12

See Important Note
Regarding Charts
Page 1

W 77° 25'

© Copyright White
Sound Int'l Ltd. 2002

W 77° 20'

N 26° 45'

For continuation see chart on page 52 or page 56

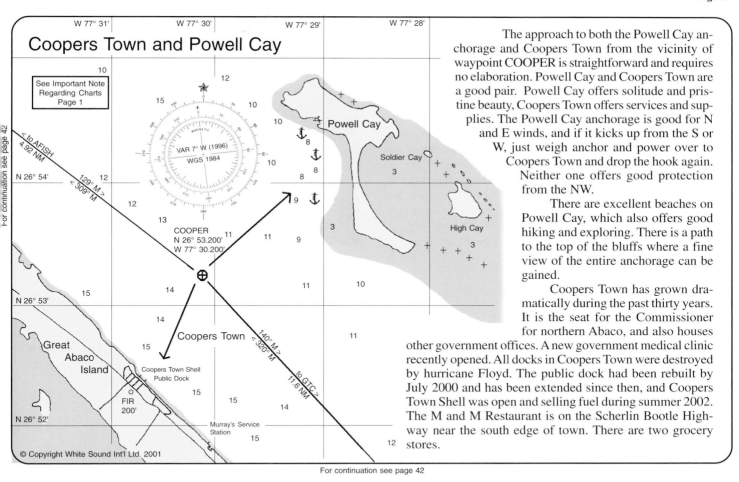

For continuation see page 42

Coopers Town and Powell Cay

See Important Note Regarding Charts Page 1

VAR 7° W (1996)
WGS 1984

COOPER
N 26° 53.200'
W 77° 30.200'

Powell Cay

Soldier Cay

High Cay

Great Abaco Island

Coopers Town

Coopers Town Shell Public Dock

FIR 200'

Murray's Service Station

< to AFISH 4.92 NM

to GTC 11.6 NM

© Copyright White Sound Int'l Ltd. 2001

For continuation see page 42

The approach to both the Powell Cay anchorage and Coopers Town from the vicinity of waypoint COOPER is straightforward and requires no elaboration. Powell Cay and Coopers Town are a good pair. Powell Cay offers solitude and pristine beauty, Coopers Town offers services and supplies. The Powell Cay anchorage is good for N and E winds, and if it kicks up from the S or W, just weigh anchor and power over to Coopers Town and drop the hook again. Neither one offers good protection from the NW.

There are excellent beaches on Powell Cay, which also offers good hiking and exploring. There is a path to the top of the bluffs where a fine view of the entire anchorage can be gained.

Coopers Town has grown dramatically during the past thirty years. It is the seat for the Commissioner for northern Abaco, and also houses other government offices. A new government medical clinic recently opened. All docks in Coopers Town were destroyed by hurricane Floyd. The public dock had been rebuilt by July 2000 and has been extended since then, and Coopers Town Shell was open and selling fuel during summer 2002. The M and M Restaurant is on the Scherlin Bootle Highway near the south edge of town. There are two grocery stores.

Coopers Town with Powell Cay and the reef in the background from the southwest.

Cooperstown Shell

Shell

- gasoline and diesel
- electricty and water
- 7' 9" at dock at low tide
- VHF 16

Coopers Town from the southeast.

Manjack and Crab Cays

The large bight formed by Manjack (pronounced Munjack or sometimes Nunjack) and Crab Cays provides a delightful anchorage, though it is not protected from the south through the west. Entry is straightforward. Vessels drawing more than 4' should not go east of Rat Cay. The mangrove creek is shallow, but is easily explored by dinghy at high tide. There is one home on Manjack Cay; it is serviced by the private dock on the north side of the Manjack/Crab anchorage. The beach along the northeast side of Manjack is pretty and there is some good diving and snorkeling just offshore. The two anchorages at the NW end of Manjack are both attractive. The northernmost one is open to the northwest and north, and the other is open to the west and southwest. A shallow rocky bar extends NW from the rocks at the SE side of

Several boats in the anchorage at Manjack and Crab Cays. This photo was taken from the SE. Generally boats drawing more than four feet should not go east of Rat Cay.

the entrance to the latter, so stay close to the NW side. The dock on the north side is part of a land development in which there are roads which lead to a very beautiful beach along the north shore of Manjack Cay. There is also a park in a mangrove swamp area and a nature walk. Visitors are welcome.

For continuation see page 42

N 26° 50'

scattered heads
(not surveyed)

Manjack Rocks

Manjack Beach

SEA

OF

ABACO

ATLANTIC

OCEAN

N 26° 50'

scattered heads
(not surveyed)

Manjack Cay

Coconut Tree Bay

Manjack Bluff

Manjack Cay

Rat Cay

Manjack Harbour
(shallow)

Manjack Cay

N 26° 49'

Crab Cay Bluff

Crab Cay

Fiddle Cay

VAR 7° W (1996)
WGS 1984
MAGNETIC

See Important Note
Regarding Charts
Page 1

© Copyright White Sound Int'l Ltd. 2002

W 77° 24'

W 77° 23'

W 77° 22'

W 77° 21'

N 26° 48'

For continuation see page 42

The anchorage at the north end of Manjack Cay offers good protection for everything except northwest and north winds. Its beach is spectacular.

This is the limestone rock bluff near the southwest extremity of Crab Cay, and is typical of the limestone base of the Bahamian islands. The Bahama Banks were built of calcium carbonate over a period of 200 million years; they

now tower about 1 1/2 miles above the floor of the sea. The calcium carbonate was extracted from the sea in a variety of ways, including the growth and death of shell fish, the growth of coral reefs, and the creation of oolitic sand. The present islands were built up higher than the rest of the banks when sea level was up to 100' higher than it is today. When the earth cooled and the polar ice caps re-formed, sea level declined leaving the limestone islands. Limestone is a soft rock which has been carved by the waves of the sea at the periphery of the islands and cays, dissolved by rainfall, and weathered by winds.

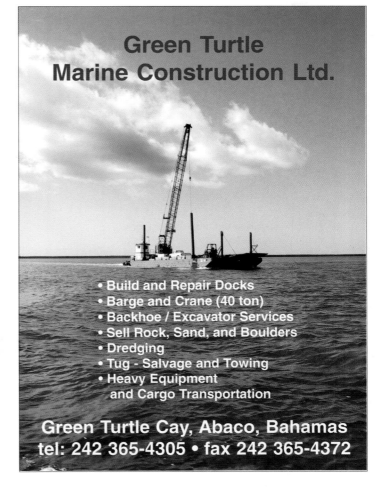

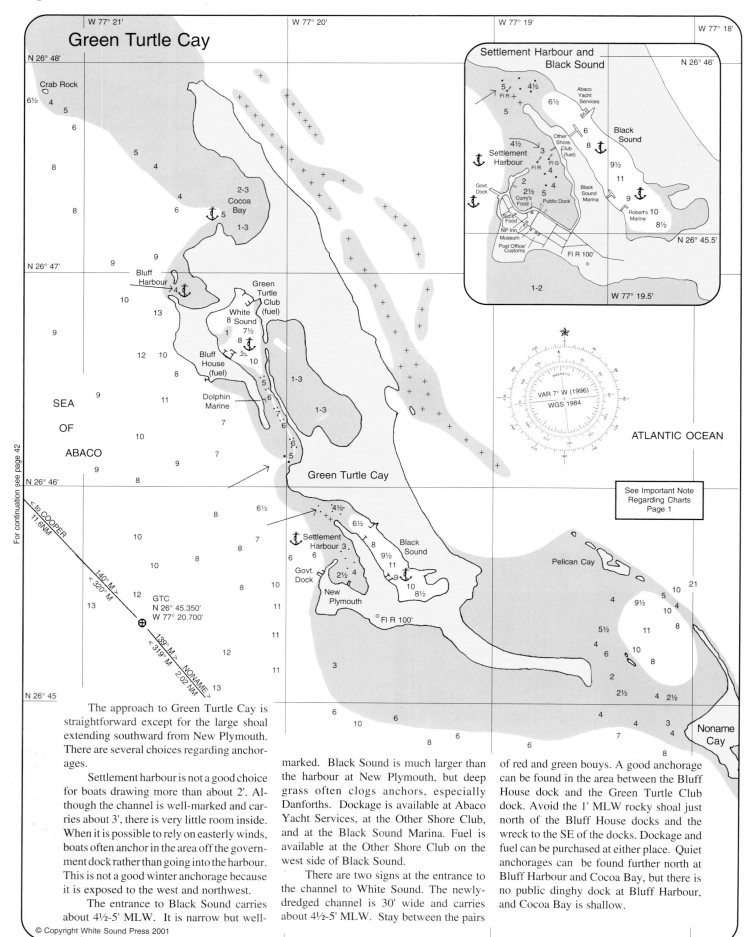

Green Turtle Cay

Settlement Harbour and Black Sound

SEA
OF
ABACO

ATLANTIC OCEAN

See Important Note
Regarding Charts
Page 1

VAR 7° W (1996)
WGS 1984

GTC
N 26° 45.350'
W 77° 20.700'

Green Turtle Cay

Pelican Cay

Noname Cay

For continuation see page 42

The approach to Green Turtle Cay is straightforward except for the large shoal extending southward from New Plymouth. There are several choices regarding anchorages.

Settlement harbour is not a good choice for boats drawing more than about 2'. Although the channel is well-marked and carries about 3', there is very little room inside. When it is possible to rely on easterly winds, boats often anchor in the area off the government dock rather than going into the harbour. This is not a good winter anchorage because it is exposed to the west and northwest.

The entrance to Black Sound carries about 4½-5' MLW. It is narrow but well-

marked. Black Sound is much larger than the harbour at New Plymouth, but deep grass often clogs anchors, especially Danforths. Dockage is available at Abaco Yacht Services, at the Other Shore Club, and at the Black Sound Marina. Fuel is available at the Other Shore Club on the west side of Black Sound.

There are two signs at the entrance to the channel to White Sound. The newly-dredged channel is 30' wide and carries about 4½-5' MLW. Stay between the pairs

of red and green bouys. A good anchorage can be found in the area between the Bluff House dock and the Green Turtle Club dock. Avoid the 1' MLW rocky shoal just north of the Bluff House docks and the wreck to the SE of the docks. Dockage and fuel can be purchased at either place. Quiet anchorages can be found further north at Bluff Harbour and Cocoa Bay, but there is no public dinghy dock at Bluff Harbour, and Cocoa Bay is shallow.

Entrance to White Sound, Green Turtle Cay

Approach from the SW. Head to the left of the beach.

Go between the signs.

Turn to the NNW following the green and red buoys.

Continue approx. NNW for about .5 NM and enter the anchorage.

Aerial of entrance to White Sound, Green Turtle Cay, 11 July 2002.

Approaches to Settlement Harbour, New Plymouth, Black Sound, and White Sound, Green Turtle Cay.

Entrance to Black Sound, Green Turtle Cay

Approach from WSW; note that the deep water channel is on the north (port side when entering) side of the opening. A rocky shoal extends across the rest of the opening.

Pilings with red and green arrows mark the channel, which turns to the SE (starboard when entering).

Turn to starboard (marked by pilings with arrows) and enter Black Sound. Abaco Yacht Services is to port, the Other Shore Club and Black Sound Marina to starboard.

NEW PLYMOUTH AND GREEN TURTLE CAY

Green Turtle Cay is a small island with a population of about 450, but it offers visiting yachtsmen exceptional variety with several different anchorages, and an excellent array of restaurants, hotels, marine services, and shopping facilities. Restaurants in New Plymouth include the New Plymouth Inn, the Plymouth Rock, Laura's Kitchen, the McIntosh Restaurant and Bakery, and the Wreckin' Tree Bakery and Restaurant. At White Sound the Green Turtle Club and Bluff House both offer excellent dining. See the business directory on pages 150-151 for a complete list.

Hotels include the Bluff House and the Green Turtle Club at White Sound, and the New Plymouth Inn, which is located in the center of town. There are also cottages and houses for rent.

Complete boatyard services are available at Abaco Yacht Services on Black Sound, which has a large Travelift. Marine fuel is available at the Other Shore Club, the Green Turtle Club, and the Bluff House. Abaco Yacht Services is a Yamaha dealer; Dolphin Marine is an OMC distributor and an Evinrude/Johnson dealer which maintains a large inventory of parts. Roberts Marine is an Evinrude/Johnson dealer located on Black Sound.

There are three grocery stores—Sid's, Lowe's, and Curry's—and two hardware stores—Roberts Hardware and New Plymouth Hardware. There are several gift shops in town.

The Albert Lowe Museum houses artifacts and photographs which tell the story of the history of New Plymouth and of Abaco. It has ship's models built by the late Albert Lowe, and paintings by Albert's talented and well-known artist son, New Plymouth native Alton Lowe. The Memorial Sculpture Garden features bronze busts of persons who have played important roles in Bahamian history, and a centerpiece sculpture depicting the arrival of loyalists from the United States. Also, there is a gallery with paintings on display in a section of Alton Lowe's hilltop home, which is located east of New Plymouth.

Green Turtle Cay is small enough so that one can cover a good part of the island on foot, but bicycles can be rented. See the business directory for Green Turtle Cay on pages 150-151 for those who currently rent bicycles.

New Plymouth from the northwest. Photo by Steve Dodge

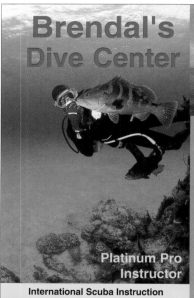

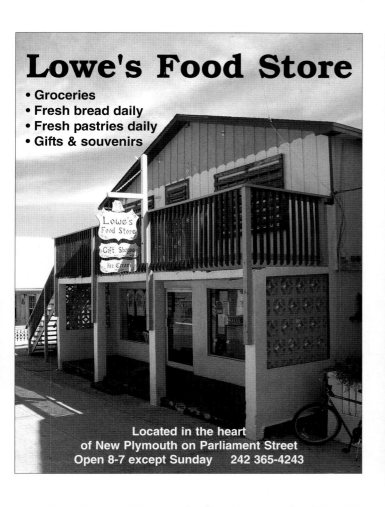

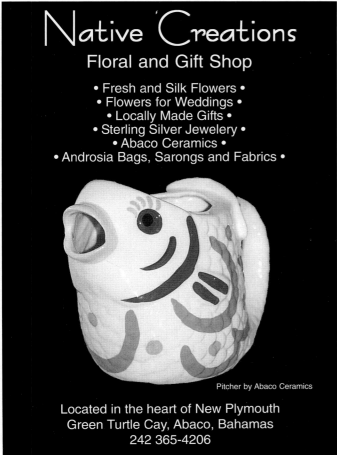

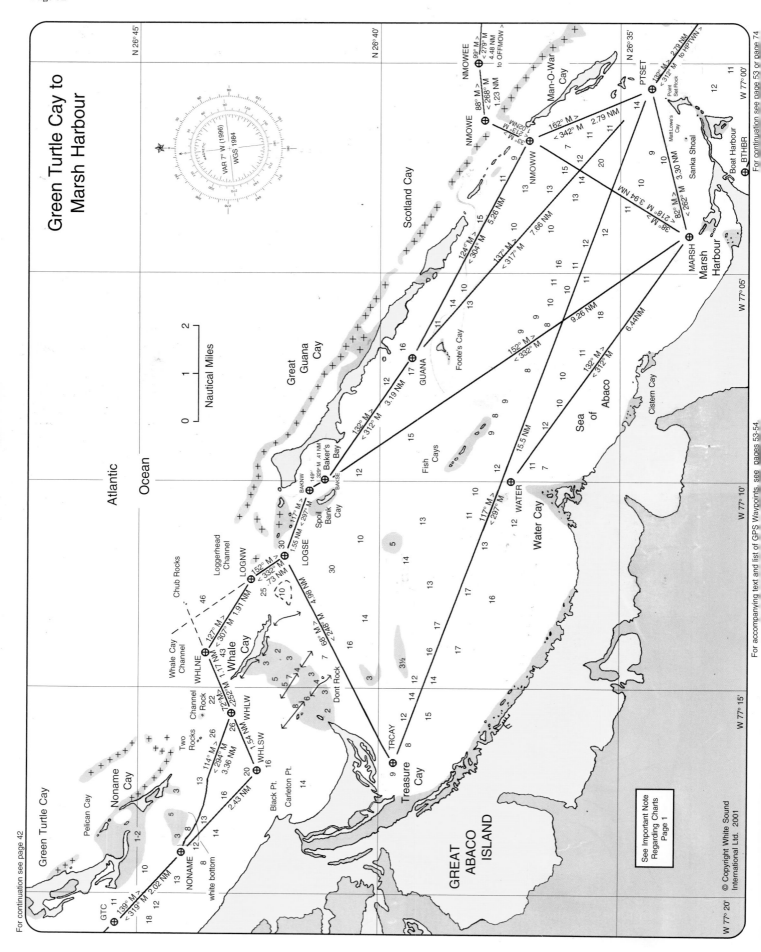

Green Turtle Cay to Marsh Harbour

Atlantic Ocean

Nautical Miles
0   1   2

VAR 7° W (1996)
WGS 1984

For continuation see page 42

For continuation see page 53 or page 74

For accompanying text and list of GPS Waypoints, see pages 53-54.

See Important Note
Regarding Charts
Page 1

GREAT ABACO ISLAND

For continuation see page 116 or page 119

Marsh Harbour to Little Harbour

(nautical chart showing the area from Marsh Harbour to Little Harbour, with labeled cays including Johnny's Cay, Hope Town, Elbow Cay, White Sound, Tilloo Cay, Pelican Cays, North Bar Channel, Lynyard Cay, Little Harbour, Witch Point, Snake Cay, Cornish Cay, Lubbers Quarters Cay, Boat Harbour, Marsh Harbour, and numerous course lines with bearings and distances)

Nautical Miles

See Important Note Regarding Charts Page 1

VAR 7° W (1996)
WGS 1984

© Copyright White Sound Int'l Ltd. 2002

N 26° 30'   N 26° 25'   N 26° 20'

W 77° 03'   W 76° 58'

GREEN TURTLE CAY TO MARSH HARBOUR

The area from Green Turtle Cay to Marsh Harbour is probably the most popular cruising area in Abaco—perhaps the most popular in the entire Bahamas. It is about 20 miles long and about 5 miles wide and offers the cruiser incredible variety—snug harbours, beautiful beaches, good diving, excellent restaurants, quaint villages, ocean cruising, fancy marinas, good anchorages, fancy marinas, and good shopping. All continuous suggested course lines on the chart carry at least 6' MLW.

Boats drawing more than about 4' transiting the area must avoid the shallow bank extending from Treasure Cay (which is actually located on the mainland of Great Abaco Island) to Whale Cay. The prefered route in moderate weather is outside Whale Cay. The inside routes (shown as discontinuous lines) are deeper this year than last and now carry about 3-4' MLW. For more detailed information regarding Whale Cay passage, see pages 56-57.

After re-entering the Sea of Abaco there are shoals extending from Spoil Bank Cay, created when a cruise ship channel was dredged at Baker's Bay at the north end of Great Guana Cay in 1989. There are some additional small shoals between this cay and Treasure Cay. There are no other major obstacles to navigation in the area.

There is a daytime anchorage at No Name Cay, which is uninhabited. Head for a point near the northern end of the cay on a heading of about 40 degrees to avoid the bars extending SE from Green Turtle Cay and W from the SE end of No Name Cay. When about 1/4 mile offshore, turn to starboard and anchor off the entrance to the island's lagoon. A shallow rocky bar at the entrance of the lagoon bares at low water—so exploration is by dinghy only at half tide or better.

There is another daytime anchorage to the west of the north tip of Whale Cay, which is also uninhabited. Like the anchorage at No Name Cay, it is exposed from the S to the NW.

Treasure Cay is a resort community. It has a marina, condominiums, privately owned villas and homes, stores, various services, and

continued on page 54

MARSH HARBOUR TO LITTLE HARBOUR

The Sea of Abaco narrows at its southern end, but continues to offer great variety for the visitor. Two of Abaco's principal communities—Marsh Harbour and Hope Town—are at the northern perimeter of this area, which also has beautiful beaches, Pelican Cays Land and Sea Park, and three viable passages between the Sea of Abaco and the Atlantic Ocean. At its southern perimeter is Little Harbour, home of the art community founded by the late Randolph Johnston and now maintained by his son Pete.

There are several shoals in the area. The largest are Lubbers Bank, which extends about 2½ miles NW of Lubbers Quarters Cay, and Tilloo Bank, which extends 1½ to 2 miles W from Tilloo Cay. Also, most of the area west of Channel, Gorling, Sandy, and Cornish Cays is shallow. All suggested course lines on this chart carry about 6' MLW, with the exception of the course through Lubber's Quarters Channel, which carries about 5½', a 5½' bump on the route between White Sound and Boat Harbour, the approach to Hope Town Harbour which has several 5-5½' bumps, and the entrance to Little Harbour, which carries only 3½'.

Boat Harbour is one of the largest and finest marinas in The Bahamas. It offers complete marina services. For more information see pp. 94-97.

Hope Town has a fully protected harbour. There are two marinas, one of which has fuel service. For more information, see pages 98-104.

White Sound has two restaurants and one full-service marina (including fuel) with easy access to the ocean beach. There is no room to anchor in the dredged channels in White Sound, but there is a fair weather anchorage just outside. For more information, see pages 106-109.

Lubbers Quarters Channel carries about 5½' MLW and requires careful piloting to avoid the shallow grassy shoals on each side of the suggested course lines. Tilloo Cut carries about 5½' MLW and is usually a viable passage to the Atlantic Ocean. There are some good fair weather anchorages in the area. For more detail, see pages 110-112.

There is a popular summer anchorage just north of Tilloo Bank and close to Tilloo Cay. Boats drawing more than about 2' need to go west of Tilloo Bank. See pages 114-115 for a detailed description

continued on page 54

Green Turtle Cay to Marsh Harbour, continued from page 53

one of the most beautiful beaches in the world. Transient boats are welcome at the marina, or may pick up a mooring or anchor in the fully protected basin on the way to the marina. For more information, see page 58.

Great Guana Cay also has one of the most beautiful beaches in the world. It is long, wide, and sparsely developed. A favorite anchorage at Guana Cay is Baker's Bay. It was developed as "Treasure Island" for cruise ship visitors, but the "Big Red Boat" stopped visiting in 1993. There is less activity now--and more serenity. Great Guana Cay has two more viable anchorages. Settlement harbour offers excellent protection from the prevailing easterlies, but is exposed from the S through the W. Orchid Bay Marina, located on the south side of Settlement Harbour near the entrance, has a breakwater and offers good protection at new docks. Fisher's Bay, the harbour immediately north of the settlement, offers better protection from the SW, but is exposed to the NW. A dock for dinghies at the head of this harbour is maintained by Guana Beach Resort. A dock on the north shore services Dolphin Beach Resort and the new Blue Water Grill as well as a new dive shop which maintains moorings for transients in Fisher's Bay and Settlement Harbour. For more information, see pages 62-67.

The Man-O-War, Marsh Harbour-Hope Town area forms the Hub of Abaco. For a larger scale chart of the area and some more detailed information, see pages 74-75.

The harbour at Man-O-War Cay offers complete protection, and Man-O-War Marina has slips for transients. Complete repair and maintenance services are available from Edwin's Boat Yard, which has a sail loft as well. There are two grocery stores, and several clothing and gift shops. The harbour is a busy place, and it can sometimes be difficult to find swinging room. For more information, see pages 68-72.

Marsh Harbour is the largest protected deep water anchorage in Abaco. It is the third largest city in The Bahamas, and is growing rapidly. It has five banks, numerous restaurants, and a wide variety of stores. For more information see pages 76-93.

Waypoints: *Green Turtle Cay to Marsh Harbour* (generally north to south):

WPT	Description of Position	Latitude	Longitutde
GTC	west of Green Turtle Cay	N 26° 45.350'	W 77° 20.700'
NONAME	1 NM WSW Noname Cay	N 26° 44.002'	W 77° 19.017'
WHLSW	Whale Cay Channel SW end	N 26° 42.380'	W 77° 17.000'
WHLW	W of N tip Whale Cay	N 26° 43.009'	W 77° 15.426'
WHLNE	Whale Cay Channel NE end	N 26° 43.510'	W 77° 14.250'
LOGNW	Loggerhead Channel NW end	N 26° 42.560'	W 77° 12.400'
LOGSE	Loggerhead Channel SE end	N 26° 41.960'	W 77° 11.930'
TRCAY	near entrance Treasure Cay	N 26° 39.570'	W 77° 16.800'
BAKNW	northwest side Baker's Bay	N 26° 41.430'	W 77° 10.300'
BAKSE	southeast side Baker's Bay	N 26° 41.110'	W 77° 10.020'
GUANA	SW Guana Cay settlement	N 26° 39.310'	W 77° 07.080'
WATER	½ NM N Water Cay	N 26° 37.200'	W 77° 10.000'
NMOWW	Abaco Sd. end NMOW Chan.	N 26° 36.900'	W 77° 01.860'
NMOWE	Atlantic end NMOW Chan.	N 26° 37.820'	W 77° 01.360'
NMOWEE	1¼ NM E of NMOWE	N 26° 38.000'	W 77° 00.000'
PTSET	¼ mile NE Point Set Rock	N 26° 34.370'	W 77° 00.550'
MARSH	near entrance Marsh Harbour	N 26° 33.520'	W 77° 04.110'
BTHBR	near entrance Boat Harbour	N 26° 32.410'	W 77° 02.550'

Marsh Harbour to Little Harbour, continued from page 53

of the Middle Passage through Tilloo Bank as well as the entire region of the Pelican Cays Land and Sea Park, where there are moorings for daytime use by small boats (under 25') and a daytime anchorage in Pelican Harbour NW of the reef. North Bar Channel is the best passage to the Atlantic in this area. See pages 114-115.

Boats proceeding south to Little Harbour should stay about 1/3 mile off the coast of Great Abaco Island in order to avoid shoals extending W from Lynyard Cay. The entrance to Little Harbour carries only about 3½' MLW, and boats drawing more will need tide help. It is possible to anchor west of Tom Curry's Point in the Bight of Old Robinson or in the lee of the point on which the old lighthouse is located to wait for the tide. For more information, see pages 116-117.

Waypoints: *Marsh Harbour to Little Harbour* (generally north to south):

WPT	Description of Position	Latitude	Longitutde
PTSET	1/4 mile NE Point Set Rock	N 26° 34.370'	W 77° 00.550'
MARSH	Near entrance to Marsh Hrbr	N 26° 33.520'	W 77° 04.110'
HPTWN	Near entrance to Hope Town	N 26° 32.608'	W 76° 58.063'
WSMK	Near entrance White Sound	N 26° 31.130'	W 76° 58.870'
BTHBR	Near entrance to Boat Hrbr	N 26° 32.410'	W 77° 02.550'
LQN	N end Lubbers Quarters Chan	N 26° 30.330'	W 76° 59.110'
LQMID	Mid Lubbers Quarters Chan	N 26° 29.990'	W 76° 59.460'
LQS	S end Lubbers Quarters Chan	N 26° 29.100'	W 76° 59.720'
WITCHN	N of Witch Point	N 26° 30.630'	W 77° 02.550'
WITCHE	E of Witch Point	N 26° 29.550'	W 77° 01.550'
MIDNW	Middle Channel NW end	N 26° 25.830'	W 77° 01.010'
MIDSE	Middle Channel SE end	N 26° 25.280'	W 77° 00.090'
TBANK	SW of end of Tilloo Bank	N 26° 25.160'	W 77° 01.220'
PELICY	SW of the N Pelican Cay	N 26° 25.150'	W 76° 59.290'
SANDY	SE of Sandy Cay	N 26° 23.590'	W 76° 59.090'
NBAR	Atlantic End North Bar Chan	N 26° 23.410'	W 76° 58.470'
PELIPT	NE Pelican Point	N 26° 23.110'	W 76° 59.730'
LTHBW	Abaco Sd. end Little Hrbr Chan	N 26° 20.470'	W 76° 59.660'
LTHBE	Atlantic end Little Hrbr Chan	N 26° 19.900'	W 76° 59.390'

The road leading to Man-O-War Marina in the late afternoon.

Dont Rock (shown above from south) is located between the entrance to Treasure Cay and Loggerhead Channel on the southern edge of the sand bank which extends from Treasure Cay to Whale Cay. Wave action has eroded the rock at water level on all sides, and at low tide it looks like a huge mushroom. It serves as the southern landmark for the "Dont Rock Passage," which carries about 4' MLW. The Sand Bank Cays serve as the northern landmark for this route. There is good snorkeling around the rock.

The most famous landmark in Abaco is the Elbow Reef Lighthouse located in Hope Town. Built in 1863 by the British Imperial Lighthouse Service, its huge fresnel lens magnifies the light from a kerosene mantle and its five flashes every fifteen seconds are visible for about twenty miles.

Whale Cay Channel, Loggerhead Channel, the Dont Rock and inside Whale Cay Passages

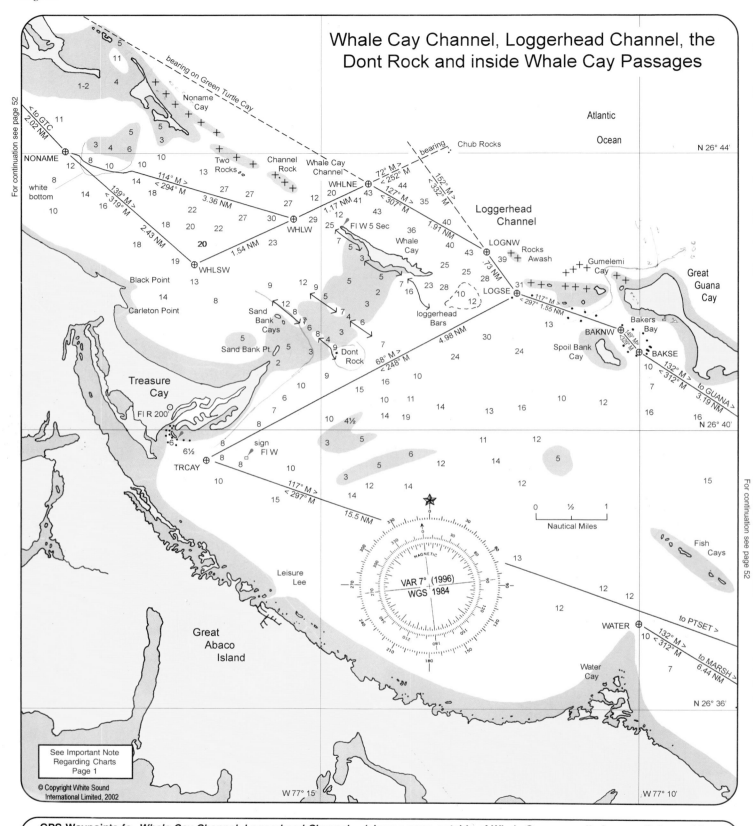

© Copyright White Sound
International Limited, 2002

GPS Waypoints fo *Whale Cay Channel, Loggerhead Channel, ..* **(along course outside of Whale Cay, generally from north to south):**

NONAME	1 NM WSW No Name Cay	N 26° 44.002'	W 77° 19.017'
WHLSW	southwest (Abaco Sound) end of Whale Cay Channel	N 26° 42.380'	W 77° 17.000'
WHLW	west of north tip of Whale Cay	N 26° 43.009'	W 77° 15.426'
WHLNE	northeast (Atlantic Ocean) end of Whale Cay Channel	N 26° 43.510'	W 77° 14.250'
LOGNW	northwest (Atlantic Ocean) end of Loggerhead Channel	N 26° 42.560'	W 77° 12.400'
LOGSE	southeast (Abaco Sound) end of Loggerhead Channel	N 26° 41.960'	W 77° 11.930'
BAKNW	northwest side of Baker's Bay; middle dredged channel	N 26° 41.430'	W 77° 10.300'
BAKSE	southeast side of dredged basin at Baker's Bay	N 26° 41.110'	W 77° 10.020'
TRCAY	southeast of entrance to Treasure Cay	N 26° 39.570'	W 77° 16.800'
WATER	½ NM N Water Cay	N 26° 37.200'	W 77° 10.000'

WHALE CAY CHANNEL, LOGGERHEAD CHANNEL, THE DONT ROCK AND INSIDE WHALE CAY PASSAGES

The Whale Cay area is clearly the most difficult and treacherous part of the Abacos. Certain weather conditions may make it impossible to traverse the area for several days, though at other times transit can be easily accomplished in one hour even in a slow boat.

The difficulties are the result of the fact that a shallow bank extends all the way from Whale Cay to "Treasure Cay" on the mainland of Great Abaco Island, and the passage across it is difficult for vessels drawing more than about 3-4'. This makes it necessary for most cruising boats to pass outside Whale Cay. Although both Loggerhead Channel (southeast of Whale Cay) and the Whale Cay Channel (northwest of Whale Cay) are wide, the Whale Cay Channel, especially, is fairly shallow (about 12') and is susceptible to a rage sea condition (breaking waves all the way across) when ocean swells come from the northeast. This most often occurs during a strong northeaster, but can also be the result of storms hundreds of miles away, which can cause a rage during deceptively sunny and light wind days in Abaco.

The single greatest problem is deciding whether or not the Whale Cay and Loggerhead Channels are passable. Of the two, the Whale Cay Channel is the most critical. Boats contemplating the passage often consult with one another in the morning on the VHF, so it is often possible to get information about conditions just by listening, or by calling "any boat in the Whale Cay area." The cruiser's net, which airs each morning at 8:15 am on VHF 68, usually reports conditions at Whale Cay. Also, Mr. Everette Roberts, Manager of Abaco Yacht Services at Black Sound, has agreed to provide advice regarding conditions in Whale Cay Channel to cruising boats. Stop in to consult with him at Black Sound, Green Turtle Cay, and inspect his boatyard/marina operation.

If conditions are appropriate for going around Whale Cay, follow the course lines on the chart. Coming from waypoint GTC (about 1 mile west of New Plymouth Harbour), head toward the Sand Bank Cays and Dont Rock on a heading of about 139° M. At the waypoint NONAME you may continue on 139° M to WHLSW and then turn to WHLW, or change course to head for just below the northern tip of Whale Cay on a course of 114° M and go directly to WHLW. This will keep you clear of the shoal extending SW from No Name Cay but rather close to it, so watch your cross track error and alter course to the SW if the water becomes shallow. Note the suggested courseline. This "shortcut" saves .61 NM. When you reach the waypoint WHLW Chubb Rocks (white water) bears 72° M. Turn (or continue) to head for them. This course will take you

through Whale Cay Channel approximately halfway between Channel Rock and the NW point of Whale Cay in 12'-14' water. When Green Turtle Cay bears 307° M, you will have reached the next waypoint, WHLNE. Turn to put Green Turtle Cay on your stern and assume the reciprocal heading, 127°M. You will be heading toward Gumelemi Cay, which will be difficult to distinguish from Great Guana Cay, which lies immediately behind Gumelemi. Hold this course until you are about 1/4-1/3 mile beyond the point at which the SE tip of Whale Cay is abeam (Chubb Rocks should be off the port quarter), and then, at LOGNW, turn to starboard and head toward the two piles which form a range for the course in through Loggerhead Channel. Take care not to go too far SE before making this turn—be wary of Rocks Awash! Your heading should be 152°M, and you should be headed toward a point just to the north of the Fish Cays, which appear as 4-5 lumps on the horizon SE of the land mass of Great Abaco Island. You should pass a single pile marking the SW side of the cruise ship channel. Continue to the next turning point, LOGSE, which is marked with buoys, and change course to 117°M, proceeding toward Baker's Bay (waypoint BAKNW) with the low spoil bank cays off the starboard bow. The cruise ship channel is well marked here, with several successive sets of buoys or piles (some are missing). Premier Cruise Lines discontinued use of this channel in 1993, so there should be no cruise ship traffic in the area. GPS waypoints are provided for all turning points on the route around Whale Cay. Use the reciprocal headings when going from SE to NW.

The inside passages are not necessarily viable alternatives to the outside passage on rough days, because high wind conditions usually make the inside passages impassable also. Neither one is straightforward because of shifting sand, and they should be negotiated only when visability is good on a rising tide. The Dont Rock passage had silted in during the 1990s, but has become deeper during the past three years. In July 2002 it again carried about 3-4' MLW.

The passage along the southwest shoreline of Whale Cay carries about 3' MLW, and therefore 5-6' at high tide. To go from south to north stay about 100 yards off the shore near the division line between the light and the dark water, passing close to the small rocky point, which is southeast of the mid-point of Whale Cay. Give a wider berth to the next point, a sandy one (about 200-250 yards), and then turn back toward Whale Cay to avoid a very shallow bar to the west. Proceed northwestward past the northern tip of Whale Cay, which has a small navigation light on a pole. Watch for shoals, and be prepared to alter course to avoid them. This inside route is generally recommended only for vessels drawing less than 3-4'.

Whale Cay from the northeast with Sand Banks and Treasure Cay beyond. Loggerhead Channel is on the left in this photo, and Whale Cay Channel to the right. Par of the channel inside Cay between Wh Sand Banks photo—r wate

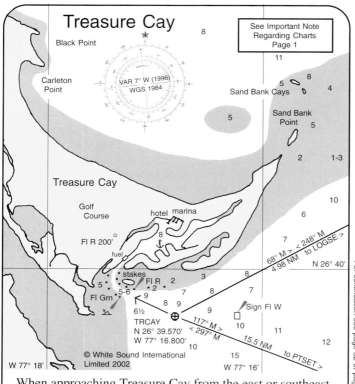

When approaching Treasure Cay from the east or southeast, head for the low part of Great Abaco Island . There is a radio tower near this point. From Man-O-War Cay the heading should be 290° M. Pass the sign, head for the stakes, and then go between them through the entrance channel. Make a sweeping turn to starboard. Controlling depth is abour 6' MLW. Dockage is available at the marina (150 slips). Moorings are available in the basin to starboard on the way in, or anchor there. Register for either at the Marina Office. Fuel is available at the fuel dock on the port side of the main entrance channel.

For continuation see page 52 or page 56

Treasure Cay

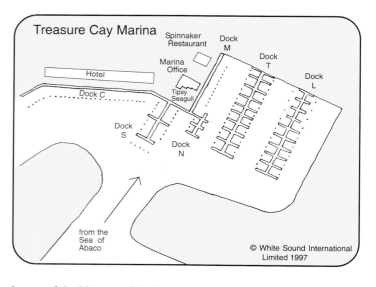

TREASURE CAY

Treasure Cay started as a hotel/marina development and has grown into a medium-sized vacation community. The main attraction at Treasure Cay is its beach, which is surely one of the loveliest in the world—it extends for about 3 miles in a beautiful semi-circle. There are sailboats and windsurfers for rent. The marina is full service and a marine store has supplies for boats as well as clothing items. There is a grocery store, a doctor's office, a bank, a hardware store, and even a marine upholstery shop. Abaco Ceramics, located on the entrance road, is a special attraction for shoppers. There are villas, private homes, and condominiums for rent.

The Tipsy Seagull bar at the marina, located adjacent to the swimming pool, offers drinks and snacks. The hotel, which is located west of the marina, has 64 rooms and 32 suites, all of which have recently been refurbished. Eighteen of the rooms and 11 of the suites are "deluxe." The Spinnaker Restaurant is conveniently located north of the marina office. Treasure Cay also has an 18-hole golf course and several tennis courts.

Walking the beach is pleasant, and those who want a good bit of exercise can walk all the way to the northern end and through to a path leading to the rocky point extending northeast This point was named Carleton Point in 1983 in

honor of the bicentennial of the arrival of the first loyalists settlers in Abaco. They left New York and the United States because they opposed independence; they travelled to Carleton to found a new British colony which they believed would prosper because it would gain the British trade which the new United States would lose. The settlement lasted only a few years. A bronze plaque cemented in the rocks at Carleton Point commemorates this first settlement in Abaco.

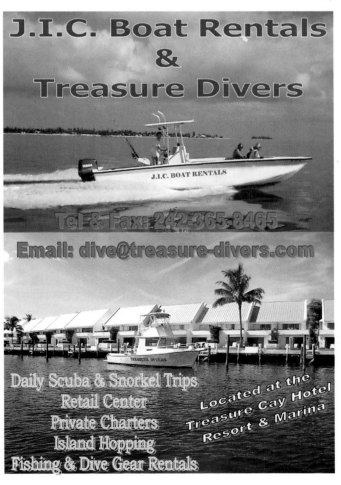

Great Guana Cay

The approaches to Settlement Harbour and to Fisher's Bay west of it are both straightforward and direct. Settlement Harbour is obviously exposed to the south and southwest. The bottom is grass, making it difficult to get a Danforth anchor to hold. The old Guana Beach Resort dock is located at the NW corner of the harbour. Orchid Bay Marina is in the SE corner. A breakwater protects Orchid Bay Marina's docks.

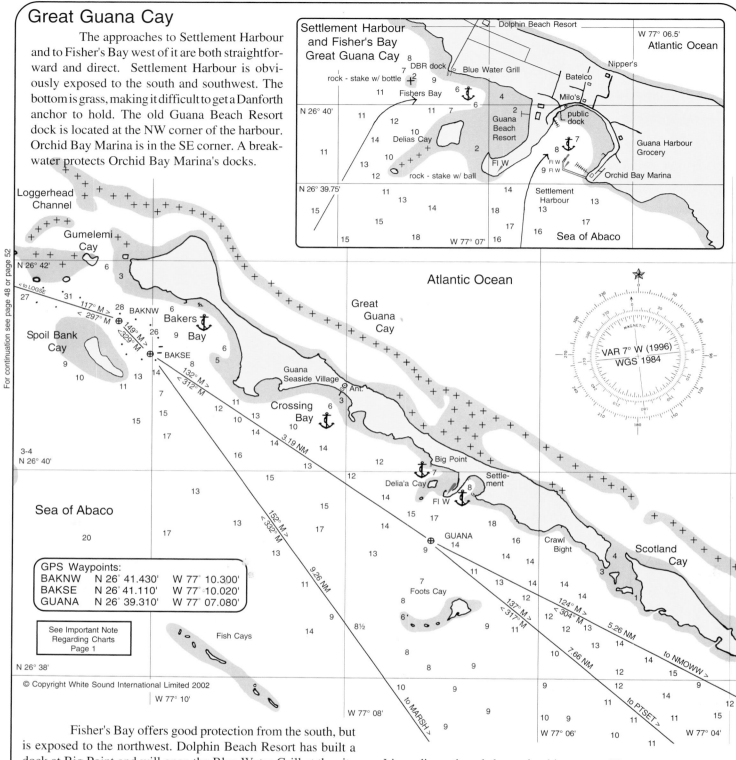

Fisher's Bay offers good protection from the south, but is exposed to the northwest. Dolphin Beach Resort has built a dock at Big Point and will open the Blue Water Grill at the site early in 2003. Moorings for transients maintained by Troy at the dive shop are available. There is a submerged rock off Big Point at the north side of the harbour. It is usually marked with a white pipe. A shallow rocky bar runs from Delia's Cay southwest to the off-lying rock. All boats should avoid trying to cross the bar and should go to the southwest of the off-lying rock, which is usually marked with a pole with a ball at the top.

The northwestern end of Great Guana Cay is also of interest to cruisers. Baker's Bay was developed several years ago as a cruiseship destination, but in early 1993 Premier Cruise

Lines discontinued the cruiseship stops. There were too many cancelled visits because of rough weather in Loggerhead Channel. Baker's Bay can be a good stop for lunch or for overnight. The anchorage is beautiful, and it is very comfortable in the prevailing winds. It does not offer protection from the south through the northwest. The spoil bank cay created by dredging the channel and mooring basin for the cruiseship is an excellent place for shelling.

Crossing Bay, just to the southeast of Baker's Bay, is the site of a restaurant and resort—Guana Seaside Village. It has a long dock with 3' MLW; dredging is planned. Until then, deeper draft vessels should plan to anchor off and dinghy to their dock.

GREAT GUANA CAY

The settlement at Great Guana Cay is one of the smallest in the central part of Abaco—the 1990 census reported only 95 persons living on the cay. The cay's principal asset has long been its beautiful ocean beach, which is one of the widest in Abaco and extends almost the entire 5½ mile length of the island. The beach made Guana a popular stop for cruisers for many years. The Guana Beach Resort was the only bar and restaurant on the island, and groceries were available at Guana Harbour Grocery in the settlement.

During the past seven years Guana has experienced a boom, and several new developments have made the cay even more attractive for visitors. The opening of Nipper's Beach Bar and Grill during summer 1996 brought large numbers of cruisers, tourists, and local residents to the cay. Nipper's is located a short walk from the settlement high on a dune overlooking the beach and the reef. Ocean Frontier Hideaways now offers overnight accomodations next door to Nippers.

The opening of Orchid Bay Marina in 1999 provided well protected dockage at Guana for the first time. It is also a residential development with lots for sale, and a restaurant opened on the site in 2002.

Dolphin Beach Resort, located just northwest of the settlement on the ocean beach, continues to expand and will soon include two restaurants as well as 20 rooms/cottages—The Blue Water Grill is expected to open at Big Point on Fisher's Bay early in 2003. Dolphin Beach is a residental development as well. There is another relatively new resort 1½ miles northwest of the settlement at Crossing Bay. Guana Seaside Village consists of a hotel, restaurant and bar. Its property stretches from the Atlantic Ocean to the Sea of Abaco. Newly opened accomodations in the settlement include Sea Side Villas and Harbour View Haven. Both offer modern facilities, beautiful views and excellent access to town.

Guana Beach Resort and its Sunset Grill are now under new management and are open for business. The property no longer includes the dock on Settlement Harbour, but does still have the dinghy dock on Fisher's Bay. Accomodations as well as food and drinks are available. The future of the old Guana Beach Resort dock is unclear.

In addition to Guana Harbour Grocery there is a liquor store in town and there are two or three shops which sell T-shirts, postcards, books, and other gift items. Haircutting and beauty services are provided by Ruth Sands, and Edmund Pinder is a fishing guide who is also in the real estate business. Ice is available from the liquor store.

If you want to walk, swim, snorkel, or picnic, cross to the ocean side at the settlement, and then walk southeast on the beach to High Rocks, where the reef is just off the beach. It will be obvious when you reach High Rocks.

The northern end of Great Guana Cay was developed by Treasure Cay Limited in 1989-1990 for use by cruise ship visitors and named "Treasure Island." The facility is now closed.

Great Guana Cay from Settlement Harbour to Baker's Bay from the southeast.

Harbour View Haven

Our new (December, 2000) one and two bedroom units feature Queen-size beds, full kitchens, large living and dining areas, and an unmatched view of Great Guana Cay's beautiful harbour. An efficiency unit with kitchenette is also available.

- Central Air Conditioning
- Satellite TV, Radio/CD/Tape Player
- Private Gazebo and Garden, BBQ Grills

Tel: (242) 365-5028   Fax: (242) 365-5083
Email: harbourviewhaven@abacoinet.com
Web: guanacayvillas.com

Sea Shore Villas

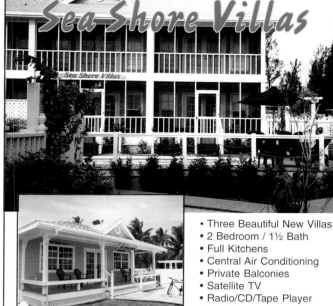

The new gift Shop and Laundromat

- Three Beautiful New Villas
- 2 Bedroom / 1½ Bath
- Full Kitchens
- Central Air Conditioning
- Private Balconies
- Satellite TV
- Radio/CD/Tape Player
- Gift Shop
- Laundromat

Tel: (242) 365-5006 (gift shop)
Tel: (242) 365-5028
Fax: (242) 365-5083
Email: seashorevillas@abacoinet.com
Web: guanacayvillas.com

Guana Harbour Grocery

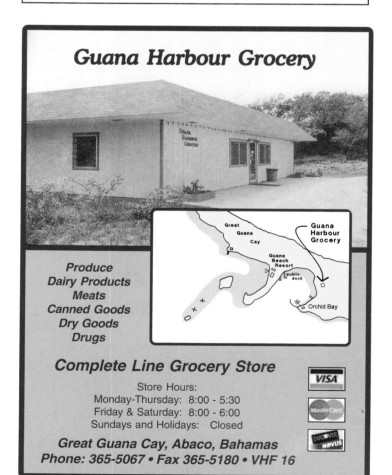

Produce
Dairy Products
Meats
Canned Goods
Dry Goods
Drugs

Complete Line Grocery Store

Store Hours:
Monday-Thursday: 8:00 - 5:30
Friday & Saturday: 8:00 - 6:00
Sundays and Holidays: Closed

VISA
MasterCard
DISCOVER NOVUS

Great Guana Cay, Abaco, Bahamas
Phone: 365-5067 • Fax 365-5180 • VHF 16

Oceanfrontier Hideaway
a unique vacation experience

A Mountain Cabin at the Beach?
Why not?!

- Located on Guana Cay's Breathtaking Beach
- Sleeps up to 6 with Two bedrooms and a Loft
- Kitchenette and Bath
- Adjacent to Nippers Bar and Grill for excellent food, friendly people and plenty of fun!
- Two minutes from settlement
- Snorkeling, beachcombing, swimming just a few yards away

For Reservations Call
1 519 389-4846
or Fax 1 519 389-3027

E-mail: info@oceanfrontier.com
Web: www.oceanfrontier.com

Blue Water Grill

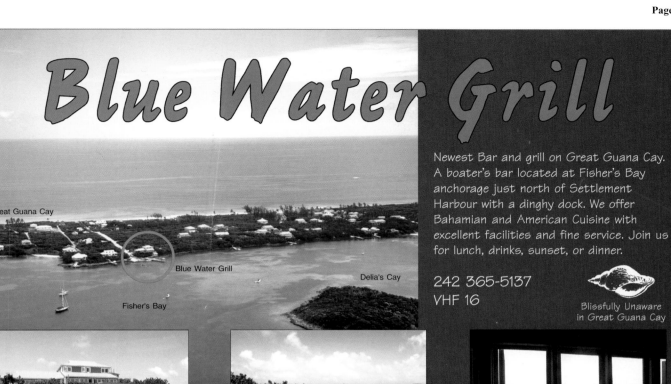

Great Guana Cay

Blue Water Grill

Fisher's Bay

Delia's Cay

Newest Bar and grill on Great Guana Cay. A boater's bar located at Fisher's Bay anchorage just north of Settlement Harbour with a dinghy dock. We offer Bahamian and American Cuisine with excellent facilities and fine service. Join us for lunch, drinks, sunset, or dinner.

242 365-5137
VHF 16

Blissfully Unaware
in Great Guana Cay

Nipper's
Beach Bar and Grill

the new pool

- *Over-looking the most beautiful beach in the Abacos and the world's third largest barrier reef*
- *Snorkeling 75 yards off the beach*
- *Featuring Bahamian Home Cooking with a Pig Roast every Sunday*
- *On the north side of Great Guana Cay at the settlement, Abaco, Bahamas*

Michael and Johnnie Roberts • VHF 16 • 365-5143

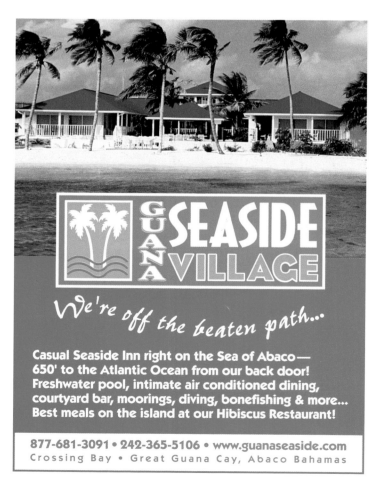
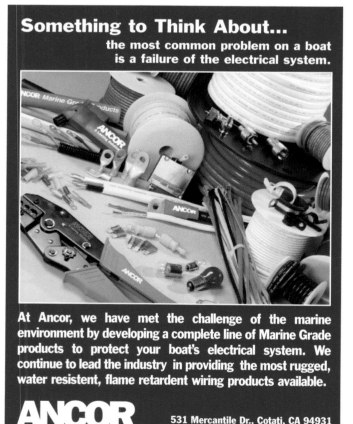

North Man-O-War Channel from the southwest. It is the widest and deepest passage between the Sea of Abaco and the Atlantic Ocean in central Abaco. Note the southeast tip of Fish Hawk Cay and a portion of Fowl Cay Reef on the left, and the northwest tip of Man-O-War Cay with the rock which almost always breaks, as well as a portion of the barrier reef off Man-O-War Cay on the right. A boat is entering the channel. See the charts and descriptions on page 68, and also on pages 12-13, 14.

South Man-O-War Channel from the southwest. This passage is narrower than North Man-O-War Channel and entry is not straightforward. Note the southeastern tip of Man-O-War Cay on the left and the barrier reef offshore. The opening is clearly visible. The boat entering is beginning its turn to port to avoid a 6' MLW coral patch. Vessels approaching this channel from the south must use extreme caution to avoid Elbow Reef; it is recommended that all vessels coming from the south go to the waypoint OFFSMOWE before approaching SMOWE. See the charts and descriptions on pages 12-13, 14, 68 and 74.

Man-O-War Cay and its Approaches

The north Man-O-War Channel is wider than the south Man-O-War Channel and is the best passage between the Sea of Abaco and the Atlantic Ocean in this area. Its shallowest part is 17' deep. From offshore approach the waypoint NMOWE from the north or east or, if coming from the south, from OFFMOW and NMOWEE (see pages 12-13, 14). Compass bearings for NMOWE are 154° M on the southeast tip of Man-O-War Cay and 227°M on the southeast tip of Fish Hawk (or Upper) Cay. From this point you will be able to see the reef breaking on both sides of the north Man-O-War Channel. Proceed on a heading of 213°M directly toward the waypoint NMOWW (toward the middle of the opening between Man-O-War and Fish Hawk Cays). This route also is on a range of 213°M on the two points at the entrance to Marsh Harbour. But these are about five miles from NMOWE and very difficult to see from a small boat. The South Man-O-War Channel has a controlling depth of about 12'. Approach the waypoint SMOWE from the north or east or, if coming from the south, from OFFELBOW and SMOWEE (see pages 12-13, 14, and 74). From SMOWE head 223° M to the waypoint SMOWW. You will be on a range of South Rock and the SW edge of Matt Lowe's Cay. At the waypoint turn to the south to avoid a 6' MLW coral patch. Turn to about 223° M again and then round South Rock to approach the harbour entrance. From the Sea of Abaco approach the harbour entrance passing either side of Sandy and Garden Cays. From Point Set Rock it is possible to use the waypoints MOW1 and MOW2 to assist if visibility is limited.

GPS Waypoints (generally N to S) -		
NMOWE	N 26° 37.820'	W 77° 01.360'
NMOWW	N 26° 36.900'	W 77° 01.860'
SMOWE	N 26° 35.997'	W 76° 58.809'
SMOWW	N 26° 35.608'	W 76° 59.136'
MOW2	N 26° 35.287'	W 77° 00.227'
MOW1	N 26° 34.771'	W 76° 59.932'
PTSET	N 26° 34.370'	W 77° 00.550'

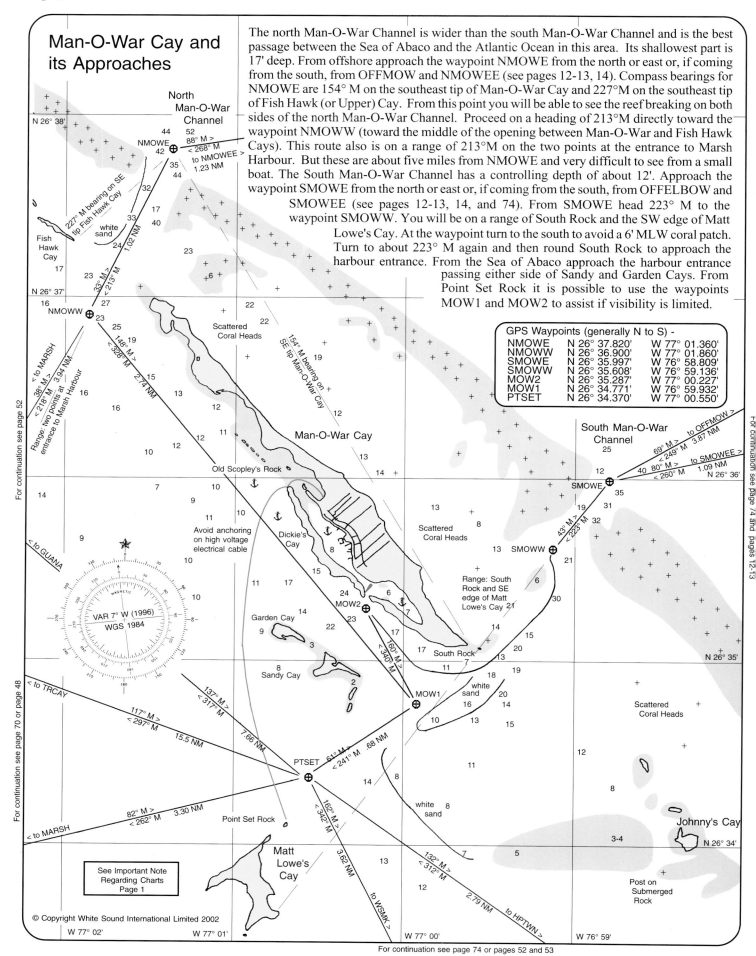

See Important Note Regarding Charts Page 1

For continuation see page 52

For continuation see page 70 or page 48

For continuation see Page 74 and pages 12-13

For continuation see page 74 or pages 52 and 53

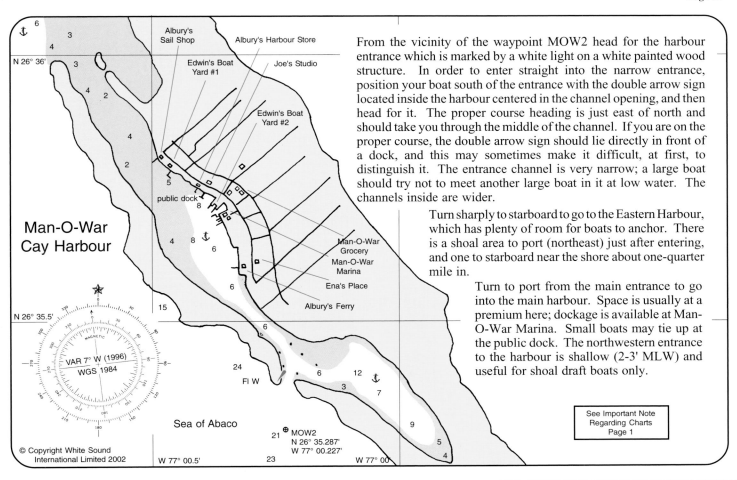

Man-O-War
Cay Harbour

VAR 7° W (1996)
WGS 1984

© Copyright White Sound
International Limited 2002

Sea of Abaco

From the vicinity of the waypoint MOW2 head for the harbour entrance which is marked by a white light on a white painted wood structure. In order to enter straight into the narrow entrance, position your boat south of the entrance with the double arrow sign located inside the harbour centered in the channel opening, and then head for it. The proper course heading is just east of north and should take you through the middle of the channel. If you are on the proper course, the double arrow sign should lie directly in front of a dock, and this may sometimes make it difficult, at first, to distinguish it. The entrance channel is very narrow; a large boat should try not to meet another large boat in it at low water. The channels inside are wider.

Turn sharply to starboard to go to the Eastern Harbour, which has plenty of room for boats to anchor. There is a shoal area to port (northeast) just after entering, and one to starboard near the shore about one-quarter mile in.

Turn to port from the main entrance to go into the main harbour. Space is usually at a premium here; dockage is available at Man-O-War Marina. Small boats may tie up at the public dock. The northwestern entrance to the harbour is shallow (2-3' MLW) and useful for shoal draft boats only.

See Important Note
Regarding Charts
Page 1

Man-O-War Cay from the south.

Approach from the south. Line up the piling with the double arrow (points left and right) in the center of the opening.

The opening is narrow; do not meet another boat here. Note the piling with the double arrow in front of the powerboat at the dock. It should be centered in the opening.

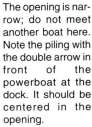

When about 50-60' from the piling with the double arrow, turn to port and proceed toward the main harbour.

MAN-O-WAR CAY

During the early twentieth century the Commissioner, who at that time was based in Hope Town, described Man-O-War Cay as a small island which had a few enterprising men. The same could be said today, though there are undoubtedly more enterprising men (and women). Man-O-War is the home base for Albury's Ferry. Marcel Albury, who runs it, is one of the most experienced pilots in Abaco. See his article on crossing the Gulf Stream to Abaco on page 15. Man-O-War has been a center for boat building and repair for many years. Edwin's Boat Yard does excellent work and maintains a good stock of marine parts. They actually have two yards—boat yard #1 is near the Sail Shop at the northwest end of town; boat yard #2 is located near the center of town. Albury Brothers Boat Building, located just northwest of Edwin's Boat Yard #2, builds sturdy round bilge deep-V fiberglass outboard boats.

Man-O-War Marina is centrally located, and offers full dockage and fuel services, in addition to ice and water, and a dive shop which also carries clothing, books, etc. The Pavilion Restaurant at Man-O-War Marina offers a complete lunch and dinner menu. Ena's Place, located on the main road southeast of the settlement, serves lunches, snacks and dinner specials. It is a take-away with tables so you can eat on the premises. Hibiscus Cafe is a restaurant located in the main part of town. No alcoholic beverages are sold anywhere on Man-O-War Cay. Two grocery stores supply the island's food needs. Albury's Harbour Grocery is on the water; Man-O-War Grocery, at the top of the hill back from Man-O-War Marina, is newly enlarged. Both deliver groceries to all docks at Man-O-War.

Joe's Studio is one of the most unique gift shops in Abaco because Joe Albury's hand-crafted items made of Abaco hardwoods are sold there. Beautiful frame models of Abaco dinghies, candlestick holders, goblets and folding chairs are all available. A very good selection of books about the Bahamas as well as jewelry, and T-shirts are available.

Another very unique shop—the Sail Shop—is located at the far northwestern edge of the settlement right on the harbour, past Edwin's Boat Yard #1. Sturdy and colorful canvas duffle bags, sewn on the premises, are available. Hats and jackets and purses are also sewn and sold there.

The ocean side of Man-O-War Cay is worth a visit—there are some beautiful beaches alternating with rock outcroppings. The northwestern and southeastern ends of the cay are well developed with private residences. Explore by walking the road, or by bicycle or golf cart. There is a clinic at Man-O-War.

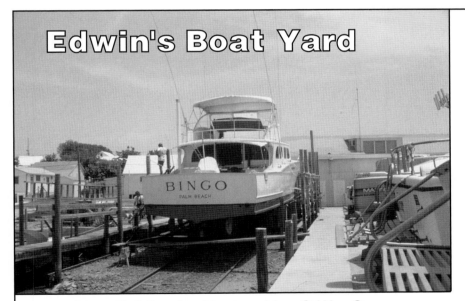
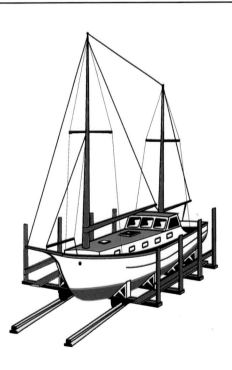

MAN-O-WAR PAVILION RESTAURANT

Come and dine in a delightful open air restaurant on the harbour's edge at Man-O-War Marina. Our menu includes tasty conch, grouper, dolphin, shrimp, chicken, burgers, peas & rice, fries, cole slaw, ice cream, pies, cake, candy and much more.

You will surely enjoy our special BBQ nights on Friday and Saturday when we serve grilled steak, ribs, chicken, fish and pork chops with our special sauce and your choice of delicious sides.
HOURS: MONDAY-SATURDAY 10:30-2:00 5:30-8:30

Man-O-War Hardware and Building Supply

Lumber • Hardware • Paints • Marine Hardware
Regular deliveries to Hope Town and Great Guana Cay.
Deliveries to all points from Green Turtle Cay to Little Harbour can be arranged.

PHONE 365-6011 • FAX 365-6039 • VHF 69
call for our quote
• Walter Sweeting •
• Arthur Elden •
• George Malone •
Man-O-War Hardware and Building Supply
Man-O-War Cay, Abaco, Bahamas

For continuation see pages 12-13

HUB OF ABACO

26° 37' N

26° 32' N

ATLANTIC OCEAN

Important Note: All boats approaching South Man-O-War Channel from the south should go to OFFELBOW and then SMOWEE in order to provide a safe berth while rounding Elbow Reef and approaching the reefs which flank south Man-O-War Channel. The reciprocal also applies for boats departing from South Man-O-War Channel and heading south.

to OFFMOW 7
to OFFMOW 3.87 NM
SMOWEE
131° M >
< 311° M
1.09 NM
to OFFELBOW 7
to OFFELBOW 3.67 NM

246° M >
< 66° M
80° M >
< 260° M
43° M
233° M
SMOWE

Hope Town
Elbow Cay
76° 58' W

Fl W (5) ev 15 sec

Johnny's Cay
Scattered Coral Heads

Scattered Coral Heads
8
26

HPTWN
5
6
6½
6
Fl Grn
4½
5
6½
6½
to WSMK
8
< 273° M
33° M >
1.9 NM

Parrot Cays
8½
6½

Porgie Rock
2
7
2
2

See Important Note Regarding Charts Page 1

For continuation see page 110 or 53

SMOWW
25
26
20
21
6
21
14
14
21
21
11
18 South Rock
White Sand
12
11
10
12

Range for South Man-O-War Channel: South Rock and SE edge Matt Lowe's Cay

Man-O-War Cay
Scattered Heads
Some Scattered Coral Heads

Post on Submerged Rock
10
3-4
4½
15
10
8
White Sand
8
7
12
9
9
10
8
9
10
11
9
10

135° M >
< 315° M 2.8 NM

162° M >
< 342° M 3.62 NM

94° M >
< 274° M 4.0 NM

Matt Lowe's Cay
14
13
14
12
12
11
11
11
10
10
14
14
15

The Sugar Loaves
Sugar Loaf Cay
18
10
14
19
14
12

1
½
0
Nautical Miles

Lubbers Bank
3
10
12

MOW1
MOW2
Fl W
21
21
9
Garden Cay
Sandy Cay
12
13
15
11
10
12

PTSET
15
22
15
14
13

Point Set Rock (white shed)
9
8
6
3½
8
12

Sanka Shoal (post)

BTHBR
12
187° M >
< 7° M
to WITCHN >

Boat Harbour Marina
Fl R
7
5½
5½
3½
7
12
11
8
9

For continuation see page 68 or page 52

Rock + (breaks)
23
19
13
16
11
13

148° M >
< 328° M 2.74 NM
137° M >
< 317° M
7.66 NM

SEA OF ABACO

7
10
10
12
13
11
9½
8
10½
9
7
8
10
9

82° M >
< 262° M 3.3 NM

3½
7

Ant 255' W over R

to NMOWE
23
16

NMOWW
38° M >
< 218° M 3.94 NM
13
11
13
13
12
13
14
11
10
9
11
10
12
8

Ant Fl R over R
9

Marsh Harbour

Great Abaco Island
77° 03' W

to GUANA
12
10
11
12
14
14
11
12
15
15
13
13
11
9½
13
17
14
16

MARSH
13
11
11

Fl Grn
Fl Grn

VAR 7° W (1996)
WGS 1984

GPS Waypoints (Generally north to south):

NMOWW	N 26° 36.900'	W 77° 01.860'
OFFMOW	N 26° 37.820'	W 76° 55.000'
SMOWEE	N 26° 36.320'	W 76° 57.650'
SMOWE	N 26° 35.997'	W 76° 58.809'
SMOWW	N 26° 35.608'	W 76° 59.136'
MOW2	N 26° 35.287'	W 77° 00.227'
MOW1	N 26° 34.771'	W 76° 59.932'
PTSET	N 26° 34.370'	W 77° 00.550'
MARSH	N 26° 33.520'	W 77° 04.110'
HPTWN	N 26° 32.608'	W 76° 58.063'
BTHBR	N 26° 32.410'	W 77° 02.550'
OFFELBOW	N 26° 34.270'	W 76° 54.250'

HUB OF ABACO

Most passages in this part of the Sea of Abaco are straight-forward with few unmarked shoals. The shoal extending westward from the small cay south of Johnny's Cay is marked with a post, as is Sanka Shoal, about ½ mile west of Matt Lowe's Cay. Lubber's Bank is clearly visible. Please see larger scale and harbour charts for Man-O-War Cay (p. 68), Marsh Harbour (p. 76), Boat Harbour (p. 94) and Hope Town (p. 99).

The straight-line route from Hope Town to Man-O-War passes over a 3-4' bank. Boats needing more water should head 306° M from Hope Town toward a point east of Point Set Rock, which has a small white shed housing electrical distribution equipment on it. When the entrance to Man-O-War bears roughly magnetic north, turn and head for it. This will keep you well west of the bank. The final approach to Man-O-War will take you over a white bank which is, however, 8' deep.

The route from Hope Town to Marsh Harbour is simple. Head 312° M from Hope Town toward Point Set Rock; leave it to port. Then head about 262° M toward Outer Point, leaving Sanka Shoal far to port. The route from Hope Town to Boat Harbour is also straightforward and simple. Leave the Parrot Cays and Lubber's Bank to the south.

The south Man-O-War Channel is a reasonable passage from Abaco Sound to the Atlantic Ocean. Its controlling depth is 12 feet. Round South Rock giving it a good berth because of the submerged rock lying about a hundred yards northeast of it. Head seaward on a course of about 45° for about ¾NM to avoid the 6' coral head ½NM northeast of South Rock. Then head north to get on the range of South Rock and the southwest edge of Matt Lowe's Cay.Then head through the channel on that range (course should be

Point Set Rock lies off Matt Lowe's Cay and has a small white shack which houses electrical junction equipment. An underwater cable carries electricity to Point Set Rock from Marsh Harbour, and other cables then carry it to Hope Town and Man-O-War Cay.

about 43°M). This course will take you between the two extensive reefs to the northwest and southeast of this channel. Alternatively, use the waypoints. Enter from the Atlantic heading toward South Rock and southeast shoreline of Matt Lowe's Cay on a heading of 223° M. See the chart on page 68 for a larger scale view of this route.

The north Man-O-War Channel is wider than the south Man-O-War Channel and is the best passage between the Sea of Abaco and the Atlantic Ocean in this area. Its shallowest point is 17 feet deep. See the chart on page 68 for a detailed description of this channel.

Some good snorkeling areas can be found northeast of Johnny's Cay (see snorkeling maps on page 123 and 126). There are some scattered heads between Johnny's Cay and the main reef, so one should not enter the area unless the sun is high so as to make the heads visible beneath the water. Johnny's Cay is private. There are also scattered heads between Man-O-War Cay and the barrier reef. Exercise extreme caution in these areas.

The anchorage at Matt Lowe's Cay from the northeast with Sugar Loaf Creek and Eastern Shores behind and to the left and Marsh Harbour in the background to the right.

For continuation see page 74 or pages 52 and 53

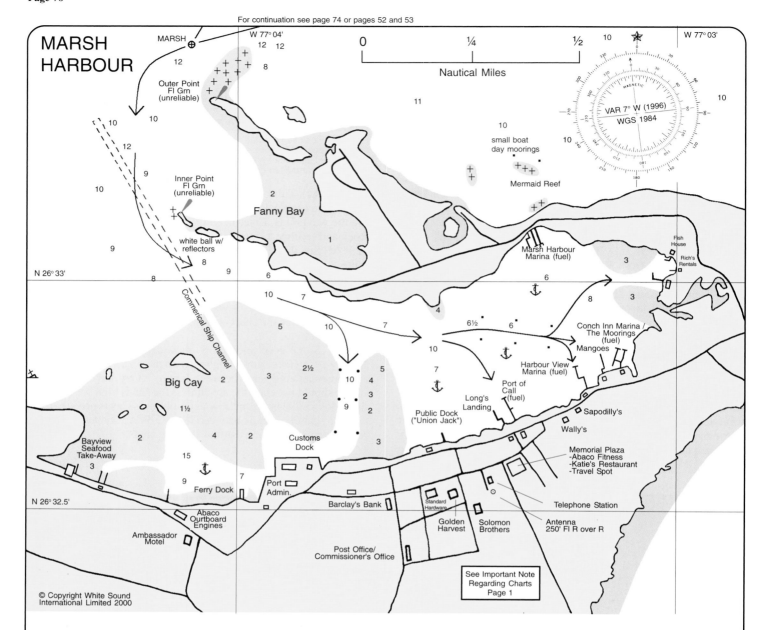

MARSH HARBOUR

The only difficult thing about entering Marsh Harbour is finding it. The landmarks are not very distinctive, and a newcomer to the area may wish to follow a rough compass course toward it until Outer Point can be distinguished. The entrance itself is simple and direct. Stay about 200 yards off the outer point and about 50 yards off the inner point, and proceed into the harbour favoring the north shore in order to avoid the large shoal area extending from Big Cay at the western end of the harbour. There is a newly dredged channel through this shoal leading to the new port facility. Still under construction during summer, 2002, both the channel and the port are expected to be operational by early 2003. Cruising boats have little reason to use this channel, unless they are clearing customs in Marsh Harbour, or planning to use the small anchorage at the western end of the harbour.

The main harbour is 8-10' deep throughout, except for the two shoals flanking the old channel leading to the customs dock, a small shoal area extending from the small

point on the north shore, and the two shoals flanking the channel leading to the old Sunsail Marina at the east end of the harbour. The holding ground is generally good. There is a "No Anchorage Zone Channel" extending from the vicinity of the small point mentioned above to a spot north of the Conch Inn Marina. It is not a deeper dredged channel; it was marked in order to better control traffic and anchoring. All the markers for this channel have been missing since about 1998—an approximate range for it is from the Texaco sign at Conch Inn Marina to Inner Point. The old channel to the old Customs Dock is clearly marked with large pilings. Anchoring is not permitted in this channel either.

Those who prefer to tie up to a dock rather than anchoring off will find excellent facilities at the Conch Inn Marina, Harbour View Marina, Mangoes, Port of Call Marina, Marsh Harbour Marina, and the new Abaco Yacht Haven at Long's Landing.

MARSH HARBOUR

Marsh Harbour is the largest town in Abaco—in fact it is the third largest in the Bahamas, exceeded in size only by Nassau and Freeport. The population is about 5000, and its many businesses and shops offer visitors the best selection in Abaco of everything from conch fritters and clothing to stereos and automobile parts.

Good restaurants abound—with Mangoes and the Conch Inn next door to each other and both offering good lunches and evening dining on the harbourfront. Wally's and Sapodilly's Bar and Grill are across the street. The Jib Room, located at Marsh Harbour Marina on the harbour's north side, is well known for its weekly specials. Angler's is located at Boat Harbour Marina. The Golden Grouper, Mother Merle's Fishnet (take-away), Katie's, and the Copper Cannon Kitchen at Long's Landing are all good modest restaurants offering local cuisine. Bayview Seafood Restaurant (take-away) is located on the waterfront in Dundas Town at the western end of the harbour. Mackerel's Native Restaurant in Dundas Town and Jamie's Place on East Bay Street are Marsh Harbour's newest—both opened recently. There is a pizzeria—Sharkees is on East Bay Street across from the Conch Inn.

There are several supermarkets in Marsh Harbour. The Golden Harvest was the closest to the harbour—just one block from the public dock (often called the Union Jack dock, named after a restaurant near the dock which burned down about twenty-five years ago). The Golden Harvest burned down in June 2001, and a sign on the site declares that a new store will be built. Unfortunately, construction had not commenced in July 2002. Sawyer's Market is located across the street and about a block west of Royal Bank. Price Rite opened in August 2001 to fill the gap created by the Golden Harvest fire. It is located on Stratton Drive next to the Classic Coin Laundromat. Solomon Brothers, a recently enlarged wholesale food distributor with a warehouse store, is located about a block southeast of the Golden Harvest site. Abaco Wholesale, on Don Mackay Boulevard, is another warehouse store which sells in reasonable quantities to individuals. Bahamas Family Market, located near the traffic light, is a grocery/gourmet food store with a produce department which is open on Sundays. A convenience grocery store is located at Conch Inn Marina—it is named the Concept Boat Rentals and Sales, Convenience Store and Boutique.

The Conch Inn Marina is Marsh Harbour's largest. It has about 75 full-service slips, a restaurant, nine harbourside rooms, a laundry, a grocery store, a dive shop and a swimming pool all on the premises. Located nearby are Mangoes, Harbour View Marina, and Port of Call Marina (formerly Triple J). Mangoes has 30 full-service slips with telephone hook-ups. There is a restaurant and boutique on the site. Harbour View has a new pool and patio deck, and is the home of Snappas Bar and Grill as well as Blue Wave Boat Rentals. Port of Call Marina is the new name for Triple J; it has new docks as well as new management. Long's Landing is located a couple of hundred feet further west—it and Port of Call are the closest to downtown Marsh Harbour. Marsh Harbour Marina with its Jib Room Bar and Restaurant is on the harbour's north side. Merlin's Marine Electronics (formerly Triple J), Sail Abaco, and Pier One Boat Rentals are all located at Marsh Harbour Marina. All marinas except Mangoes and Long's Landing offer fuel as well as dockage. Boat Harbour Marina is in the town of Marsh Harbour, but not the harbour itself—it is located east of Marsh Harbour, directly off the Sea of Abaco. It is the largest and most comprehensive marina development in Abaco. For further information regarding Boat Harbour, see page 94. Marsh Harbour Boat Yards opened at Calcutta Creek south of Boat Harbour during fall 1999. They have an 85 ton travelling marine hoist and can provide most repair and re-building services. A marine store is located on the premises.

Clothing stores include the boutique at Mangoes, Spooner's Department Store, Alexis Fashions, His and Her Jeans, Victor's

Continued on page 78

Marsh Harbour from the west northwest with Inner Point in the foreground.

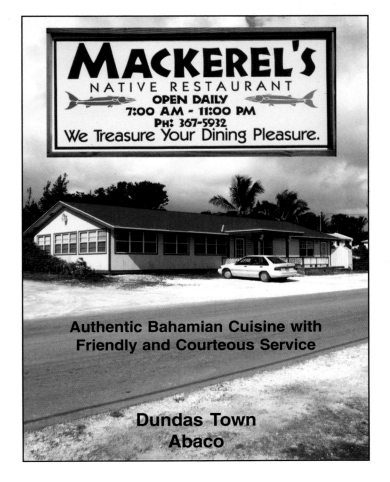

Marsh Harbour from the Southwest. A new port facility is now under construction in the area just west of the old customs dock in the foreground of this 1997 photo. For an aerial photo of the construction project, turn to page 153.

Continued from page 77

Department Store, and several others. The selection is very good. Standard Hardware, on Queen Elizabeth Drive, and Abaco Hardware, on Don Mackay Boulevard, offer broad selections of hardware and appliances, and are in the process of merging to create Abaco Home Building Centers. Both also carry some marine supplies, and B & D Marine, located at the traffic light, has an excellent selection of boat accessories and supplies, as does the marine store at Marsh Harbour Boat Yards, and National Marine on Queen Elizabeth Drive across from Standard Hardware. Please see the classified business directory for Marsh Harbour to learn the full extent of the goods and services available in this bustling Out Island town. It can be found on pages 148-150. Also see the street maps of Marsh Harbour on pages 82, 84 and 86.

Marsh Harbour is a port of entry for vessels coming to the Bahamas from foreign ports. Customs and immigration are located at the new port facility at the west end of town. This new port will be a busy place, with two or more ships from West Palm Beach unloading each week, as well as the mail boat which arrives from Nassau early every Thursday morning.

Marsh Harbour is the seat of the Administrator for central Abaco: his office is in Dove Plaza. Several other government ministries, including agriculture, education, and labour, also have offices in Dove Plaza. See the directory of government offices on page 153 for more detailed information.

Taxicabs are readily available in Marsh Harbour (call on VHF 06), and automobiles, bicycles and minibikes can be rented, making it possible to get around easily. Newly paved roads make it possible to drive to Treasure Cay or Cooperstown or even Little Abaco Island on a day trip, or south to Cherokee Sound or Sandy Point. See the article "Exploring Abaco by Land: ..." (pp. 136-138).

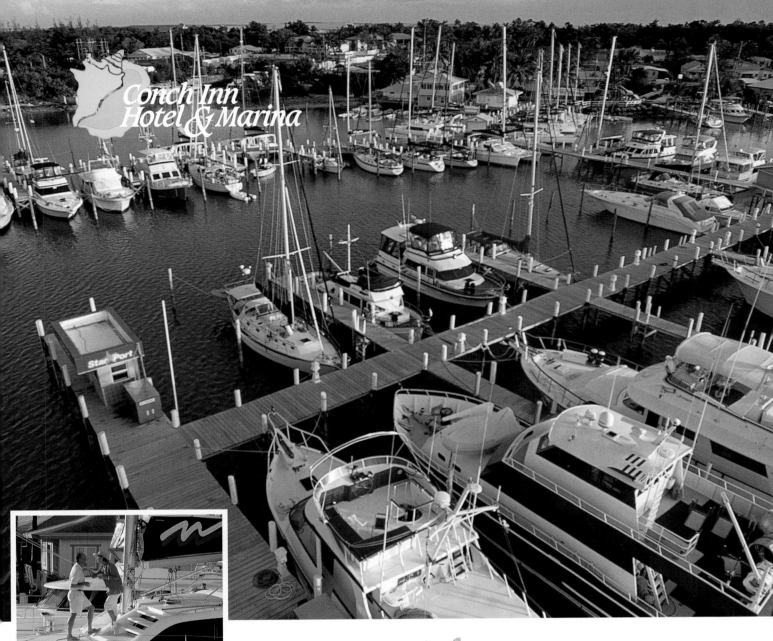

Marsh Harbour's Premier Marina

YACHT CHARTERS WITH THE MOORINGS
POWER BOAT CHARTERS WITH NAUTICBLUE
• Full Service 80-slip marina • Dive Shop • Restaurant & Bar •
• Freshwater Pool • Laundromat • Ferry Service • 5 mins. from Airport •

Each hotel room features
• 2 Double Beds • Air Conditioning • Cable TV • Refrigerator •
• Coffee Service • Private Garden Terrace •

P. O. Box AB 20469
Marsh Harbour, Abaco, The Bahamas
Phone: 242 367-4000/4003 • Fax: 242 367-4004
VHF Channels: 16 and 82
email: moorings_conchinn@oii.net
www.moorings.com

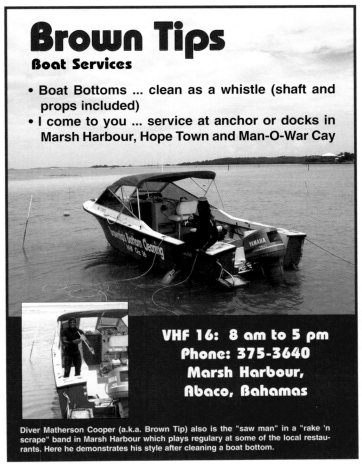
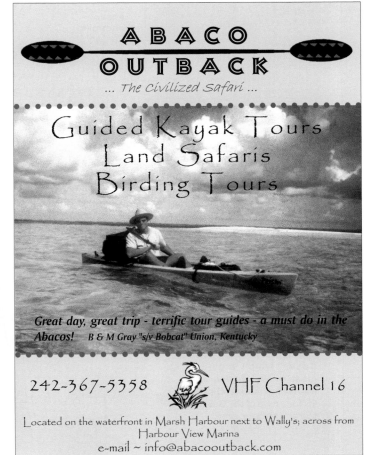

The Central Business District of Marsh Harbour

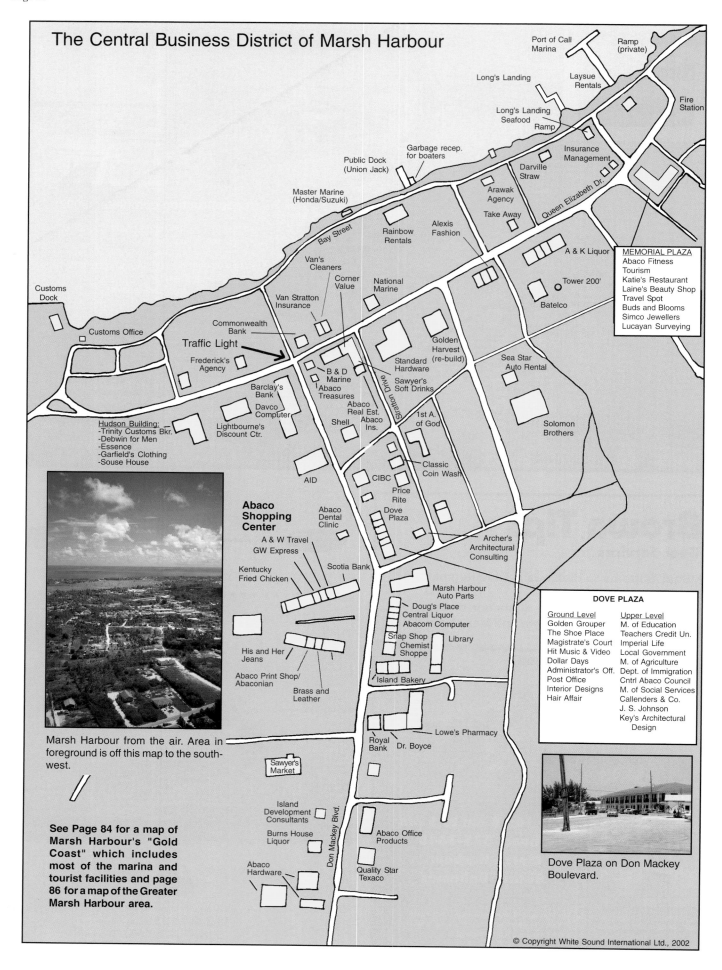

Port of Call Marina
Ramp (private)
Long's Landing
Laysue Rentals
Fire Station
Long's Landing Seafood
Ramp
Garbage recep. for boaters
Insurance Management
Public Dock (Union Jack)
Darville Straw
Queen Elizabeth Dr.
Master Marine (Honda/Suzuki)
Arawak Agency
Bay Street
Rainbow Rentals
Alexis Fashion
Take Away
A & K Liquor
Van's Cleaners
Corner Value
National Marine
Tower 200'
Batelco

MEMORIAL PLAZA
Abaco Fitness
Tourism
Katie's Restaurant
Laine's Beauty Shop
Travel Spot
Buds and Blooms
Simco Jewellers
Lucayan Surveying

Customs Dock
Van Stratton Insurance
Customs Office
Commonwealth Bank
Traffic Light
Golden Harvest (re-build)
Standard Hardware
Sea Star Auto Rental
Frederick's Agency
B & D Marine
Abaco Treasures
Sawyer's Soft Drinks
Barclay's Bank
Davco Computer
Abaco Real Est. Abaco Ins.
Shell
1st A. of God
Solomon Brothers
Hudson Building:
-Trinity Customs Bkr.
-Debwin for Men
-Essence
-Garfield's Clothing
-Souse House
Lightbourne's Discount Ctr.
Stratton Drive

AID
CIBC
Classic Coin Wash
Price Rite
Dove Plaza

Abaco Shopping Center
Abaco Dental Clinic
A & W Travel
GW Express
Scotia Bank
Kentucky Fried Chicken
Archer's Architectural Consulting

Marsh Harbour Auto Parts
Doug's Place
Central Liquor
Abacom Computer
Snap Shop
Library
Chemist Shoppe
His and Her Jeans
Abaco Print Shop/ Abaconian
Brass and Leather
Island Bakery

Marsh Harbour from the air. Area in foreground is off this map to the southwest.

Lowe's Pharmacy
Royal Bank
Dr. Boyce

DOVE PLAZA

Ground Level	Upper Level
Golden Grouper	M. of Education
The Shoe Place	Teachers Credit Un.
Magistrate's Court	Imperial Life
Hit Music & Video	Local Government
Dollar Days	M. of Agriculture
Administrator's Off.	Dept. of Immigration
Post Office	Cntrl Abaco Council
Interior Designs	M. of Social Services
Hair Affair	Callenders & Co.
	J. S. Johnson
	Key's Architectural Design

See Page 84 for a map of Marsh Harbour's "Gold Coast" which includes most of the marina and tourist facilities and page 86 for a map of the Greater Marsh Harbour area.

Sawyer's Market
Island Development Consultants
Burns House Liquor
Don Mackey Blvd.
Abaco Office Products
Abaco Hardware
Quality Star Texaco

Dove Plaza on Don Mackey Boulevard.

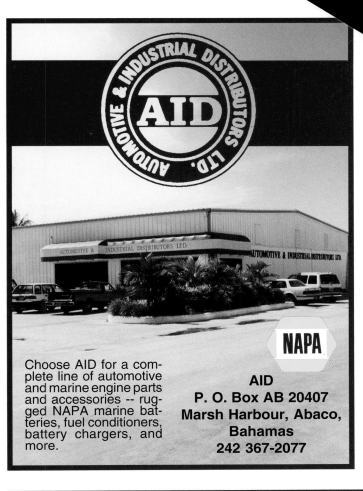

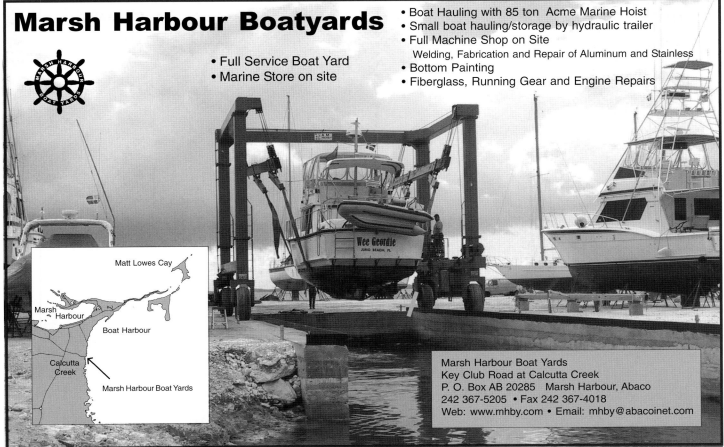

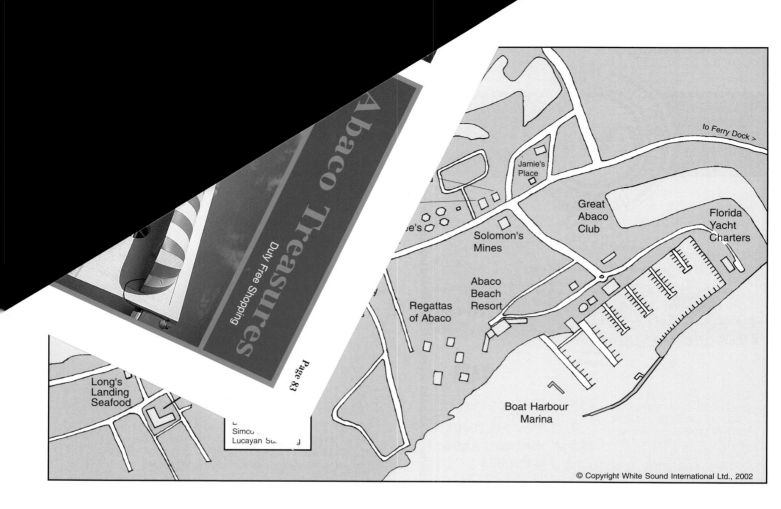

Map labels:
- to Ferry Dock >
- Jamie's Place
- Great Abaco Club
- Florida Yacht Charters
- Solomon's Mines
- ...e's
- Abaco Beach Resort
- Regattas of Abaco
- Boat Harbour Marina
- Long's Landing Seafood
- Simco...
- Lucayan Su...

Abaco Treasures
Duty Free Shopping
Page 83

© Copyright White Sound International Ltd., 2002

Bistro

Harbourside Restaurant
At the Conch Inn

Invites you to partake in a
wonderful dining experience ...

Breakfast, Lunch & Dinner,
Come & relax by the water side
while we cater to your eating needs!!

Phone: 242 367-4444   VHF 16
Live music weekly by Impact

TELEPHONE 367-5523

JaVa

ORIGINAL ART CERAMICS
GOURMET COFFEE ★ LATTE ★ TEA ★ COFFEE BEANS ★ OIL & CAPPUCCINO ★ BOOKS & ... BAKED GOODS

JAVA

- Gourmet Coffees •
- Expresso •
- Cappuccino •
- Latte •
- Tea •
- Baked Goods •
- Coffee Beans •
- Original Art •
- Books •
- Gift Items •

Royal Harbour
Building
East Bay Street
(east of Conch Inn)

367-5523

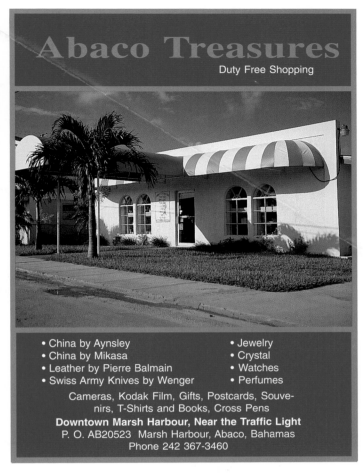

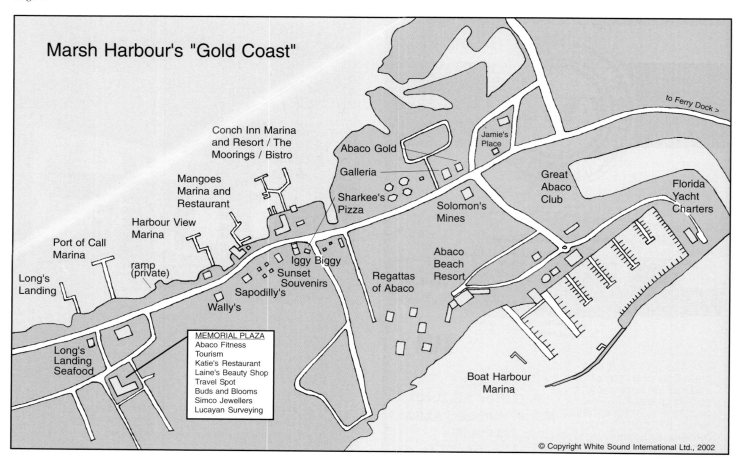

Marsh Harbour's "Gold Coast"

to Ferry Dock >

Conch Inn Marina and Resort / The Moorings / Bistro

Abaco Gold

Galleria

Jamie's Place

Mangoes Marina and Restaurant

Sharkee's Pizza

Solomon's Mines

Great Abaco Club

Florida Yacht Charters

Harbour View Marina

Port of Call Marina

ramp (private)

Iggy Biggy

Sunset Souvenirs

Sapodilly's

Wally's

Regattas of Abaco

Abaco Beach Resort

Long's Landing

Long's Landing Seafood

MEMORIAL PLAZA
Abaco Fitness
Tourism
Katie's Restaurant
Laine's Beauty Shop
Travel Spot
Buds and Blooms
Simco Jewellers
Lucayan Surveying

Boat Harbour Marina

© Copyright White Sound International Ltd., 2002

Bistro

Harbourside Restaurant
At the Conch Inn

Invites you to partake in a
wonderful dining experience ...

Breakfast, Lunch & Dinner,
Come & relax by the water side
while we cater to your eating needs!!

Phone: 242 367-4444   VHF 16
Live music weekly by Impact

TELEPHONE 367-5523

Java

ORIGINAL ART CERAMICS · BOOKS
GOURMET COFFEE · LATTE · TEA · COFFEE BEANS · EXPRESSO · CAPPUCCINO · BAKED GOODS

JAVA
• Gourmet Coffees •
• Expresso •
• Cappuccino •
• Latte •
• Tea •
• Baked Goods •
• Coffee Beans •
• Original Art •
• Books •
• Gift Items •

Royal Harbour
Building
East Bay Street
(east of Conch Inn)

367-5523

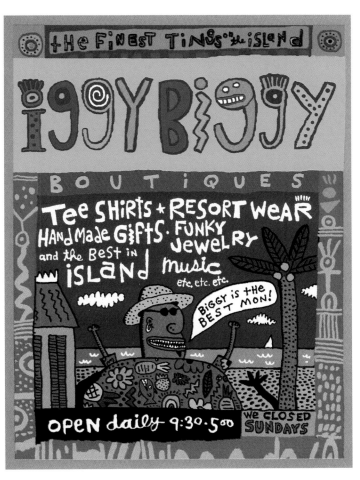

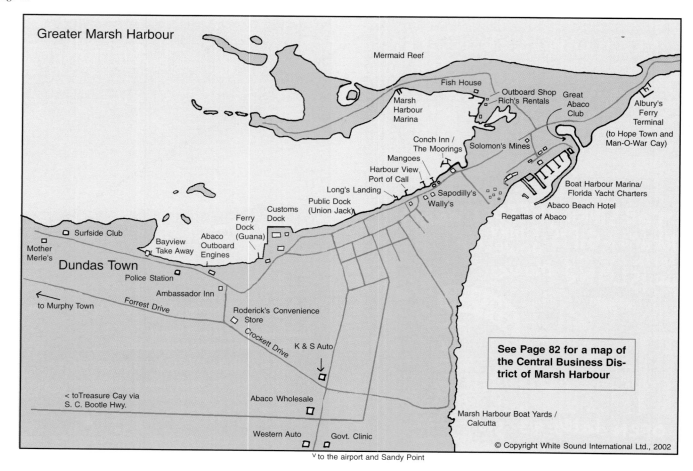

Greater Marsh Harbour

Mermaid Reef

Fish House

Outboard Shop
Rich's Rentals

Great Abaco Club

Albury's Ferry Terminal
(to Hope Town and Man-O-War Cay)

Marsh Harbour Marina

Conch Inn / The Moorings

Solomon's Mines

Mangoes
Harbour View
Port of Call

Long's Landing
Public Dock
(Union Jack)

Sapodilly's
Wally's

Boat Harbour Marina/
Florida Yacht Charters

Abaco Beach Hotel

Regattas of Abaco

Customs Dock

Ferry Dock (Guana)

Abaco Outboard Engines

Surside Club

Bayview Take Away

Mother Merle's

Dundas Town

Police Station

Ambassador Inn

to Murphy Town

Forrest Drive

Roderick's Convenience Store

Crockett Drive

K & S Auto

See Page 82 for a map of the Central Business District of Marsh Harbour

< toTreasure Cay via S. C. Bootle Hwy.

Abaco Wholesale

Marsh Harbour Boat Yards / Calcutta

Western Auto

Govt. Clinic

© Copyright White Sound International Ltd., 2002

ᵛ to the airport and Sandy Point

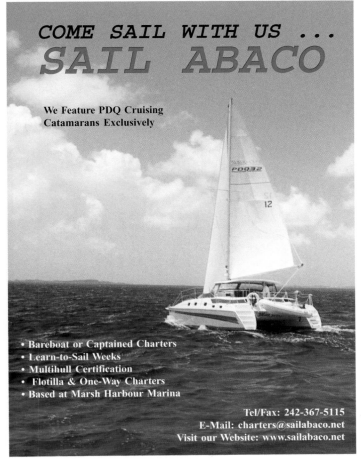

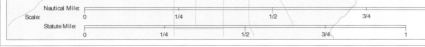

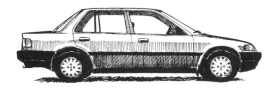

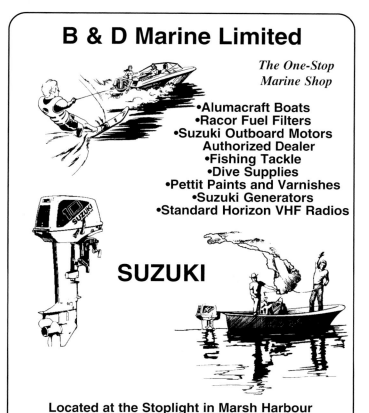

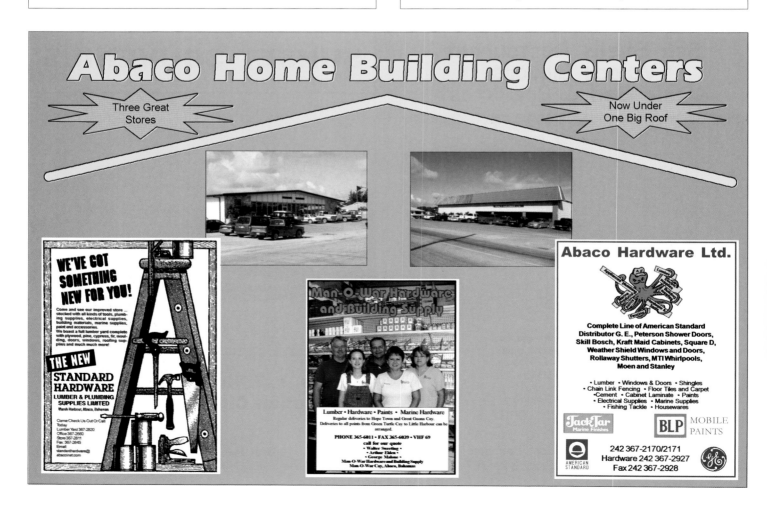

ABACO INSURANCE AGENCY LTD.

Walker's Cay
Carter Cays
Great Sale Cay
Green Turtle Cay
Great Guana
Man-O-War
Hope Town
Mores Island
Cherokee Sound
Crossing Rocks
Sandy Point
Hole in the Wall

When you put your most important asset in the hands of an Insurance Company, you'd better know something about them!

Your assets are safe with us.

Call our agents

Daron Roberts & Ginnie Sawyer

Abaco Insurance Agency Ltd., Marsh Harbour

Tel (242) 367-2549   Fax (242) 367-3075

Agents for:

ROYAL & SUNALLIANCE

BAHAMAS FIRST

Offices in Marsh Harbour, Treasure Cay, Hope Town, and Green Turtle Cay.

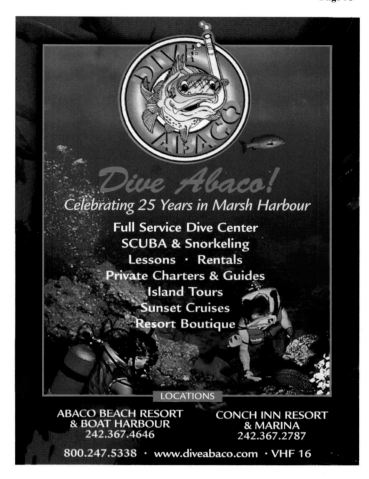

Dive Abaco!
Celebrating 25 Years in Marsh Harbour

Full Service Dive Center
SCUBA & Snorkeling
Lessons · Rentals
Private Charters & Guides
Island Tours
Sunset Cruises
Resort Boutique

LOCATIONS

ABACO BEACH RESORT
& BOAT HARBOUR
242.367.4646

CONCH INN RESORT
& MARINA
242.367.2787

800.247.5338 · www.diveabaco.com · VHF 16

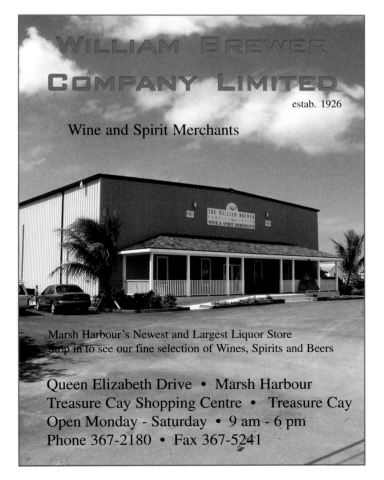

WILLIAM BREWER COMPANY LIMITED

estab. 1926

Wine and Spirit Merchants

Marsh Harbour's Newest and Largest Liquor Store
Stop in to see our fine selection of Wines, Spirits and Beers

Queen Elizabeth Drive • Marsh Harbour
Treasure Cay Shopping Centre • Treasure Cay
Open Monday - Saturday • 9 am - 6 pm
Phone 367-2180 • Fax 367-5241

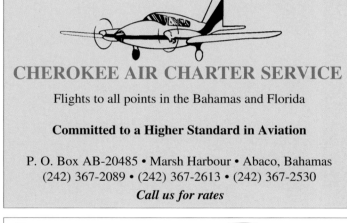

CHEROKEE AIR CHARTER SERVICE

Flights to all points in the Bahamas and Florida

Committed to a Higher Standard in Aviation

P. O. Box AB-20485 • Marsh Harbour • Abaco, Bahamas
(242) 367-2089 • (242) 367-2613 • (242) 367-2530
Call us for rates

Pier One Boat Rentals

19' SeaPro with 130 HP • Also 20', 21' and 22' boats
Located at the Jib Room / Marsh Harbour Marina

All boats equipped with Bimini Tops, VHF Radio, anchor, dive ladder, life jackets, flares, first aid kit, fire extinguisher, and compass

Call 242 367-3587 • Cellular 359-6982 • VHF 16
Pier One Boat Rentals • P. O. Box AB- 21008
Marsh Harbour, Abaco, Bahamas

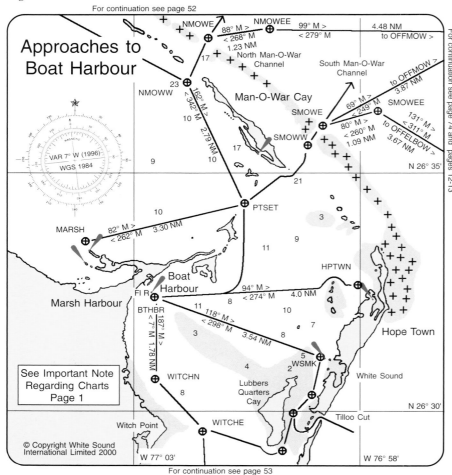

For continuation see page 52

Approaches to
Boat Harbour

NMOWE   NMOWEE
88° M >   99° M >   4.48 NM
< 268° M   < 279° M   to OFFMOW >
1.23 NM
North Man-O-War
Channel   South Man-O-War
Channel
to OFFMOW >
3.87 NM

23   162° M >
< 342° M   Man-O-War Cay   69° M >   SMOWEE
< 249° M
NMOWW   2.79 NM   SMOWE   131° M >   to OFFELBOW >
10   80° M >   < 311° M   3.67 NM
17   SMOWW   < 260° M
1.09 NM
9   10   N 26° 35'

21

PTSET

10

MARSH   82° M >   3.30 NM   3
< 262° M   11   9

Boat
Harbour   HPTWN

FI R   94° M >   4.0 NM
Marsh Harbour   8   < 274° M   10
BTHBR   11   118° M >   8
< 7° M   < 298° M   3.54 NM
3   7
1.78 NM
5
WSMK   Hope Town
See Important Note   4   2
Regarding Charts   WITCHN   Lubbers
Page 1   8   Quarters   White Sound
Cay   N 26° 30'

Witch Point   WITCHE   Tilloo Cut

© Copyright White Sound
International Limited 2000   W 77° 03'   W 76° 58'

VAR 7° W (1996)
WGS 1984

For continuation see pages 74 and pages 12-13

For continuation see page 53

BOAT HARBOUR MARINA

Boat Harbour Marina is conveniently located on the southeast shoreline of Great Abaco Island in the town of Marsh Harbour. Access to Marsh Harbour's business district is very good (about five minutes by car), and access by water to Hope Town, White Sound, Man-O-War Cay, or to the Atlantic Ocean via Tilloo Cut, South Man-O-War Channel or North Man-O-War Channel is easy and direct.

The waypoint BTHBR (N 26° 32.410'; W 77° 02.550') is located about 100 yards SE of the piling with the flashing red light, which is located about 100 yards ESE of the entrance to the marina. Approach the waypoint from the east on a course of 270° M, or from White Sound on a course of 298° M. Approach it from the south from the waypoint WITCHN on a course of 7° M. See intermediate scale charts of the Hub of Abaco (p. 74), the Lubbers Quarters area (p. 110), and Man-O-War Cay and its Approaches (p. 68) for more detail.

Boat Harbour offers gasoline, diesel, and complete marina services, has two bars and restaurants, the Great Abaco Beach Hotel, a liquor store and a dive shop all on the premises. A Solomon's Mines gift shop are located a short walk from the marina.

Boat Harbour Marina and Abaco Beach Resort from the southwest with Man-O-War Cay in the background. The fuel dock is to starboard after entering.

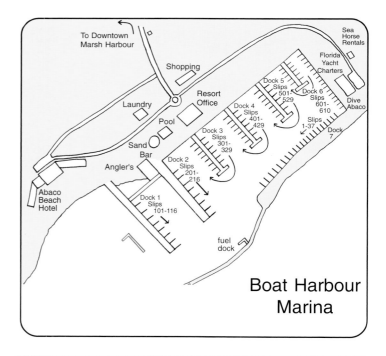

Boat Harbour
Marina

SO CLOSE
Yet so far away...

Miami
Bahamas
Key West

Set sail from our headquarters at the **Miami Beach Marina**, in the Art Deco district of chic **South Beach**. Cruise **Biscayne Bay** and the **Florida Keys** or venture across the Gulfstream to the islands of the Bahamas.

Thinking of purchasing a yacht or an alternative to chartering? Inquire about our new **"Peace of Mine in Paradise"** program, where you can own a yacht for a fraction of the cost; use it frequently, and have it maintained by us in your choice of our three beautiful locations. It's an investment the whole family can enjoy!

Discover an out-island adventure in the **Abacos**. Fly in and sail out of **Marsh Harbour** from the luxurious Abaco Beach Resort. Cruise the idyllic Sea of Abaco aboard new air conditioned **Hunter** sailboats. **Mainship** trawlers or cruising catamarans.

Enjoy a relaxing vacation afloat and earn your **ASA certification** with your "mate" on one of our romantic **Couples Cruising course.**

Enjoy spectacular sailing, exquisite coral reefs and the carefree spirit of **Key West**. Begin or end your charter from the heart of Old Town; where gourmet restaurants, Hemingway haunts, artist galleries and the nightly Sunset Celebration await you. One-way trips from Miami to **Key West** available.

Authorized dealer for Hunter sailboats & Mainship trawlers. Licensed yacht brokerage. Open every day!

HUNTER
MARINE CORPORATION

FLORIDA YACHT
CHARTERS (Bahamas) Ltd.
FLORIDAYACHT.COM

Mainship
TRAWLERS

AT ABACO BEACH RESORT
Boat Harbour Marina • Marsh Harbour, Abaco
floridayacht@oii.net
(242) 367-4853

AT THE MIAMI BEACH MARINA
1290 5th St • Miami Beach, FL 33139
charter@floridayacht.com
(800) 537-0050 • (305) 532-8600

For continuation see page 74 or pages 52 and 53

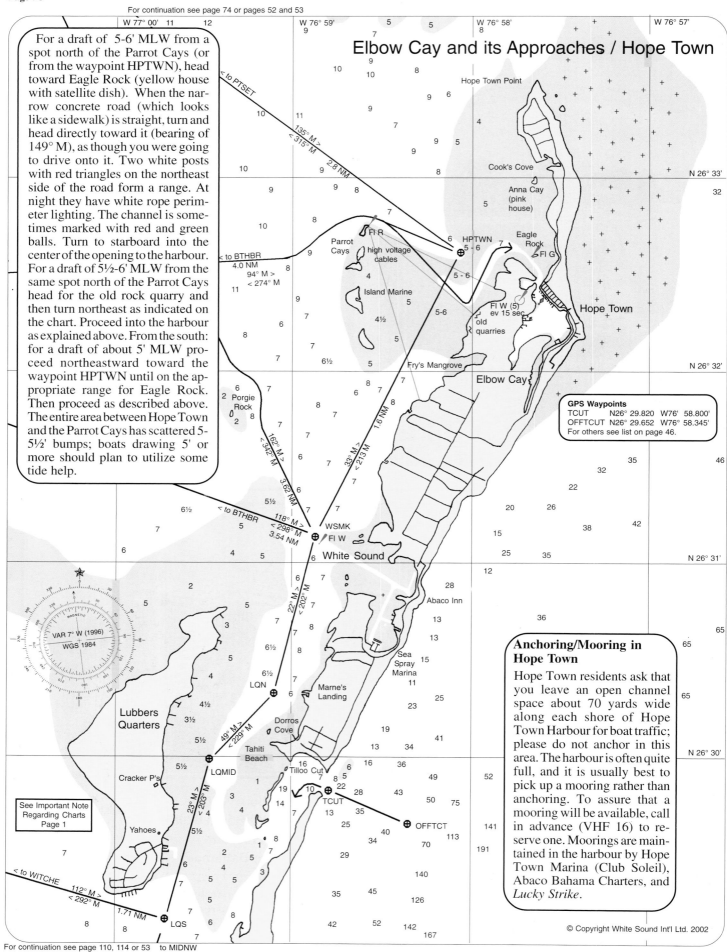

Elbow Cay and its Approaches / Hope Town

For a draft of 5-6' MLW from a spot north of the Parrot Cays (or from the waypoint HPTWN), head toward Eagle Rock (yellow house with satellite dish). When the narrow concrete road (which looks like a sidewalk) is straight, turn and head directly toward it (bearing of 149° M), as though you were going to drive onto it. Two white posts with red triangles on the northeast side of the road form a range. At night they have white rope perimeter lighting. The channel is sometimes marked with red and green balls. Turn to starboard into the center of the opening to the harbour. For a draft of 5½-6' MLW from the same spot north of the Parrot Cays head for the old rock quarry and then turn northeast as indicated on the chart. Proceed into the harbour as explained above. From the south: for a draft of about 5' MLW proceed northeastward toward the waypoint HPTWN until on the appropriate range for Eagle Rock. Then proceed as described above. The entire area between Hope Town and the Parrot Cays has scattered 5-5½' bumps; boats drawing 5' or more should plan to utilize some tide help.

GPS Waypoints
TCUT   N26° 29.820 W76' 58.800'
OFFTCUT N26° 29.652 W76' 58.345'
For others see list on page 46.

VAR 7° W (1996)
WGS 1984

See Important Note Regarding Charts Page 1

Anchoring/Mooring in Hope Town

Hope Town residents ask that you leave an open channel space about 70 yards wide along each shore of Hope Town Harbour for boat traffic; please do not anchor in this area. The harbour is often quite full, and it is usually best to pick up a mooring rather than anchoring. To assure that a mooring will be available, call in advance (VHF 16) to reserve one. Moorings are maintained in the harbour by Hope Town Marina (Club Soleil), Abaco Bahama Charters, and *Lucky Strike*.

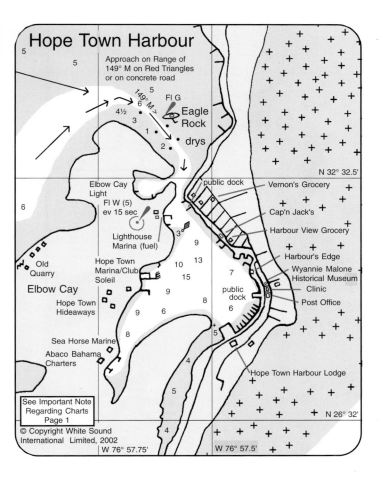

Hope Town Harbour

Approach on Range of 149° M on Red Triangles or on concrete road

149° M

Fl G

Eagle Rock

drys

4½

N 32° 32.5'

Elbow Cay Light
Fl W (5) ev 15 sec

public dock

Vernon's Grocery

Cap'n Jack's

Harbour View Grocery

Lighthouse Marina (fuel)

Harbour's Edge

Old Quarry

Hope Town Marina/Club Soleil

Wyannie Malone Historical Museum

Clinic

Elbow Cay

public dock

Post Office

Hope Town Hideaways

Sea Horse Marine

Abaco Bahama Charters

Hope Town Harbour Lodge

N 26° 32'

See Important Note Regarding Charts Page 1

© Copyright White Sound International Limited, 2002

W 76° 57.75'   W 76° 57.5'

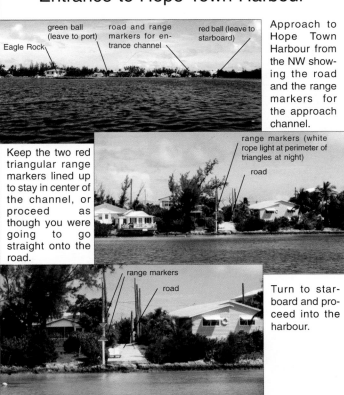

Entrance to Hope Town Harbour

green ball (leave to port)

Eagle Rock

road and range markers for entrance channel

red ball (leave to starboard)

Approach to Hope Town Harbour from the NW showing the road and the range markers for the approach channel.

range markers (white rope light at perimeter of triangles at night)

road

Keep the two red triangular range markers lined up to stay in center of the channel, or proceed as though you were going to go straight onto the road.

range markers

road

Turn to starboard and proceed into the harbour.

HOPE TOWN

Hope Town is clearly one of the most picturesque settlements in the Bahamas. Its candy-striped lighthouse was built by the British Imperial Lighthouse Service in 1863, and still uses a small kerosene-fueled mantle and a huge rotating glass fresnel lens to send a beam of light which can be seen for up to 20 miles. The town has many charming old houses, some of them beautifully restored. The ocean beach, just to the east, has powdery pink sand and is protected by an extensive offshore reef. Founded by loyalists in c. 1785, the community maintains the Wyannie Malone Historical Museum, which has many interesting artifacts, photographs, and documents.

Hope Town provides many services for visitors. There are two grocery stores—Harbour View Grocery and Vernon's Grocery. Vernon's includes the Upper Crust Bakery where pies and bread are baked daily. Vernon's business slogans—"Let Them Eat Key Lime Pie" and "Pies 'R' Us" exemplify his delightful sense of humor. Harbour View Grocery is on the waterfront, and has its own dock. Both stores are well stocked; what one does not have can likely be found at the other.

There are three marinas—Lighthouse Marina near the harbour entrance, Hope Town Marina further in along the harbour's west side, and Hope Town Hideaways just beyond Hope Town Marina. Lighthouse Marina offers fuel, wet and dry storage, and has a well-stocked marine store. Hope Town Marina has wet storage and the Club Soleil Resort and Restaurant. Hope Town Hideaways is a small resort and has a pool.

The Hope Town Harbour Lodge is also a resort/restaurant complex, and has recently been completely refurbished. It offers snorkeling just off its ocean beach and pool bar. Other bars and restaurants include Harbour's Edge, located on the water north of the main (upper) public dock, and Cap'n Jack's, located further north on the water. Munchies offers take-away food, and has a small eating area on the premises. Rudy's Place, located just outside of town serves dinner, and the Abaco Inn and Boat House Restaurant (at Sea Spray Marina and Resort), both located at White Sound, serve breakfast, lunch, and dinner. All offer excellent food and friendly service—and provide the visitor with exceptional variety in a small town.

continued on page 100

Hope Town

continued from page 99

There are several excellent gift and souvenir shops—the Ebb Tide Shop, Kemp's Souvenir Center, Iggy Biggy, El Mercado and Fantasy Boutique. The Ebb Tide offers Androsia Batik clothing, and all have a good assortment of other clothing, jewelry, T-shirts, books, and various gift items. Iggy Biggy specializes in art prints, paintings, island clothing, and jewelry.

Bicycles can be rented at Harbour's Edge Restaurant and the Hope Town Harbour Lodge, and golf carts are available from Island Cart Rentals (366-0448), Hope Town Cart Rentals (366-0064) and T&N Carts (366-0069). White Sound is a 3-mile ride; Tahiti Beach is another 1½ miles. Hope Town Point is a short ride or walk north of town. Motorized vehicles (including golf carts) are not allowed in town.

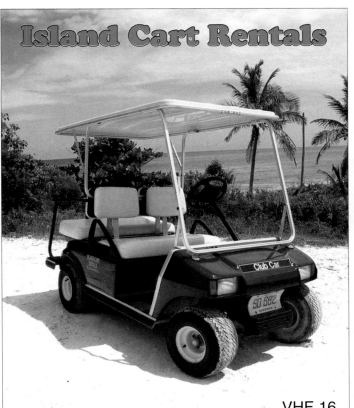

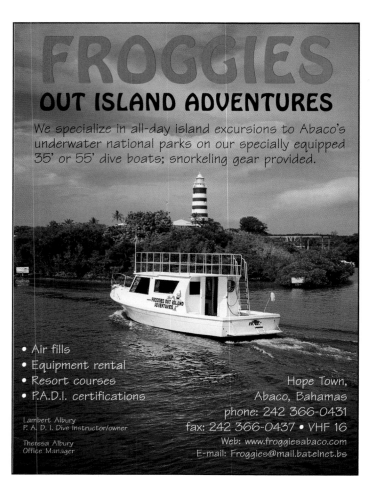

Get off your Boatt

You've been cruising around in the warm sun and suddenly, there it is - the perfect spot. The crystal waters beckon. The kids can't wait to dive in. Everyone wants to see the wonders beneath. But who has room on the boat for 2, 3, 4 or more sets of scuba gear? And what about all those scuba tanks? How many do you need for each diver? (too many, right?) And they need to be filled, and stowed, and refilled, and carried.....

Wouldn't it be great if everyone could dive together without the hassles of heavy tanks and limited air supply?

The most convenient way to dive.

Brownie's Third Lung has been the leading manufacturer of family diving systems since 1969. Our floating systems can take 2, 3 or 4 divers to recreational depths and run for up to 4 hours on a single tank of gas. Still not tired? With your Brownie, there's no need to come back in to refill cylinders. Just refuel and you're back in business.

It's time to Browniedive!

Once you're in the water, the fun really begins. You'll be amazed at the comfort and freedom of diving without tanks. Brownie Diving feels more like freediving or snorkeling than scuba.

Share the fun.

Each diver has plenty of hose to get out and explore, yet all divers remain connected so no one will get separated from the group. The float cover is brightly colored and easily seen, and the dive flag warns other boaters to keep a safe distance from the group below.

Easy to dive. Easy to handle.

And you won't be cramped on your boat. Everything you'll need for 4 divers comes in a small protective case and a couple of gear bags. That's less space than a *single* set of scuba gear and 2 tanks - and it won't chip your gelcoat. You can inflate, deploy and dive in less than 10 minutes. Boating should be fun. Relax and enjoy the water.

Brownie's Third Lung

In Ft. Lauderdale: 954-524-2112
For a dealer near you: 954-462-5570
fax: 954-462-6115
info@browniedive.com, info@tankfill.com

*SCUBA certfication required for purchase and operation of all Brownie's floating systems.

www.browniedive.com

World's Finest Hookah
33 Years
1969-2002

Or, refill tanks right on your boat

Still want to get wet, but not ready to give up your tanks? No problem. Brownie's manufactures compressors so compact, they fit on almost any size boat. All systems are fully marinized with stainless steel fittings and hardware to withstand marine conditions.

All of our Yacht Pro systems are completely automated. You only need to connect your cylinders and flip the switch - it does everything else, including shutting itself down when the tanks are full. Advanced filtration system ensures the cleanest air available. Handy cartridges make scheduled maintenance a snap.

Boating should be fun.
Relax and enjoy the water.

Tank Fill
BROWNIE'S

www.tankfill.com

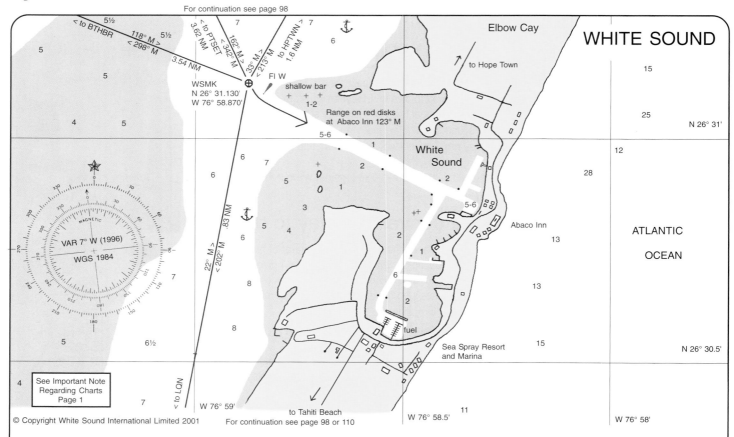

For continuation see page 98

WHITE SOUND

Elbow Cay

to Hope Town

White
Sound

Abaco Inn

ATLANTIC

OCEAN

fuel

Sea Spray Resort
and Marina

WSMK
N 26° 31.130'
W 76° 58.870'

Fl W

shallow bar
1-2

Range on red disks
at Abaco Inn 123° M

VAR 7° W (1996)
WGS 1984
MAGNETIC

See Important Note
Regarding Charts
Page 1

© Copyright White Sound International Limited 2001

to Tahiti Beach

For continuation see page 98 or 110

N 26° 31'

N 26° 30.5'

W 76° 59'   W 76° 58.5'   W 76° 58'

Boats transiting the area should stay west of the White Sound mark which indicates the channel entrance and also the western end of the White Sound Bar. This rocky bank lies just to the north of the channel and has a depth of only about 1' at MLW, so even small outboard boats should stay west of the mark.

Enter White Sound in the dredged channel which carries about 5-6' at mean low water. It is marked by the White Sound mark (Fl W) at its northwestern end and a range consisting of two large red disks on the Abaco Inn at its southeastern end. Enter on a bearing of 123° M. The range is lit by red lights at night. Proceed directly to the Abaco Inn dock, or turn to starboard and follow the marked channel to Sea Spray Marina and Resort.

Complimentary dockage is available for restaurant and bar patrons at the Abaco Inn. Space is limited, so boats should Mediterranean moor—drop an anchor off the bow, back off, and tie the stern to the dock. Power and water are not available.

The channel to Sea Spray Marina branches off the main channel with about a ninety degree turn to starboard and is marked with stakes with red and green targets. Just after entering the branch channel, there is a rock pile outside the channel off to starboard. The channel leads west of a free-standing rock breakwater which protects the fuel dock. Gasoline and diesel fuel are available. Slips are serviced with power and water, and ice, bait, etc. are available.

Anchoring in the dredged channels of White Sound is prohibited, and vessels drawing more than 2½ feet will be unable to find secure anchorage outside the channels in White Sound. Good anchorages in prevailing easterlies can be found just outside White Sound, both north and south of the entrance. It is a short dinghy ride into either Abaco Inn or Sea Spray Resort and Marina.

WHITE SOUND

White Sound has a residential community of about forty homes and two small resorts. The Abaco Inn is situated on a narrow strip of land between White Sound and the Atlantic Ocean, and has rooms facing each. It offers informal gourmet dining on open air patios with sensational views of breaking surf to the east and placid White Sound to the west. Its swimming pool is built into a rock outcropping on the ocean side, and its bar is a friendly place.

Sea Spray Marina and Resort offers 40 slips with power and water, gasoline and diesel fuel, a small boutique, an easy walk to the ocean beach, and is the only marina in Abaco with its own bakery service. It is owned and operated by Ruth Albury. Ruth's mother-in-law, Belle Albury, is the baker—fresh bread and pies may be ordered daily (Mon-Sat). The Boat House Restaurant offers breakfast, lunch, and dinner, and is fully air conditioned. There is a freshwater pool and deck overlooking White Sound adjacent to the Garbonzo Bar. Complimentary transportation to and from Hope Town is provided for marina, resort and restaurant guests.

The ocean beaches at White Sound are beautiful; the beach to the north of the Abaco Inn is better for swimming than the one to the south, which has shallow coral and rock. Because there is no offshore reef here, the area offers some of the best surfing in the Bahamas, with at least six good breaks all within half a mile of the Abaco Inn. The walk to Tahiti Beach is about 1½ miles and offers some spectacular views of both White Sound and Tilloo Cut. Hope Town is a 3-mile walk. Bicycles are available for rent at the Abaco Inn.

White Sound was severely damaged by hurricane Floyd in September 1999; the area is now recovering nicely. Visitors are asked not to walk on the recovering dunes between the Abaco Inn and Sea Spray Resort. Access to the ocean beach is available through a right of way a little south of the Abaco Inn.

The White Sound Channel from the west with the Atlantic Ocean in the background. The Abaco Inn is located at the end of the channel; range markers with round red targets provide an easy way to enter in the middle of the channel. The range is lit at night with red lights. A branch channel goes south to Sea Spray Marina.

North Channel Marker

Round red range marks (red lights at night) on Abaco Inn

South Channel Marker

White Sound Mark (flashing white -visible 2 miles)

White Sound Mark and entrance channel showing range marks and channel markers from the WNW.

Abaco Inn

22 very private rooms
Clubhouse Restaurant/Lounge
Beaches, a pool, and plenty of hammocks

The Abaco Inn is nestled on a sand dune between the Atlantic Ocean to the east and White Sound and the Sea of Abaco to the west, two miles from historic Hope Town. Superb swimming, snorkeling, SCUBA, sailing, fishing, and boating. Elegant but casual dining. Come be our guests for lunch, cocktails, dinner, a weekend, a week, or a month or two.

Abaco Inn
Hope Town, Abaco, Bahamas
1 800 468-8799
Island Direct: 242 366-0133
VHF 16
Web: www.abacoinn.com
E-mail: info@abacoinn.com

Sea Spray Resort - Villas and Marina

White Sound, Elbow Cay
Abaco, Bahamas

Sea Spray Marina and Resort is located in the quiet southern corner of beautiful White Sound, 3½ miles south of Hope Town. Our property stretches from the modern marina on protected White Sound to the beach on the Atlantic Ocean, just a few hundred yards away. We have 30 and 50 amp electrical service and water at our docks, and 1 bedroom/1 bath and 2 bedroom/2 bath villas. The Boat House Restaurant serves breakfast, lunch and dinner, and there is a new pool and deck overlooking the marina. Owned and operated by Ruth Albury.

Marina Specials
August 1 - April 30

Villa Specials
August 2 - November 15

- Full Service Deep Water Marina
- Villas with Ocean and Harbour Views
- Boat Rentals
- Fresh Water Pool and Deck
- Bakery on Site
- Boat House Restaurant
- Garbonzo Bar
- Texaco Starport

Sea Spray Resort and Marina
White Sound • Elbow Cay • Abaco • Bahamas
242 366-0065 • fax 242 366-0383 • VHF 16
Email: seasprayres@oii.net • Web: www.seasprayresort.com

CasaBlanca

(The White House)

Available for rent at White Sound, Elbow Cay, Abaco, beginning 1 March 2003

Three bedrooms, two baths, large great room, central air conditioning, dock. Located on hill overlooking Sea Spray Marina and Resort at southern end of White Sound, Elbow Cay, three miles south of Hope Town.

Call White Sound Press 386 423-7880 for further information.

Sweeting's Grocery
at White Sound

• Meats •	Hours:
Fresh each week;	M-Th 7:30am - 6:00 pm
special orders accepted	Fri-Sat 7:30 am - 8:00 pm
• Dairy Products •	Closed Sunday
• Fruits and Vegetables •	
• Beverages, Water, Ice •	Visa/Mastercard

North Side of White Sound, Elbow Cay
VHF 16   366-0391

TIDE WATCHES
by Ripcurl

- Convenient
- Reliable
- Water Resistant - 660 feet
- Stainless Steel

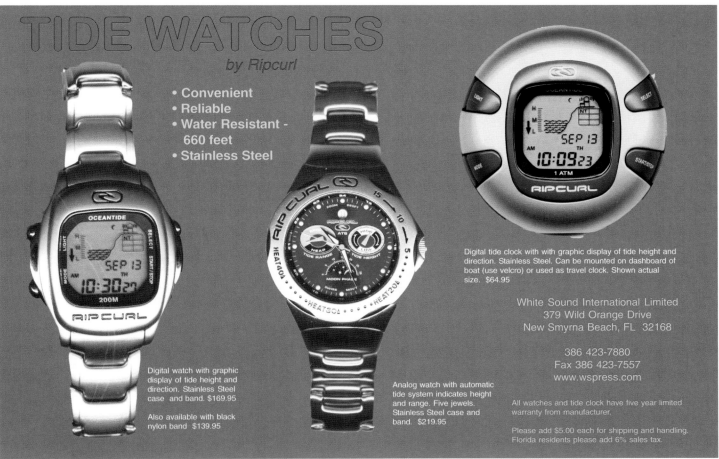

Digital watch with graphic display of tide height and direction. Stainless Steel case and band. $169.95

Also available with black nylon band $139.95

Analog watch with automatic tide system indicates height and range. Five jewels. Stainless Steel case and band. $219.95

Digital tide clock with with graphic display of tide height and direction. Stainless Steel. Can be mounted on dashboard of boat (use velcro) or used as travel clock. Shown actual size. $64.95

White Sound International Limited
379 Wild Orange Drive
New Smyrna Beach, FL 32168

386 423-7880
Fax 386 423-7557
www.wspress.com

All watches and tide clock have five year limited warranty from manufacturer.

Please add $5.00 each for shipping and handling. Florida residents please add 6% sales tax.

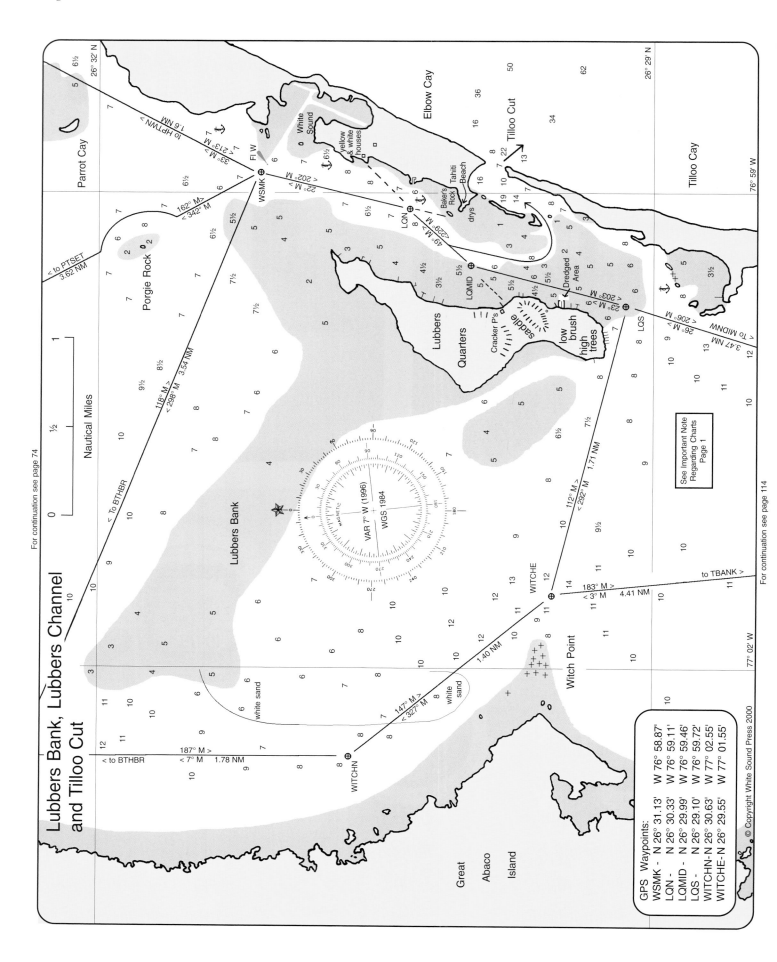

Lubbers Bank, Lubbers Channel and Tilloo Cut

Nautical Miles

For continuation see page 74

For continuation see page 114

See Important Note Regarding Charts Page 1

VAR 7° W (1996)
MAGNETIC
WGS 1984

GPS Waypoints:

WSMK -	N 26° 31.13'	W 76° 58.87'
LQN -	N 26° 30.33'	W 76° 59.11'
LQMID -	N 26° 29.99'	W 76° 59.46'
LQS -	N 26° 29.10'	W 76° 59.72'
WITCHN-	N 26° 30.63'	W 77° 02.55'
WITCHE-N 26° 29.55'		W 77° 01.55'

© Copyright White Sound Press 2000

Parrot Cay

Elbow Cay

Tilloo Cut

Tilloo Cay

White Sound

yellow & white houses

Baker's Rock

Tahiti Beach

Lubbers Quarters

Cracker P's

saddle

low brush

high trees

Dredged Area

Porgie Rock

Lubbers Bank

Witch Point

white sand

white sand

Great Abaco Island

WSMK

LQN

LQMID

LQS

WITCHE

WITCHN

FI W

26° 32' N

26° 29' N

76° 59' W

77° 02' W

LUBBER'S BANK, LUBBER'S CHANNEL, AND TILLOO CUT

Lubber's Quarters and the bank extending northwest of it lie athwart the Sea of Abaco, making it necessary for boats to maneuver through Lubbers Quarters Channel or to go west of the cay and the bank. The channel is shallow and has shoaled during recent years—it is now about 4½-5' MLW—and passage through it is not straightforward. Many cruising boats make the mistake of going directly down the middle of the channel because it looks OK and the outboards do it successfully. If they draw more than 2-3', and the tide is lower than high, they usually find themselves aground on a bar which is somewhat difficult to see because it is grassy rather than sandy. To carry 4½' MLW through the channel follow the course lines as drawn on the chart. Approaching from the north, go from the White Sound Mark toward Baker's Rock on a heading of 202° M, with the Parrot Cays on your stern. When the lower and smaller of the two prominent yellow and white houses on Elbow Cay bears 49°, turn to put it on your stern, heading toward the saddle on Lubbers Quarters on the reciprocal heading of 229° M. Beware of the "false saddle" which results from the high trees and low bush at the southern end of Lubbers. Stay on this course until you are rather close to Lubbers—until the western shoreline of Tavern Cay bears 203° M, then turn and head toward Tavern Cay. If you are in the right place, you will pass over the outer edge of the dredged area at the Abaco Ocean Club's community dock. Continue on this course until you are abeam the southern tip of Lubbers Quarters.

For passage from south to north sail the reciprocals—go toward the channel area heading toward a point between the northern tip of Lubbers Quarters and the Parrot Cays on a heading of 23° M. When the lower and smaller of the two prominent yellow and white houses bears 49° M, turn and head for it. When you reach the point at which your position and Baker's Rock are in range with the Parrot Cays, turn and go toward the Parrot Cays on a heading of 22° M, which will take you to the White Sound Mark.

There is a good route to the ocean through Tilloo Cut. From the north, proceed as though you were going to go through Lubber's Channel, but when about halfway between Baker's Rock and Lubber's Quarter's, turn and head toward the north tip of the curved natural deep channel which has a white sandy bottom and is therefore visible. Your heading should be about 200° M. Then follow the channel around Cooperjack Cay, passing between the cay and a rock to starboard. Proceed to the cut. Go close to the south side of the cut (only about 40 yards off the north tip of Tilloo Cay) and then turn southeast when in the ocean to avoid a shallow bar on which waves often break straight out and northeast of the cut. The depth at the cut itself is 7', but controlling depth is 5-6 feet inside just north of the north end of the natural curved channel.

There are several pleasant anchorages in this area. Just north of Baker's Rock near Tahiti Beach is a favorite summer anchorage for many boats; others can be found on either side of the entrance to White Sound, and a fourth can be found just north of the small shallow harbour on Tilloo. All of these offer little protection from the northwest.

Cracker P's Bar and Restaurant is located near the middle of the east coast of Lubbers and features fresh grilled foods. There is a nice beach, a good dock, and a play area for children. Those anchoring off are asked to stay well off to avoid fouling electrical cables. There is good protection from the northwest here.

Lubbers Quarters Cay is a developing residential community of over 50 homes. It has grown substantially since being serviced by electricity, telephones and internet about 4 years ago. An old coral path winds its way around the south end in the Abaco Ocean Club subdivision. A small marina in the subdivision is comprised of privately owned boat slips and a small public dock for its homeowners. Throughout the entire cay there is a nice mix of well-spaced homes in peaceful settings owned by foreigners as well as Bahamians.

Lubbers Quarters Channel from the southwest with Lubbers Quarters in the foreground and Tahiti Beach on Elbow Cay and Tilloo Cut in the background.

Page 112

Public dock at dredged area near southeast Lubbers Quarters. Photo is pre-hurricane Floyd. Rebuilt dock is shorter.

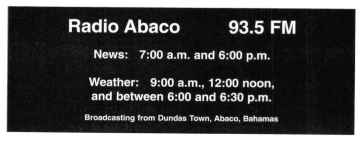

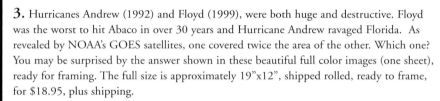

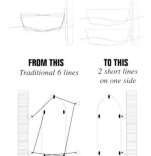

For continuation see page 110

Tavern Cay to Lynyard Cay
including North Bar Channel

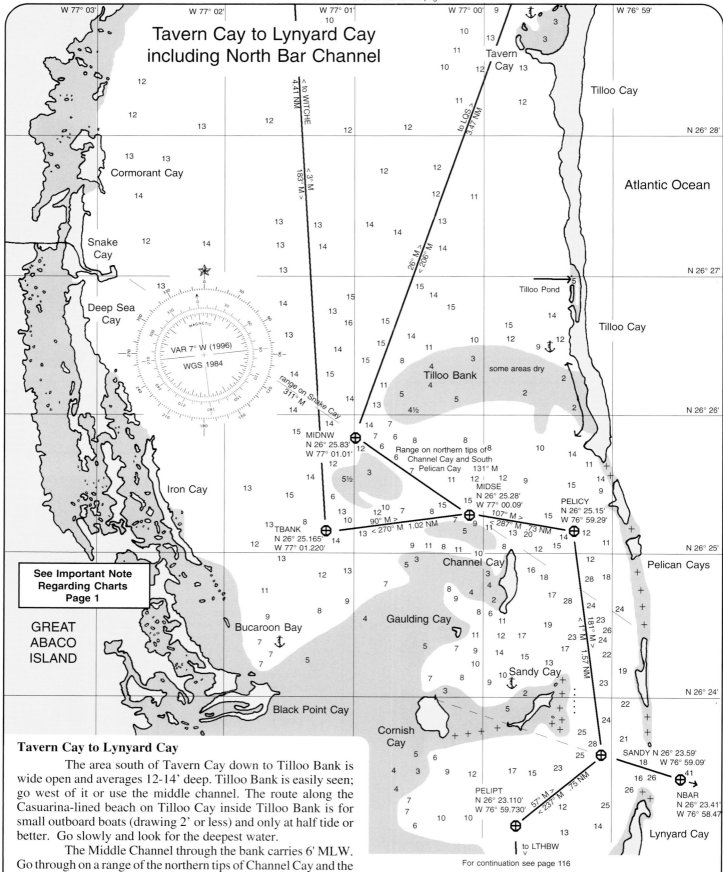

W 77° 03'   W 77° 02'   W 77° 01'   W 77° 00'   W 76° 59'

N 26° 28'
N 26° 27'
N 26° 26'
N 26° 25'
N 26° 24'

Cormorant Cay

Snake Cay

Deep Sea Cay

VAR 7° W (1996)
MAGNETIC
WGS 1984

Iron Cay

Atlantic Ocean

Tilloo Cay

Tilloo Pond

Tilloo Cay

Tilloo Bank   some areas dry

< to WITCHE 4.41 NM
183° M >   < 3° M

to LOS 3.47 NM
26° M >   < 206° M

range on Snake Cay 311° M

MIDNW
N 26° 25.83'
W 77° 01.01'

Range on northern tips of
Channel Cay and South
Pelican Cay   131° M

MIDSE
N 26° 25.28'
W 77° 00.09'

PELICY
N 26° 25.15'
W 76° 59.29'

TBANK
N 26° 25.165'
W 77° 01.220'

90° M >   < 270° M 1.02 NM
107° M >   < 287° M .73 NM

Channel Cay

Pelican Cays

Gaulding Cay

181° M > 1 NM 1.57 NM

Sandy Cay

Cornish Cay

SANDY N 26° 23.59'
W 76° 59.09'

NBAR
N 26° 23.41'
W 76° 58.47'

PELIPT
N 26° 23.110'
W 76° 59.730'

57° M >   < 237° M .75 NM

to LTHBW

Lynyard Cay

Black Point Cay

Bucaroon Bay

GREAT
ABACO
ISLAND

See Important Note
Regarding Charts
Page 1

For continuation see page 116

Tavern Cay to Lynyard Cay

The area south of Tavern Cay down to Tilloo Bank is wide open and averages 12-14' deep. Tilloo Bank is easily seen; go west of it or use the middle channel. The route along the Casuarina-lined beach on Tilloo Cay inside Tilloo Bank is for small outboard boats (drawing 2' or less) and only at half tide or better. Go slowly and look for the deepest water.

The Middle Channel through the bank carries 6' MLW. Go through on a range of the northern tips of Channel Cay and the southernmost Pelican Cay or use the GPS waypoints. Your heading should be 131° M and Snake Cay (white breakwater) should be on your stern at 311° M. Or go around the entire bank using the waypoint TBANK.

Give Sandy Cay Reef, which is marked by a high rock near the north end and a low rock near the south end, a wide berth. Snorkeling is excellent on the reef, which is part of the Pelican Cays Land and Sea Park. All fishing is prohibited in the park and

text continued on page 115

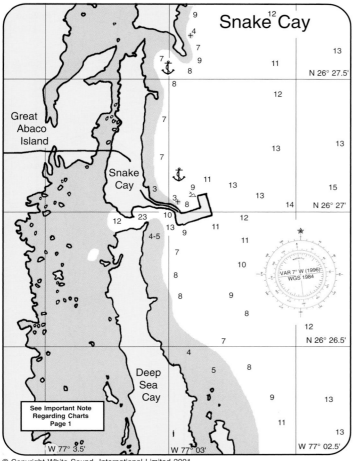

Snake ¹² Cay

Great
Abaco
Island

Snake
Cay

Deep
Sea
Cay

VAR 7° W (1996)
WGS 1984

See Important Note
Regarding Charts
Page 1

N 26° 27.5'

N 26° 27'

N 26° 26.5'

W 77° 3.5'   W 77° 03'   W 77° 02.5'

© Copyright White Sound International Limited 2001

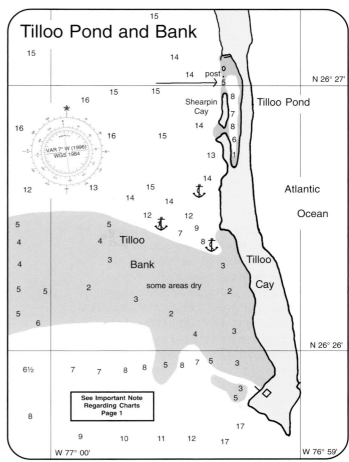

Tilloo Pond and Bank

Shearpin
Cay

Tilloo Pond

Atlantic

Ocean

Tilloo
Bank

some areas dry

Tilloo
Cay

VAR 7° W (1996)
WGS 1984

See Important Note
Regarding Charts
Page 1

N 26° 27'

N 26° 26'

W 77° 00'   W 76° 59'

© Copyright White Sound International Limited 2001

continued from page 114

no shells or coral may be taken. See the more detailed chart
on this page for the boundaries of the park. Holding ground
off the reef is poor (smooth round rocks covered with about 2"
of sand), but there are several small boat moorings (for boats
24' or less) located just east of the reef. Anchoring on the reef
is prohibited; it damages the coral. Larger boats should anchor
in Pelican Harbour to the west of Sandy Cay and dinghy to the
small boat moorings. Holding ground in Pelican Harbour is
less than ideal, and there is a swell in the area. This is a daytime
anchorage only; Pelican Harbour is not really a harbour. See
the separate snorkeling/diving sketch chart on page 126 for
more detailed information about the reef.

North Bar Channel is one of the best passages from
the Sea of Abaco to the Atlantic Ocean, providing about 16-
17' of water at its shallowest point. The range for this channel
consists of two white concrete posts, one on Sandy Cay and the
other on Cornish Cay. When entering on the range, the heading
should be 295° M. This course should take you about midway
between the north tip of Lynyard Cay and Channel Rock,
avoiding the rocky shoal area just off Lynyard Cay.

Several settled weather or daytime anchorages can
be found in appropriate weather on the west side of Tilloo Cay
and at Snake Cay (see charts above). Anchoring in Tilloo Pond
is not recommended; it is small and a Bahamian moor is
necessary to hold the boat in position if the wind shifts. It can,
of course, be used in an emergency, and it offers excellent
shelter. The cut leading to the lagoon behind Snake Cay and
Deep Sea Cay is deep with excellent protection, but it is also
very small and strong tidal currents exist, so if one chooses to
be anchored here during a reverse of tidal flow, a Bahamian
moor is absolutely necessary.

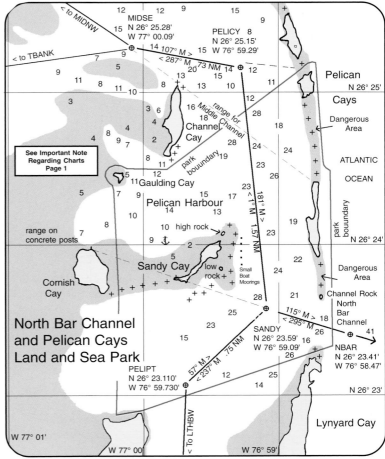

North Bar Channel
and Pelican Cays
Land and Sea Park

Pelican
Cays

Dangerous
Area

ATLANTIC

OCEAN

park boundary

Dangerous
Area

Channel Rock
North
Bar
Channel

MIDSE
N 26° 25.28'
W 77° 00.09'

PELICY 8
N 26° 25.15'
W 76° 59.29'

Middle Channel Cay

Gaulding Cay

Pelican Harbour

range on
concrete posts

high rock

Small
Boat
Moorings

Sandy Cay

low
rock

Cornish
Cay

SANDY
N 26° 23.59'
W 76° 59.09'

NBAR
N 26° 23.41'
W 76° 58.47'

N 26° 23'

PELIPT
N 26° 23.110'
W 76° 59.730'

See Important Note
Regarding Charts
Page 1

Lynyard Cay

W 77° 01'   W 77° 00'   W 76° 59'

© Copyright White Sound International Limited 2000

For continuation see page 114 or page 53

Approaches to Little Harbour

Approach from north: The beach just to the east of the entrance can be seen from a distance of several miles. Head toward its eastern end on a heading of 186° M. When you are about ½ mile from Tom Curry's Point, turn and head toward it. When the white house at the SW corner of the harbour is centered in the harbour opening, head for it. Proceed until you are on the range line between the other prominent house (white roof) and Tom Curry's Point, and then turn and head toward the house. This course should carry you through the marked channel between the buoys over the white sand bottom. The darker water on either side is shallow and grass covered. The channel turns 35° to port and opens into the harbour. The shallowest part of the channel is about 3½' at Mean Low Water; half tide is needed to carry 5' draft through. Temporary daytime anchorages to wait for tide can be found west of the tip of Tom Curry's Point or northwest of the old lighthouse building (a small dilapidated structure without a traditional lighthouse tower). After entering Little Harbour, anchor or pick up one of Pete's Pub's moorings.

To enter Abaco Sound from the Atlantic Ocean at Little Harbour approach the lighthouse on a northwesterly course (315° M) until the prominent house on Bridges Cay bears 344° M, and then head for it. This course will carry you between the rocky shoal extending from the lighthouse point and the reef to the northeast in about 14' MLW. GPS waypoints for this courseline are provided on the chart.

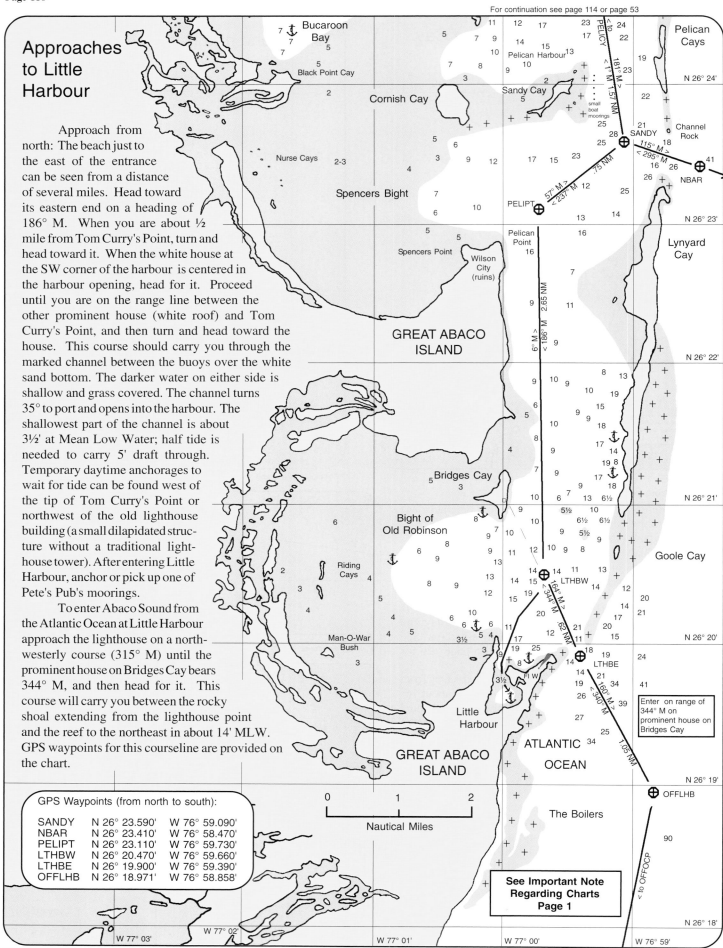

Enter on range of 344° M on prominent house on Bridges Cay

GPS Waypoints (from north to south):

SANDY	N 26° 23.590'	W 76° 59.090'
NBAR	N 26° 23.410'	W 76° 58.470'
PELIPT	N 26° 23.110'	W 76° 59.730'
LTHBW	N 26° 20.470'	W 76° 59.660'
LTHBE	N 26° 19.900'	W 76° 59.390'
OFFLHB	N 26° 18.971'	W 76° 58.858'

See Important Note Regarding Charts Page 1

For continuation see page 119 or page 120

Entrance to Little Harbour

The opening is between the beach and Tom Curry's Point.

Get on a range with Tom Curry's point on the transom and the group of houses on the bow.

The channel is marked with buoys, and the deepest water is the light green water (approx. 3½' MLW).

Turn about 35° to port and enter the anchorage.

Pete's Pub and Gallery
Little Harbour

Mailing Address:
Pete's Pub and Gallery
P. O. Box AB 20282
Marsh Harbour, Abaco, Bahamas

Cell Phone: 242 366.3503
Fax: 242 367.3144
Email: petespub@abacoinet.com

Open 7 Days a Week

For continuation see page 116 or 53

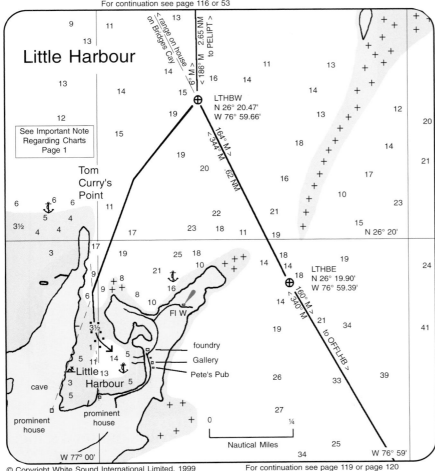

Little Harbour

LTHBW
N 26° 20.47'
W 76° 59.66'

Tom Curry's Point

See Important Note Regarding Charts Page 1

LTHBE
N 26° 19.90'
W 76° 59.39'

foundry
Gallery
Pete's Pub

Little Harbour

cave

prominent house

prominent house

Nautical Miles

Little Harbour from the northeast.

For continuation see page 119 or page 120

Little Harbour

Little Harbour is a beautiful, small, fully-protected anchorage. Randolph and Margot Johnston made Little Harbour their home during the middle 1950s, and founded an art colony there. Randolph, who died in late 1992, was an internationally known artist renowned for his lost wax casting in bronze, and his wife Margot worked with ceramics. Their son Pete now runs Pete's Pub and Gallery, and makes life size marine bronzes and jewelry inspired by local motifs. Two galleries are open to visitors from about 10:00 to about 4:00 or by special appointment (closed Sundays). Pete is usually very accomodating. Pete's Pub is an open air bar on the beach. It serves hot dogs and hamburgers, fish, ribs, chicken, lobster and bouillabaisse. No other shopping or services are available.

The walk to the lighthouse and the ocean side is well worth it, and the caves on the west side of the harbour in which the Johnstons lived when they first came to Little Harbour, are interesting. The small reef to the east of the entrance is convenient for snorkeling, and the larger open water reef off Lynyard Cay is quite beautiful. The Bight of Old Robinson, to the west, has numerous interesting shallow creeks, some with blue holes.

Bronze dolphin mounted on driftwood by Pete Johnston, Pete's Pub and Gallery, Little Harbour, Abaco, Bahamas.

The anchorage at Lynyard Cay.

Lynyard Cay to Hole-in-the-Wall

North Bar Channel and the opening between Little Harbour and Lynyard Cay are both viable routes between the Sea of Abaco and the Atlantic Ocean. See pages 114-115 and 116-117 respectively for more information. Once in the ocean, care should be taken to give a wide berth to the Boilers, a reef lying off the coast of Great Abaco Island between Little Harbour and Ocean Point. Cherokee Sound offers limited protection to the west of Cherokee Point, where there is often a surge, and the route to the small inner anchorage only carries about 3' MLW. For more detail see page 120.

The coastline of Great Abaco Island from Cherokee Sound to Hole-in-the-Wall is forbidding and hostile, offering no secure anchorages or protection for boats. It is about 27 NM from Cherokee Sound to Hole-in-the-Wall. It is possible to anchor just west of Hole-in-the-Wall to gain protection from the prevailing easterlies, but this anchorage is completely exposed to the S and SW.

Waypoints: Lynyard Cay to Hole-in-the-Wall and beyond

LTHBW	Abaco Sd. end Little Hrbr Ch.	N 26° 20.470'	W 76° 59.660'
LTHBE	Atlantic end Little Hrbr Ch.	N 26° 19.900'	W 76° 59.390'
OFFLHB	1¼ NM SSE Little Harbour	N 26° 18.971'	W 76° 58.858'
OFFOCP	1¼ NM ESE Ocean Point	N 26° 17.079'	W 76° 59.349'
OFFCHS	.4 NM S Cherokee Point	N 26° 15.663'	W 77° 03.152'
HOLEWL	2 NM SE Hole-in-the-Wall	N 25° 50.000'	W 77° 09.000'
SWPNT	3 NM WSW South West Pt.	N 25° 48.000'	W 77° 17.000'

Eleuthera:

BRIDGN*	N end Bridge Pt. reef opening	N 25° 34.298'	W 76° 43.344'
EGGREF	.8 NM west of Egg Reef	N 25° 31.102'	W 76° 55.031'

Nassau:

NASSAU	north Nassau Hbr. entrance	N 25° 05.447'	W 77° 21.340'

Grand Bahama Island:
See pages 12-13 and 16-19

*This waypoint is at the north end of the Bridge Point opening in Devil's Backbone Reef. Local knowledge and good visibility are required for this passage the first time. For charts and waypoints for Eleuthera, Nassau, and the rest of the Bahamas, see the 5th edition of Maptech's Chartkit *The Bahamas*.

Hole-in-the-Wall Lighthouse from the northwest .

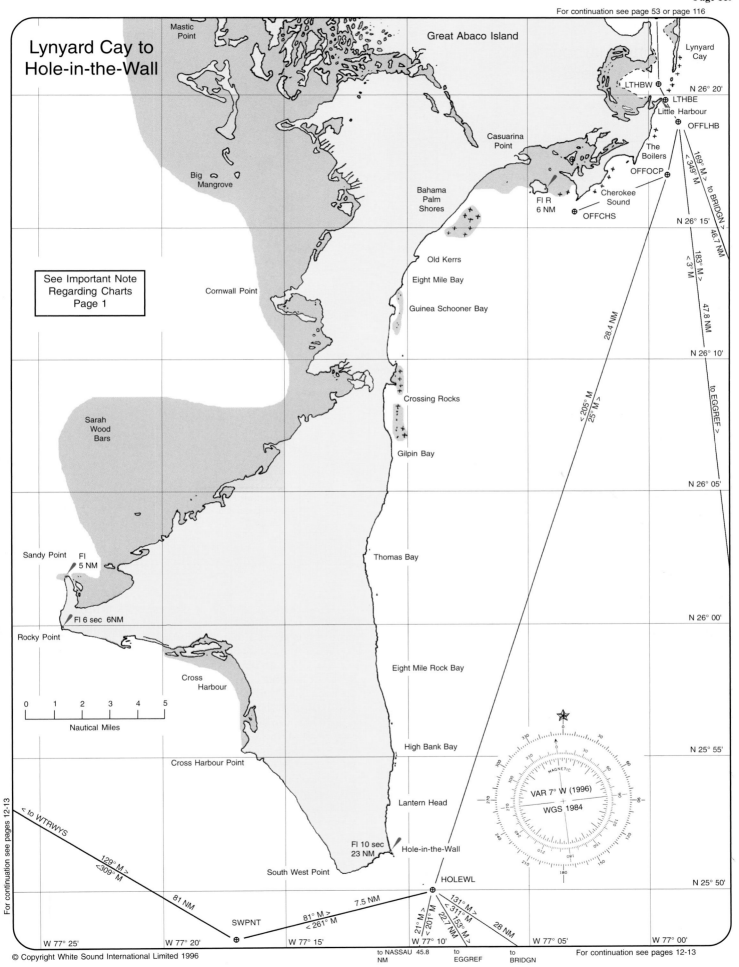

Lynyard Cay to Hole-in-the-Wall

For continuation see page 53 or page 116

Great Abaco Island

Mastic Point

Lynyard Cay

LTHBW

N 26° 20'

LTHBE

Little Harbour

OFFLHB

Casuarina Point

The Boilers

169° M

349° M

to BRIDGN

Big Mangrove

OFFOCP

Cherokee Sound

46.7 NM

Bahama Palm Shores

Fl R 6 NM

183° M

3° M

See Important Note Regarding Charts Page 1

OFFCHS

N 26° 15'

47.8 NM

Cornwall Point

Old Kerrs

Eight Mile Bay

Guinea Schooner Bay

N 26° 10'

28.4 NM

205° M

25° M

to EGGREF

Crossing Rocks

Sarah Wood Bars

Gilpin Bay

N 26° 05'

Thomas Bay

Sandy Point

Fl 5 NM

N 26° 00'

Fl 6 sec 6NM

Rocky Point

Eight Mile Rock Bay

Cross Harbour

0 1 2 3 4 5

Nautical Miles

High Bank Bay

N 25° 55'

Cross Harbour Point

Lantern Head

MAGNETIC

VAR 7° W (1996)

WGS 1984

Fl 10 sec 23 NM

Hole-in-the-Wall

HOLEWL

131° M

311° M

South West Point

21° M

201° M

153° M

22.7 NM

28 NM

N 25° 50'

129° M

309° M

81 NM

SWPNT

81° M

261° M

7.5 NM

W 77° 25'

W 77° 20'

W 77° 15'

to NASSAU 45.8 NM

to EGGREF

to BRIDGN

W 77° 10'

W 77° 05'

W 77° 00'

For continuation see pages 12-13

For continuation see small scale area chart page 53 or larger scale chart on page 116

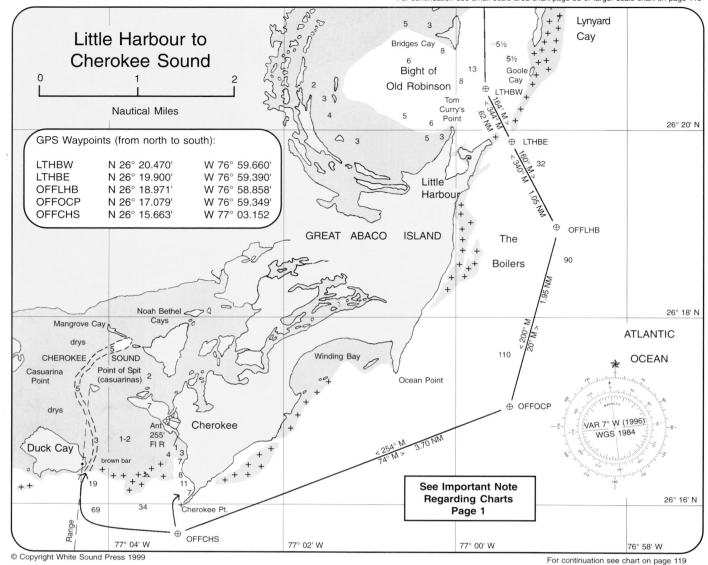

Little Harbour to Cherokee Sound

0   1   2

Nautical Miles

GPS Waypoints (from north to south):

LTHBW	N 26° 20.470'	W 76° 59.660'
LTHBE	N 26° 19.900'	W 76° 59.390'
OFFLHB	N 26° 18.971'	W 76° 58.858'
OFFOCP	N 26° 17.079'	W 76° 59.349'
OFFCHS	N 26° 15.663'	W 77° 03.152'

GREAT ABACO ISLAND

Lynyard Cay

Bridges Cay

Bight of Old Robinson

Goole Cay

LTHBW

Tom Curry's Point

LTHBE

Little Harbour

The Boilers

OFFLHB

ATLANTIC OCEAN

Noah Bethel Cays

Mangrove Cay

drys

CHEROKEE   SOUND

Casuarina Point

Point of Spit (casuarinas)

Winding Bay

Ocean Point

drys

Cherokee

Ant 255' Fl R

Duck Cay

brown bar

VAR 7° W (1996)
WGS 1984

Range

Cherokee Pt.

OFFOCP

OFFCHS

See Important Note Regarding Charts Page 1

© Copyright White Sound Press 1999

For continuation see chart on page 119

77° 04' W   77° 02' W   77° 00' W   76° 58' W

26° 20' N
26° 18' N
26° 16' N

LITTLE HARBOUR TO CHEROKEE SOUND

Vessels proceeding southward from Little Harbour should stay well clear of the Boilers, a breaking reef extending about ½ mile offshore from Great Abaco Island located about 1½ miles south of the Little Harbour channel. The waypoints and suggested course lines shown on the chart keep boats about 1 mile offshore. Cherokee Sound, located 5 miles SW of Little Harbour, is an extensive region of shallow water with a small settlement. Entrance to either one of the two possible anchorages there should be attempted in flat or moderate conditions only as breaking seas extend across both entrances in an easterly blow or when there is a strong surge.

From the waypoint OFFCHS proceed on a heading of about 0° toward the radio antenna located in the settlement. This should keep you well clear of Cherokee Point. Round the point, turning to starboard and head for the beach with the limestone cliff. The anchorage is just west of the beach with 7-11' MLW. This provides good shelter from the prevailing easterlies, but offers little protection from the SW to W, and there is often a surge in this area. Shoal draft vessels may be able to get to the dock which may well be the longest in The Bahamas, but still has only 1-2' MLW at its end. Stay fairly close to shore in order to avoid the reef to port. Proceed slowly toward the dock and look for the deepest water. Plan your visit for a tide which offers sufficient water for departure as well as arrival.

A second anchorage in the center of Cherokee Sound offers better protection, but access is not straightforward, and the anchorage is about a mile away from the settlement. Approach Duck Cay from the south on a range which lines up the lighthouse on Duck Cay with the W shoreline of Point of Spit, which has a stand of casuarinas. When about 100-150 yards off Duck Cay, turn about 20-25° to starboard and pass between Duck Cay and the brown bar to starboard. You should pass over two or three black spots. Then turn gradually to port to assume a course which will leave Point of Spit well to starboard. The shallowest spot is near where you make this turn—it is between a grassy patch (west side) and a sand bar (east side)—and its carries about 3' MLW. The remainder of the route to the anchorage is a narrow dredged channel clearly visible in good light which carries about 5' MLW. The anchorage is about 7' MLW and is just SE of Mangrove Cay and W of Noah Bethel Cays. From this anchorage you can take the dinghy to small boat docks on the creek which borders the NW side of the town.

The settlement at Cherokee Sound is small, but there is a grocery store, a radio-telephone station, and a road which goes to Marsh Harbour. Cherokee Sound was formerly a center for boat building and a thriving fishing community. The people are friendly and welcome visitors.

Snorkeling/Dive/Fishing
Chart Section

South Abaco Sound   122-123
Walkers Cay Dive Chart   124
Buoy Locations at Green Turtle Cay   125
Three Reefs Near Hub of Abaco   126-127

Sailboat at Fowl Cay Reef off Fowl Cay, 11 July 2002. Man-O-War Cay, Garden and Sandy Cays, Elbow Cay, Lubbers Quarters, Matt Lowe's Cay and Point Set Rock can all be seen in the background.

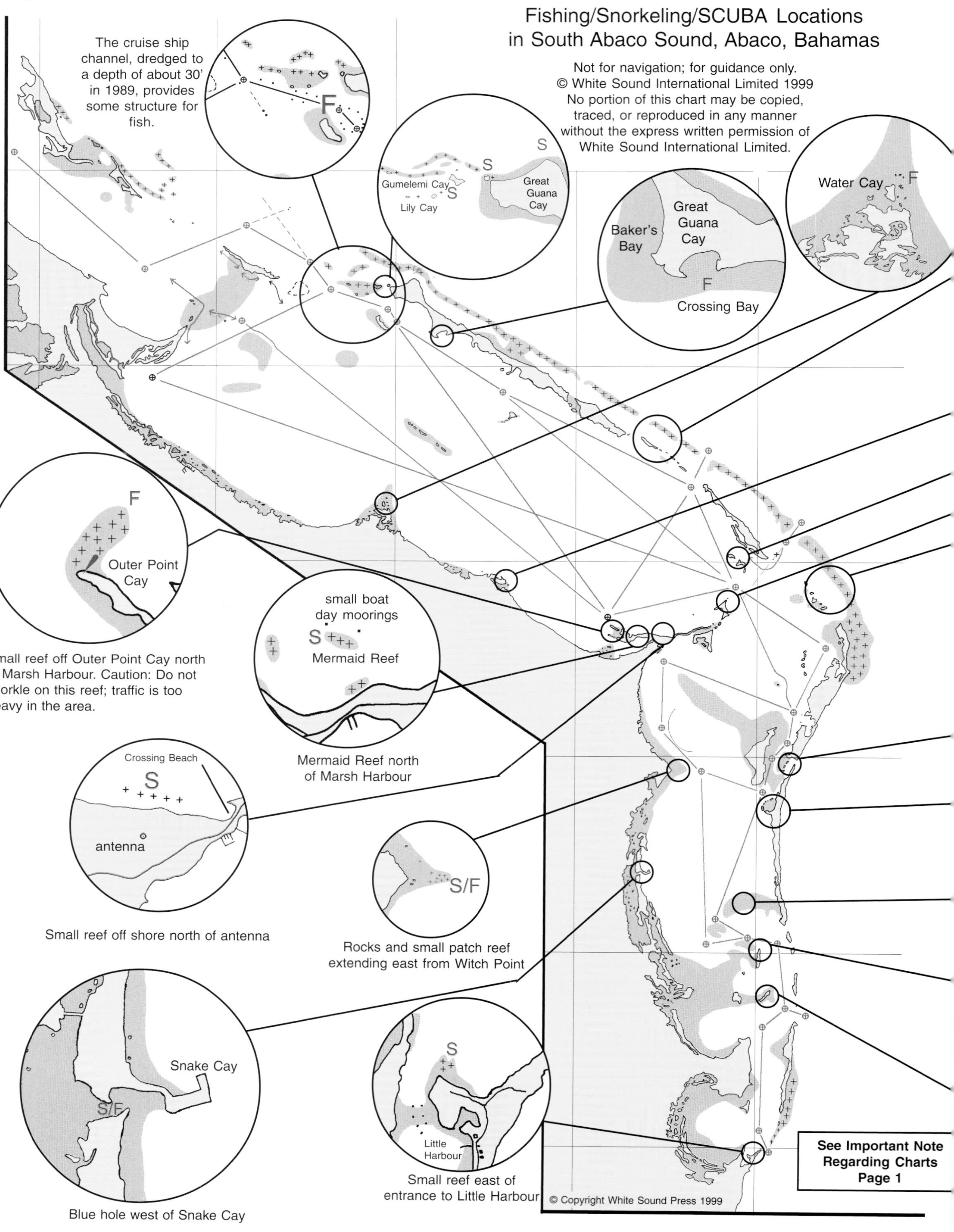

Fishing/Snorkeling/SCUBA Locations
in South Abaco Sound, Abaco, Bahamas

Not for navigation; for guidance only.
© White Sound International Limited 1999
No portion of this chart may be copied,
traced, or reproduced in any manner
without the express written permission of
White Sound International Limited.

The cruise ship
channel, dredged to
a depth of about 30'
in 1989, provides
some structure for
fish.

F

S

Gumelemi Cay
Lily Cay
S
S
Great
Guana
Cay

S

Water Cay
F

Great
Guana
Cay
Baker's
Bay
F
Crossing Bay

F

Outer Point
Cay

Small reef off Outer Point Cay north
of Marsh Harbour. Caution: Do not
snorkle on this reef; traffic is too
heavy in the area.

small boat
day moorings
S
Mermaid Reef

Mermaid Reef north
of Marsh Harbour

Crossing Beach
S
+ + + + +
antenna

Small reef off shore north of antenna

S/F

Rocks and small patch reef
extending east from Witch Point

Snake Cay
S/F

Blue hole west of Snake Cay

S

Little
Harbour

Small reef east of
entrance to Little Harbour

© Copyright White Sound Press 1999

See Important Note
Regarding Charts
Page 1

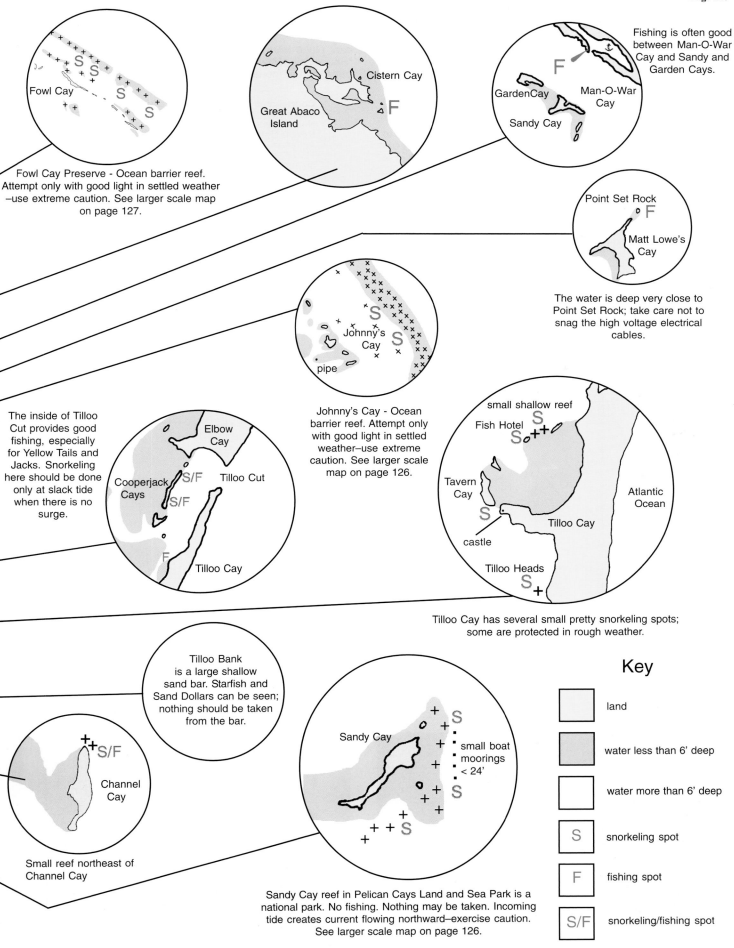

Fowl Cay Preserve - Ocean barrier reef. Attempt only with good light in settled weather —use extreme caution. See larger scale map on page 127.

Cistern Cay

Great Abaco Island

Fishing is often good between Man-O-War Cay and Sandy and Garden Cays.

GardenCay

Man-O-War Cay

Sandy Cay

Point Set Rock

Matt Lowe's Cay

The water is deep very close to Point Set Rock; take care not to snag the high voltage electrical cables.

Johnny's Cay

pipe

Johnny's Cay - Ocean barrier reef. Attempt only with good light in settled weather—use extreme caution. See larger scale map on page 126.

small shallow reef

Fish Hotel

Tavern Cay

castle

Tilloo Cay

Atlantic Ocean

Tilloo Heads

The inside of Tilloo Cut provides good fishing, especially for Yellow Tails and Jacks. Snorkeling here should be done only at slack tide when there is no surge.

Elbow Cay

Cooperjack Cays

Tilloo Cut

Tilloo Cay

Tilloo Cay has several small pretty snorkeling spots; some are protected in rough weather.

Tilloo Bank is a large shallow sand bar. Starfish and Sand Dollars can be seen; nothing should be taken from the bar.

Channel Cay

Small reef northeast of Channel Cay

Sandy Cay

small boat moorings < 24'

Sandy Cay reef in Pelican Cays Land and Sea Park is a national park. No fishing. Nothing may be taken. Incoming tide creates current flowing northward—exercise caution. See larger scale map on page 126.

Key

land

water less than 6' deep

water more than 6' deep

S   snorkeling spot

F   fishing spot

S/F   snorkeling/fishing spot

Walker's Cay Dive Chart

This chart was developed from information and a sketch chart provided by Jon Longair of Treasure Island, Florida. He wrote: "We watched and followed [the dive] boat in and out of the marina all week and they all went the same way as depicted on the map. The big mistake is trying to follow the dive boat out the middle of the reef. Do not even try. There is a week's worth of diving right inside what we called the horseshoe. All around "Pillars," "Utopia," and "Jon's Point." If you had a week there you would never need to leave that area. Most of the other dive locations were deeper but I did not think that they were that much better if at all. The reef is treacherous though. You can be in 50' of water and step out of the side of your boat on to a 3' deep mound. The steepness of the reef is also what makes it so beautiful. Go slow and watch the colors. The area in front of Walker's is now a preserve. There is no fishing, lobstering, or spearing, even with a pole spear or Hawaiian sling. Just enjoying the pristine beauty God created. I have not dived the world but I can say without hesitation that this is the most magnificent place I have ever been. Also, tell readers not to miss the "Shark Rodeo" with the Walker's dive boat. It was worth every penny of the money they charge."

Coordinates for Walker's Cay Dive Sites

Name (Depth)	latitude	longitude
Near Kevin's Crack	27° 18.980'	78° 25.590'
Kevin's Crack (60/90')	27° 18.890'	78° 26.600'
Aquarium (85')	27° 18.980'	78° 25.540'
190' Blue Canyon (80/190')	27° 18.760'	78° 25.610'
80-130' Canyon (80/130')	27° 18.710'	78° 25.610'
Small Ledge - Lobsters (80')	27° 18.890'	78° 22.500'
Shark Canyon (90')	27° 18.180'	78° 22.580'
Walker's Cay Dive Buoy (80')	27° 17.880'	78° 22.500'
Jon's Point	27° 17.271'	78° 22.958'
Pillars (48')	27° 17.266'	78° 22.551'
Utopia (48')	27° 17.218'	78° 22.572'
Larry's Sharks (60')	27° 17.910'	78° 21.980'

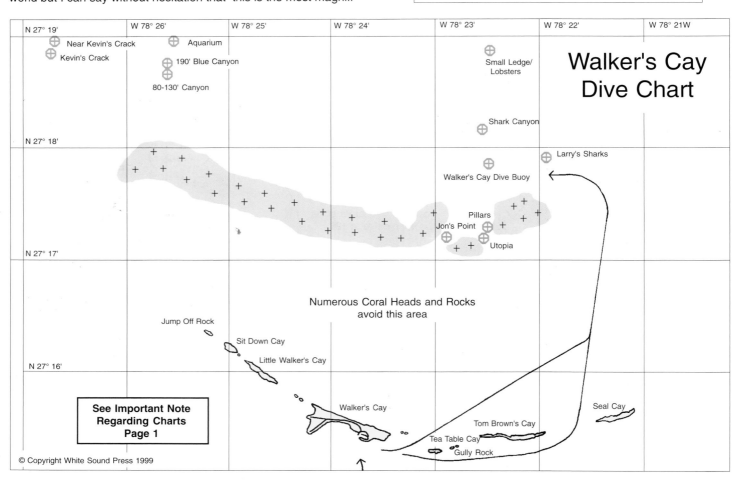

© Copyright White Sound Press 1999

See Important Note Regarding Charts Page 1

Juvenile Quenn Angelfish.

photo © Mike Adair, Sports Photography, 2001

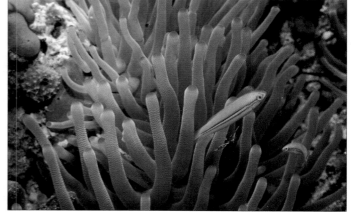

Flamefish.

photo © Mike Adair, Sports Photography, 2001

Manjack Cay, Green Turtle Cay and No Name Cay

Moorings have been installed at several popular coral reef sites near Green Turtle Cay. Please tie up to the mooring buoys rather than anchoring, which damages the fragile living corals.

Coral reefs are comprised of slow growing hard and soft corals that are actually living animals called coral polyps that can be crushed or damaged by anchors. When visiting the reef, be sure to avoid all other contact with the coral from fins, hands and dive equipment.

This project, which resulted in the installation of eighteen moorings on reefs in the vicinity of Green Turtle Cay, was spearheaded by Reef Relief of Key West, Florida.

Moorings and Dive Sites, #1-#18

1) Munjack North
These shallow coral reefs are known for their consistently clear water and an abundance of sea life. From Green Turtle Cay, if the winds are out of an easterly direction, it is easiest to get to these reefs by transiting to them using the Sea of Abaco (west side of the Cays). Head around the north side of Munjack Cay taking care to avoid the many small coral outcroppings that become more numerous closer to the reef. Approach the buoys from the west side only. Buoys # 1 and # 2 are within sight of each other and mark the presence of dangerous shallows to the east of a line drawn between them. On a Navigational chart, buoys # 1 and # 2 are on the north side of Munjack Channel.

2) Munjack
While snorkeling, care should be taken to avoid contact with the coral, especially if there are ocean swells passing over the reef. There are many small patch reefs to see around the buoys if the ocean is breaking on the shallow reefs to the east. To visit buoy #3 from here, be sure to avoid the large shallow reef on the south side of Munjack Channel. Backtrack toward Munjack Cay before heading toward buoy #3.

3) Mid Munjack
This is one of the most difficult buoys to locate for the first time because this area is cluttered with shallow coral and should only be transited when the sunlight illuminates the bottom. This buoy is very close to the magnificent beaches on the eastern side of Munjack Cay and is frequently used by boaters using the beach. A long shallow nearshore coral reef lies between the buoy and the beach which must be avoided. Approaching from buoy #2 (see North Munjack #2), parallel the Munjack shoreline on the east side of the shallow nearshore reef. This buoy can only be approached from the west. Even though this reef has some nuisance algae, beautiful boulder corals dominate the sea scape, providing shelter to a myriad of sea life.

4) Rocky Bay Hump
Approaching from North Green Turtle Channel, this buoy marks the beginning of many very shallow coral patch reefs that extend all the way to North Munjack and can only be avoided with proper sea and sunlight conditions. This buoy is designed for small boat use. There is an abundance of sand in this area where larger boats can safely anchor to visit this reef. This small buoy, dominated by algae and surrounded by sand, offers a very safe snorkeling experience. The seagrass beds on the northwest side of the reef are very healthy: avoid anchoring here. From this location, Crab Cay and Green Turtle Cay North buoys are easily accessible if conditions do not permit safe passage to the buoys north of here. There are a few shallows heading toward the Crab Cay buoy that should be avoided. The area to the east of Crab Cay is very shallow.

5) Crab Cay
The best snorkeling is to the east of the buoy.

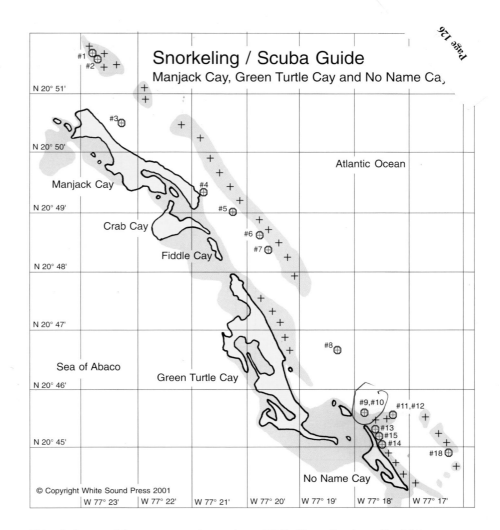

Snorkeling / Scuba Guide
Manjack Cay, Green Turtle Cay and No Name Cay

Atlantic Ocean

Manjack Cay

Crab Cay

Fiddle Cay

Sea of Abaco

Green Turtle Cay

No Name Cay

© Copyright White Sound Press 2001

This shallow reef is very expansive and offers hours of snorkeling enjoyment in good weather.

6) North Green Turtle
This buoy is located on top of a spectacular isolated coral rise that protrudes off a beautiful white sandy bottom. The diving and snorkeling is excellent at this location.

7) Raven's Cliff
Located to the south of a shallow coral plateau, the final approach to this buoy must be from the west to the east. Dolphins and sharks have been observed on this reef that offers both diving and snorkeling.

8) Green Turtle South
This buoy is often approached from South Green Turtle Channel. Once in the vicinity of the buoy, there are several reefs to visit. Sand dominates the bottom and offers good holding for anchors if the buoy is taken. The fish life in this area is spectacular. Diving is very good and deeper than on the buoys to the north. Snorkeling is also very good on top of these shallow reefs.

9 & 10) Sea Gardens 1 & 2
These buoys are the closest to New Plymouth and are frequently used by people in small inflatable boats. Located just off of Pelican Cay, this coral reef is home to thousands of purple sea fans and soft corals. This is a very good spot for children or those who feel safer snorkeling close to shore.

11 & 12) Sand Channels
This large coral reef protrudes upward from the 35 foot sea floor to within inches of the surface. Two buoys mark this reef which should be approached with caution. When the waves are breaking the surface, snorkeling here is dangerous. Diving is excellent on this reef which has been featured in many dive magazines.

13) No Name Cay Inner Reef # 1
This buoy is easily accessible by open fisherman-type boats and offers snorkeling access to the shallow nearshore reefs to the west. Isolated coral heads and beautiful sea grass meadows are found around this buoy.

14 & 15) No Name Cay Inner Reef # 2 & # 3
These buoys can only be reached by small boats. Pass very close to the north end of No Name Cay (within less than 200 feet) through a small channel. If the channel is not visible, turn back. Buoy # 14 is not advisable on a westerly wind due to the close proximity of a coral head. Buoy # 15 is located in a very diverse area. Sand, sea grass, large boulders and shallow coral are all found near this well-protected buoy.

16) No Name Outer Reef North
This buoy is within sight of the buoys at the Sand Channels and is located in a grotto on the shallow outer reef. Approach from the west, taking care to avoid the shallow reef to both sides of the buoy. This is a spectacular reef for both diving and snorkeling.

17) No Name Outer Reef South
This buoy is approached just like buoy # 16. This reef is called the Golden Grotto and has a small coral nursery established by Reef Relief to save broken pieces of storm-damaged Elkhorn coral. The broken corals were stabilized on a large coral pinnacle on the north side of the grotto.

18) No Name South (The Pinnacles)
This buoy offers a great deep dive (65') and excellent snorkeling. It can only be used in calm weather or when the winds are out of the northwest. Southeasterly or easterly winds build up seas that make this buoy unusable. Best to save this buoy for a calm day. The top of this coral reef is in excellent condition: please do not anchor here.

Snorkeling / Scuba Guide to Three Reefs near the Hub of Abaco

sketch charts by Dave Gale

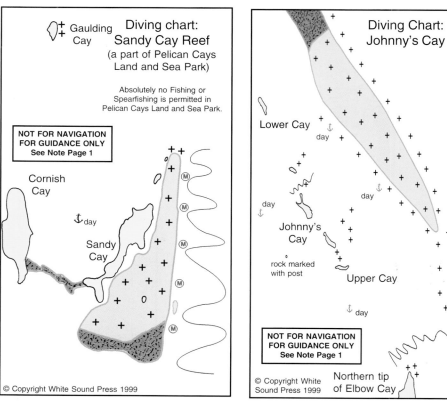

Diving chart: Sandy Cay Reef
(a part of Pelican Cays Land and Sea Park)

Gaulding Cay

Absolutely no Fishing or Spearfishing is permitted in Pelican Cays Land and Sea Park.

NOT FOR NAVIGATION
FOR GUIDANCE ONLY
See Note Page 1

Cornish Cay

Sandy Cay

© Copyright White Sound Press 1999

Diving Chart: Johnny's Cay

Lower Cay

Johnny's Cay

rock marked with post

Upper Cay

NOT FOR NAVIGATION
FOR GUIDANCE ONLY
See Note Page 1

© Copyright White Sound Press 1999

Northern tip of Elbow Cay

Three of the best reefs in Abaco for snorkeling and diving are Sandy Cay Reef, Johnny's Cay Reef, and Fowl Cay Reef. All are reasonably accessible to small boats. But the sun should be high (around midday) so that the scattered coral heads in the vicinity of the reefs can be clearly seen. Boats should approach reefs slowly with extreme caution, and should maintain a sharp lookout for coral heads. Do not attempt to snorkel any of these areas if large ocean swells or breaking waves are present.

Sandy Cay Reef is within the boundaries of the Pelican Cays Land and Sea Park, and Fowl Cay Reef is part of the Fowl Cay Bahamas National Trust Preserve. All fishing is prohibited at both sites, and no coral or shells may be taken.

There are fifteen new morrings at Sandy Cay Reef. All of these are not yet indicated on the chart on this page. The ten moorings close to the reef are for small boats; the five away from the reef can be used by larger boats, the occupants of which can then take their dinghy to the closer moorings to see the reef.

There are nineteen new moorings at Fowl Cay Preserve. These are shown on the chart on the facing page and GPS coorindates are provided for them. All these moorings have been placed by Friends of the Environment, a not-for-profit organization based in Hope Town.

Boats should never anchor on any reef because the corals may be killed or damaged by the anchor or the rode. If you choose not to use a mooring, anchor in the sand or grassy area just off the reefs.

	Water more than 6' deep with sand or grass bottom
	Land -- island, cay, or rock
	Breakers or shallow bar or head or barrier reef--to be avoided--unsafe for boat or for snorkeling
	Good snorkeling or diving reef -- pretty and shallow -- boat can go near but not over. Anchor nearby in sand; do not drop anchor in reef thereby damaging or killing corals.

D.D.S.	Deeper dive site (over 30')
Ⓜ or ●	Mooring buoy -- for use by small boats (up to 24') -- Daytime only -- placed where snorkeling and diving is good
	Possible strong current -- direction and force determined by state of tide

Sandy Cay and Sandy Cay Reef from the southwest., with the Pelican Cays and Atlantic Ocean in the background. The reef can be identified by the strip of darker water running north and south just east of the rock and breaking waves near the middle of the photo.

The southeastern extremity of Fowl Cay Reef from the northwest with Man-O-War Cay in the background. This is the shallow part of the reef represented by red/black on the chart which is dangerous for boats and divers.

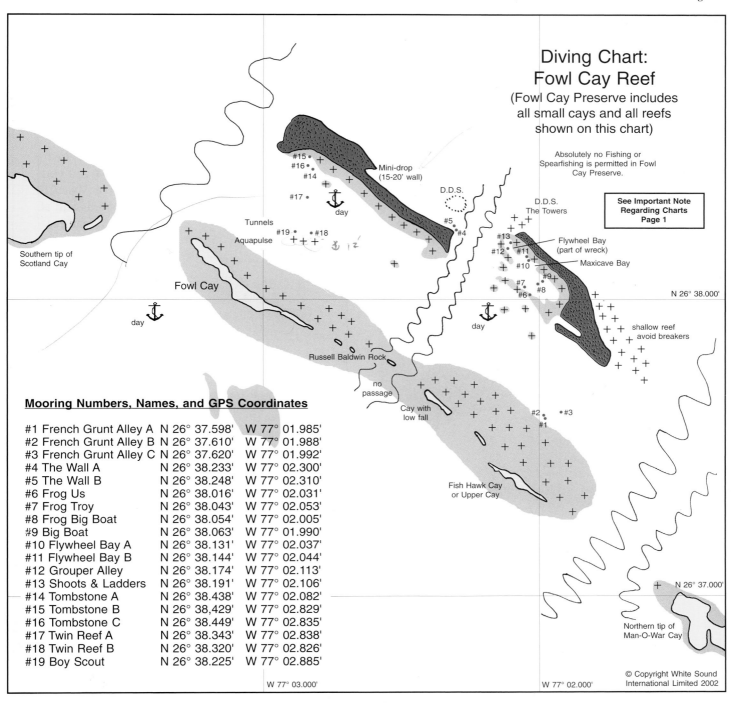

Diving Chart:
Fowl Cay Reef
(Fowl Cay Preserve includes all small cays and all reefs shown on this chart)

Absolutely no Fishing or Spearfishing is permitted in Fowl Cay Preserve.

See Important Note Regarding Charts Page 1

Southern tip of Scotland Cay

#15
#16
#14
#17 day
Mini-drop (15-20' wall)

D.D.S.
#5
#4

D.D.S.
The Towers

Tunnels
Aquapulse
#19 #18
day

#13
#12 #11
#10
#7
#6 #8
#9

Flywheel Bay (part of wreck)
Maxicave Bay

N 26° 38.000'

Fowl Cay

day

Russell Baldwin Rock

no passage

Cay with low fall

day

shallow reef avoid breakers

#2 #3
#1

Fish Hawk Cay or Upper Cay

N 26° 37.000'

Northern tip of Man-O-War Cay

© Copyright White Sound International Limited 2002

Mooring Numbers, Names, and GPS Coordinates

#1 French Grunt Alley A N 26° 37.598' W 77° 01.985'
#2 French Grunt Alley B N 26° 37.610' W 77° 01.988'
#3 French Grunt Alley C N 26° 37.620' W 77° 01.992'
#4 The Wall A   N 26° 38.233' W 77° 02.300'
#5 The Wall B   N 26° 38.248' W 77° 02.310'
#6 Frog Us   N 26° 38.016' W 77° 02.031'
#7 Frog Troy   N 26° 38.043' W 77° 02.053'
#8 Frog Big Boat   N 26° 38.054' W 77° 02.005'
#9 Big Boat   N 26° 38.063' W 77° 01.990'
#10 Flywheel Bay A   N 26° 38.131' W 77° 02.037'
#11 Flywheel Bay B   N 26° 38.144' W 77° 02.044'
#12 Grouper Alley   N 26° 38.174' W 77° 02.113'
#13 Shoots & Ladders   N 26° 38.191' W 77° 02.106'
#14 Tombstone A   N 26° 38.438' W 77° 02.082'
#15 Tombstone B   N 26° 38,429' W 77° 02.829'
#16 Tombstone C   N 26° 38.449' W 77° 02.835'
#17 Twin Reef A   N 26° 38.343' W 77° 02.838'
#18 Twin Reef B   N 26° 38.320' W 77° 02.826'
#19 Boy Scout   N 26° 38.225' W 77° 02.885'

W 77° 03.000'
W 77° 02.000'

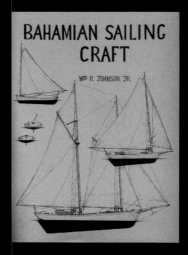

Guide to the Most Common
Whales and Dolphins of Abaco

By Diane Claridge
Bahamas Marine Mammal Survey

The Bahama Islands are home to at least twenty-three species of marine mammals, including almost one third of the world's known whales and dolphins. Since 1991, the **Bahamas Marine Mammal Survey** has been documenting the occurrence, distribution and abundance of whales and dolphins in Abaco to support conservation efforts. By photographing the pattern of natural nicks and scars on each animal's dorsal fin or tail flukes, we are able to keep track of individuals gaining an understanding of their social structure, habitat requirements and population status. The majority of species found here are deep diving toothed whales that inhabit the pelagic waters surrounding the shallow Bahama banks. Many migrate through the Bahamas, but some species are year-round residents, including some of the world's least known whales.

Our research efforts have been greatly enhanced by sighting reports that boaters have contributed over the years. As cruisers, you have a unique opportunity to observe rarely seen marine mammal species and it is important to keep an accurate log, take photographs and/or video, while respecting the animals' needs for space; and, please *never* try to touch or feed them as this may cause harm to you or the animal.

The following guide to the commonly seen whales and dolphins in the Abacos is intended to aid and encourage boaters to continue to report sightings. The species shown represent three groups of whales and dolphins, separated into their taxonomic families: oceanic dolphins, beaked whales and sperm whales. All photographs were taken in the Bahamas.

Family Delphinidae – Oceanic Dolphins

The family Delphinidae is a large diverse group of species that may not appear all that similar externally, but they share features of their internal anatomy. For example, some dolphins have a pronounced beak or rostrum while others, lack a beak entirely, but internally they all have sharp, conical teeth. These highly social animals can be found in groups ranging in size from a few individuals to several thousand; and, some species are known to live in complex societies consisting of related individuals. Eleven oceanic dolphin species are currently known from the Bahamas.

Atlantic bottlenose dolphins (*Tursiops truncatus*) are the most common marine mammals seen in Abaco. It should be noted, however, that there are at least two distinct "breeding populations" or "ecotypes" of this species: coastal or inshore bottlenose dolphins

1) A bottlenose dolphin calf surfaces alongside its mother.

2) Coastal bottlenose dolphins are the most common marine mammal species seen in Abaco.

that inhabit the shallow waters of Little Bahama Bank; and, oceanic or offshore bottlenose dolphins found in the deep waters surrounding Abaco. These populations diverged genetically several hundred thousand years ago and have since developed different physiological adaptations to their respective marine environments. The coastal ecotype is smaller in length reaching just over 8 feet and have relatively larger pectoral fins and dorsal fin which helps them to manoeuvre more readily around rocks and reefs to catch fish, and to regulate their internal body temperature (the temperature of the shallow Bank waters fluctuates much more than the deeper Atlantic Ocean). The inshore dolphins do not travel much beyond the barrier reefs of Abaco; and, while some individuals remain in the same area for years, others are known to range all over Little Bahama Bank. The deeper diving oceanic ecotype can reach 10 feet or more in length and can remain at

3) Oceanic bottlenose dolphins inhabit the pelagic waters surrounding the shallow Bahama banks.

depth for longer than their coastal cousins due to their ability to store more oxygen in their blood. They are usually seen in larger groups and appear to have an extensive range. Photographs of individual oceanic bottlenose dolphins have shown that they move between Abaco, Bimini and Exuma Sound.

Atlantic spotted dolphins (*Stenella frontalis*), shown here, are the more frequently seen of two different species of spotted dolphins found in the Abacos. Atlantic spotted dolphins are commonly seen in groups of 20-50 dolphins in the oceanic waters of Abaco where they feed on flying fish and squid. In some parts of Little Bahama Bank this species can also be found along the

4) Atlantic spotted dolphins are highly social and are usually found in groups of 20 or more individuals.

edge of the banks during the daytime where they come to rest and socialize. Pan-tropical spotted dolphins (*Stenella attenuata*) are more oceanic in their distribution and can be seen occasionally as they migrate through the islands. Spotted dolphins are not born with spots, but actually accumulate them as they mature, becoming quite mottled looking as adults. Young spotted dolphins are often confused with bottlenose dolphins, and sometimes the two species interact, which adds to the confusion. Spotted dolphins have a more slender snout, and although they can almost reach the same length as bottlenose dolphins, they are more slender in their girth or body weight.

5) Young Atlantic spotted dolphin with few spots bow-rides alongside an extensively spotted adult.

Please report your marine mammal sightings to:

Bahamas Marine Mammal Survey
P.O. Box AB-20714
Marsh Harbour
Abaco, Bahamas
Email: bmms@oii.net
Or call "Dolphin Research" VHF Ch65A

Risso's dolphins (*Grampus griseus*) are large light grey dolphins that can reach over 13 feet in length and have a relatively tall, dark dorsal fin. Adults are typically covered with overlapping white scars caused by the teeth of their con-specifics making them look quite battered. They have a rounded head, lacking a beak, but have a deep vertical crease down the centre of the forehead. As they mature, their forehead becomes prominently white, making them one of the easiest species to recognize at sea. Risso's dolphins are commonly seen in the Abacos each winter and spring, primarily on the Atlantic side of the islands. It is unknown where these groups range the rest of the year, but some individuals have been seen in Abaco repeatedly over the years.

6) Risso's dolphins have a large falcate fin and extensive scarring on their sides.

7) The prominent white forehead of the Risso's dolphins makes it a relatively easy species to recognize at sea.

Short-finned pilot whales (*Globicephala macrorhynchus*) can grow to 18 feet long and weigh over 5,000 pounds, with males being significantly larger than females. They have a bulbous forehead with no perceptible beak, a faint grey diagonal stripe faint grey "saddle" behind and below the dorsal fin. The rest of their body dorsally is jet black, which prompted whalers to name them "blackfish", a term that also includes three other species known from the Bahamas (melon-headed whales, pygmy killer whales and false killer whales). Pilot whales can be distinguished from the other blackfish species by the position of their large, broad-based dorsal fin, which is set quite far forward on their body. They live in matrilineal pods consisting of up to three generations of related females and their offspring. Pilot whales are seen in Abaco year-round but are more common during the spring and summer months. On calm days, they can be seen in tight groups lying abreast, resting at the surface for hours.

8) The bulbous head and forward position of the dorsal fin helps us to distinguish pilot whales from the other "blackfish".

9) Resting group of pilot whales.

Killer whales (*Orcinus orca*), or orcas, are probably the easiest cetacean species to recognize at sea due to their striking black and white pigmentation patterns. Orcas are the largest member of the oceanic dolphin family, with males reaching 30 feet in length and weighing 8 tons, while females reach only 23 feet and weigh 4 tons. The most conspicuous feature of these whales is the dorsal

10) The orca is one of the easiest species to identify at sea.

fin, which can grow to 6 feet in adult males, but in both sexes is tall enough to be seen at a great distance. These top predators are found in all the world's oceans but are more abundant in higher latitudes where prey resources are more plentiful. Orca pods are seen each year in Abaco usually in the late spring and summer, including one group that has returned repeatedly over the years. While they have been observed feeding on dolphins and small whales around Abaco, they are most likely in the area in response to prey on migrations such as tuna.

Family Ziphiidae – Beaked Whales

The beaked whale family is characterized by having reduced dentition, with typically only two teeth located in the lower jaw and erupting above the gum line of sexually mature males. These teeth are more appropriately described as "tusks" because they are actually used for combat with other males and not for feeding purposes. Beaked whales can be shy whales found generally in small groups that inhabit extremely deep water, making field studies difficult. As a consequence, beaked whales represent the least studied large mammals that exist today; in fact, some species have never been seen at sea, and are known only from old weathered skull fragments. Of the twenty recognized species of beaked whales found worldwide, three are known from the Bahamas, with dense-beaked whales being the most common.

Dense-beaked whales (*Mesoplodon densirostris*) are found in all the world's tropical and temperate waters and are one of the most common species seen around Abaco. These medium-sized whales reach 14-16 feet in length, with males being larger, are brownish-grey in colour and have a spindle-shaped body that tapers at both ends. They have a small dorsal fin found almost two thirds of the way back along their body and a well-defined beak or snout, which

11) An adult female dense-beaked whale surfaces showing its well-defined beak or snout.

12) Dense-beaked whales have a spindle-shaped body and their small dorsal fin is almost two-thirds of the way back.

usually breaks the water first as the whale surfaces to breath. Older whales have numerous white oval scars caused by cookie cutter sharks and multiple paired linear scars caused by the "tusks" of their con-specifics. Adult males look quite bizarre as they often have clusters of stalked barnacles growing on their protruding "tusks". There are resident groups of dense-beaked whales inhabiting the deep submarine canyons around Abaco, although adult males seem to have a greater range than females.

Family Physeteridae – Sperm Whales

The sperm whale is the only species in the family Physeteridae. However, there are two related species known as the dwarf and pygmy sperm whales, which are both small whales reaching 8 and11 feet in length, respectively. Collectively, they are characterized by a squarish head with a single nostril found on the left side of the head and all lack teeth in the upper jaw. The dwarf sperm whale is one of the most commonly seen whales in Abaco but is extremely difficult to photograph because they rarely allow a boat to approach closely.

Sperm whales (*Physeter macrocephalus*) are the largest toothed whales in the world and are the only common great whale seen year-round in the Bahamas. Males can attain a body length of 60 feet while females are considerably smaller, reaching 35-40 feet in length when mature. Sperm whales have dark brown, wrinkled-looking skin and an enormous square-shaped head that comprises one third of their total body length. Their single blowhole on the left side of the head at the front causes a distinctive "blow" which angles to the left and forward. When a sperm whale prepares to dive, it raises its massive tail, allowing us to photograph the distinctive pattern of notches in the trailing edge of the tail flukes. Sperm whales dive to great depths (>1000 metres) for more than an hour at a time where they feed on squid, their primary prey. Adult females form nursery groups that can be found in the Abacos year-round, while the mature males frequent the islands only during the winter breeding season and spend the rest of the year in more productive Arctic waters to feed.

13) The distinctive blow of the sperm whale can be seen for several miles.

14) The natural pattern of notches in the tail flukes allows us to tell individual sperm whales apart.

Fishing in Abaco

by Harry Weldon and Jon Dodge

The Abaco islands offer a beautiful and productive area for exciting fishing. The string of cays east of Great Abaco Island provide a protected to semi-protected area named the Sea of Abaco or Abaco Sound. Beyond most of the cays are rocks and reef formations up to about two miles offshore. While not continuous, a reef stretches from Walkers Cay in the north to just east of Hope Town, a distance of about 90 miles. About two to three miles offshore the bottom drops off to depths of 600 feet to over 1000 feet. The visiting fisherman to Abaco has three basic choices. Fish inside on the sound and flats, outside on the reef, or outside beyond the reef.

Fishing Inside

Almost any dock will have its resident gray snapper. Some of these will top out at three or four pounds. Trying to catch them, while entertaining, can be an exercise in frustration. The larger they are, the less likely you are to catch them. They didn't get to that size by incautious dining. The large ones have excellent eye sight and

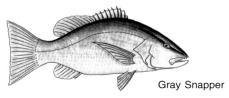

Gray Snapper

are very cautious feeders. Try using very small line (6lb or under) tied directly to the hook. With the hook fully hidden in a suitable bait, toss several pieces of cut bait in the water along with the hook and line. Allow the line to sink with the other pieces of bait. This might get you hooked up. More than likely though, the smaller snapper will take it before the larger one. Once you manage to tie into a good sized fish, the light line will snap after a quick wrap around a piling or mangrove root. This type of fishing can be lots of fun but please release all the small fry that are not going to make it to the kitchen.

Yellowtail snapper, grunt, bar jack, and many others will be found on small patches of reef or rock along any of the keys of the

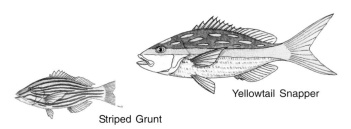

Yellowtail Snapper

Striped Grunt

Abacos. Just look for any type of hard bottom structure. On a completely flat day, the surface of the Sea of Abaco may appear as flat as glass. This does not happen often, but when it does the bottom may be viewed as if looking into an aquarium. This is a great experience in itself and it also provides an opportunity to easily see any structure on the bottom. When the wind is up it is more difficult to identify hard structure, but it is still possible to do so.

Bait fishing with spinning gear should provide food for the table and a whole lot of fun. Frozen shrimp, conch, hermit crab, and cut ballyhoo will all work with this type of fishing. Eventually the barracuda will show up and, depending on your philosophy will

either ruin the day or make it. A small live snapper with a suitable hook lightly through the back will put a barracuda on the end of your line and with six or twelve pound line give a good account of himself. Barracuda is not normally eaten by locals and unless going to the table, release him for someone else to catch.

Barracuda

If you prefer to troll, just drag a small white or yellow feather along the rocky edges of most cays. Yellowtail, bar jack, needle fish, and barracuda will be your most likely catch, but when you're near an opening to the ocean the surprise factor goes way up. If you're going to be fishing inside, take a good look at the fish at the dock before you leave. If they're active and excited over a bit of bait tossed in the water and if the snappers darken around the eyes, then they're in a feeding mood and hopefully the fish elsewhere are also ready to feed. If the snapper that were active this morning show little interest, you might want to read a book. Midday seems to be a slow time for this type of fishing but the time of year is not much of a factor, though obviously winds and tide will make a difference to you, if not to the fish.

If you're not looking for food for the table, you might want to try your hand at bonefishing. Bonefishing is done on the flats during the last of the ebb tide and the first few hours of the incoming tide. It takes a skilled eye to spot bonefish swimming in the shallow water in search of food. Look for their tails and dorsal fins which break the surface and give them away. Once the fish

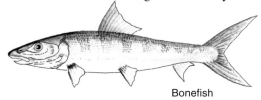

Bonefish

have been found, it is up to the angler to present the bait to the fish. The most common bait used is natural conch, crab, or shrimp. Artificial bait like the wiggle jig, which is flat and does not dig into the bottom, works well on sand or grass. Years of experience indicate that pink, which resembles shrimp, is the best color for artificial bait, but brown and yellow also seem to work well. Most bonefish are caught on spinning or fly tackle and six to twelve pound line. On the initial run, a four to six pound fish can run for a hundred yards or more- a memorable experience. Bonefish are a sport fish only and should always be released. Bonefishing is a year round sport in Abaco, but the winter months seem to provide more fish.

Fishing On the Reef

Reef fishing usually assures fish for the table. Fishing the reef is pretty much the same as fishing on the inside, it's just deeper and the fish are larger. The reefs around Abaco have a good supply of grouper, snapper, mackerel, yellowtail, and many other species that are usually easily caught. Large mutton snapper (8–15 pounds) concentrate for spawning the last of May and into June. Local fisherman have traditionally used heavy hand lines in 20-50

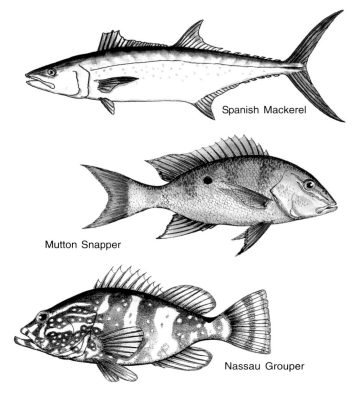

Spanish Mackerel

Mutton Snapper

Nassau Grouper

Wahoo

"drop off." Other than perhaps marlin, the best ocean fishing can be found at this line. Most boats troll skirted ballyhoo.

Weather permitting, mid-March through mid-April is normally the peak ocean fishing season, with large numbers of dolphin and tuna. By the end of June things have quieted down and

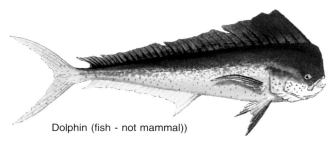

Dolphin (fish - not mammal))

with the warm water a downrigger, wire or plainer to get the bait deep will increase your success, with wahoo being a common catch. July, August, and September are only fair but catches of blackfin tuna and an occasional dolphin are always possible. Fishing picks up in October and by Christmas is normally pretty good and continues to improve through February and March. Large schools of skipjack and cero mackerel are sometimes encountered but getting them to bite can be a challenge. For the small schooling tuna, especially the blackfin, a small white feather trolled way, way back can secure a hit. The trick then is landing the fish before a shark takes the better part. Sometimes deep jigging around the

feet of water. You'll need some local knowledge, however, to find out just where they are. They're here all the time, but when they're spawning they can be found in large numbers if you know just where to fish the reef.

Reef fishing can be done two ways: trolling or bottom fishing. Cut bait, such as ballyhoo or conch, is most commonly used. When trolling or casting with artificial bait, a small yellow lure or silver spoon is a good choice. A light wire leader is also suggested because of the possibility of spanish mackerel and barracuda. Barracuda and amberjack are found on the reef and put up a great fight, but local specimens have been found to have ciguatera, or fish poisoning, and should never be eaten.

Fishing Deep

Deep-sea fishing is for those who want to venture beyond the barrier reef and try for the "Big One." Marlin, sailfish, tuna, dolphin and wahoo can be found at the drop-off, which, in the Elbow Cay

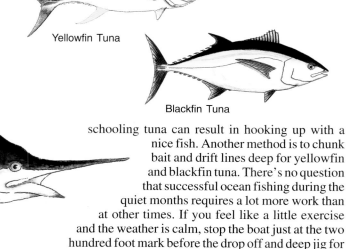

Yellowfin Tuna

Blackfin Tuna

schooling tuna can result in hooking up with a nice fish. Another method is to chunk bait and drift lines deep for yellowfin and blackfin tuna. There's no question that successful ocean fishing during the quiet months requires a lot more work than at other times. If you feel like a little exercise and the weather is calm, stop the boat just at the two hundred foot mark before the drop off and deep jig for grouper, red snapper or amberjack.

Blue Marlin

area, is approximately two to three miles east of the cay beyond the reef. The water off Hope Town goes out from the reef in steps of sixty, ninety, two hundred forty, and six hundred feet. The two hundred forty to six hundred foot break is what is referred to as the

As you can see, the cruiser or tourist who wishes to try fishing here in Abaco has a lot of options. Of course you don't have to do it all yourself. If you want your success rate to go way up, hire a local fishing guide to show you the best spots and methods to use.

Check the classified listings in the back of the book for a fishing guide in your area.

Anyone who fishes in the area should learn about local fishing rules and limits before going out. See page 11 for fishing regulations and pp 115 and 127 for the boundaries of the parks where no fishing is permitted. Remember to release any fish you cannot consume. If you're not going to eat it, please don't kill it.

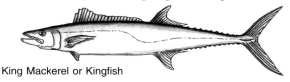

King Mackerel or Kingfish

Harry Weldon is the fishing editor for The Cruising guide to Abaco, Bahamas. He lives at White Sound on Elbow Cay. Jon Dodge also contributed to this article.

Kim Neilson of West Palm Beach, Florida, created the paintings of fish used in this article. He has lived in Florida for over fifty years, and first went to the Bahamas in 1971 to fish and dive. He started drawing and painting Bahama charts and scenes in 1972, and started Gulfstream Trading Company in 1987. He works full time producing custom T-shirt designs for sport fishing boats, and custom charts of the Bahamas, the Florida Keys, or the Caribbean. Gulfstream Trading Company, 4300 N. Flagler Drive #15, West Palm Beach, FL 33407 (studio- 561-863-7133; cell- 561-758-8536).

Where will they go from here?

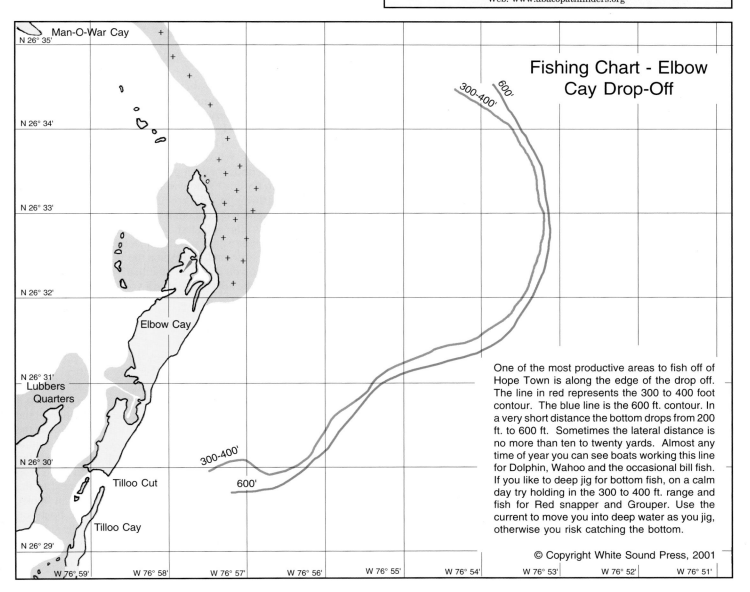

Fishing Chart - Elbow Cay Drop-Off

One of the most productive areas to fish off of Hope Town is along the edge of the drop off. The line in red represents the 300 to 400 foot contour. The blue line is the 600 ft. contour. In a very short distance the bottom drops from 200 ft. to 600 ft. Sometimes the lateral distance is no more than ten to twenty yards. Almost any time of year you can see boats working this line for Dolphin, Wahoo and the occasional bill fish. If you like to deep jig for bottom fish, on a calm day try holding in the 300 to 400 ft. range and fish for Red snapper and Grouper. Use the current to move you into deep water as you jig, otherwise you risk catching the bottom.

Beginning Fishing for the Cruising Yachtsman

Trolling from your sailboat, trawler, or powerboat

by Tom Leffler
Owner, Marsh Harbour Marina, Abaco, Bahamas

The cruising sailboat, trawler, or power boat can fish while cruising and sometimes enjoy a wonderful fresh dinner (the maybe part is why they call it fishing and not catching), Remember the motto, "If you're not fishing, you're not catching!" While cruising to, from, and around the Bahama Islands a cruising boat can fish to further enhance the enjoyment, excitement, and experience of the trip. There are various types of fishing with trolling, bottom, and spear fishing being the three main types. This article will discuss trolling; we hope to expand the article to include bottom fishing and spear fishing next year to make it more comprehensive. The article is based on several years experience fishing from a cruising sailboat, and was developed from the popular cruisers' seminars held at the Jib Room, Marsh Harbour Marina, during the winter months.

Trolling

Trolling is the method of fishing from a moving boat. A rod and reel is placed in a "rod holder" and a bait (live or lure) is towed about 100'-150' behind the vessel. By chance, a sailboat or trawler happens to travel at some of the best basic trolling speeds of 6-9 knots. The basic "blue water / open water" fish that you are targeting are tuna, dolphin, or wahoo (all good table fare) and can be caught at these speeds. This is what most of the sport fishing boats do when they go out "blue water" fishing for the day, except some target marlin or sailfish with particular size, colour, or types of bait. Trolling can also be done between the islands in 10'-30' of water while travelling, or from your dinghy while the big boat is anchored. With "inshore" trolling you will probably catch grouper, snapper, yellowtail, mutton, or spanish mackerel.

Areas

There are three basic areas to troll for fish wile cruising The Bahamas. First is the vast "blue water" between the United States and other Bahamian Islands, second is the 10'-30' waters between the islands and cays of The Bahamas, and finally the "drop-off" around the islands (usually where the bottom quickly drops off from 200' to about 1000') on the ocean side of each island. During the winter and early spring months the blue water fish tend to congregate around the "200' drop-off" looking for bait. In the early summer months (May-July) they can be on the drop-off or they begin to push further offshore hunting larger schools of bait for flying fish. Asking around about whether fish are being caught "inshore" or "offshore" can possibly give you a lead on where things are happening (the more general questions you ask usually get the straightest answers). If a fisherman tends to stay rather quiet about his successes, remember that he is spending a lot of money on equipment and fuel trying to catch fish and tends to become secretive about his fishing spots.

Items you may need

You need a few basic items if you really want to give it a try. First you will need a basic rod and reel that you can buy at most sporting goods or fishing stores—a 20-50lb. class rod and a 4/0 or 5/0 reel with 40 lb. line, a swivel release clip for between the line and the lure, a clamp on rod holder, and a gaff to pull the fish into the boat (the rod and reel can also be used for bottom fishing). Just starting out you need a couple of basic lures. If you were to buy only one, I would recommend a cedar plug. It looks like a Cuban cigar with a hood in the end and the basic one is plain old wood, not even painted!

If you would like another basic lure a pink, blue and pink, or green 6"-8" rubber skirted trolling lure with one or two hooks is a good second choice. Ask around your marina and I'm sure some fishermen can show you the basic items I've mentioned and may even have some others to recommend.

Trolling from your boat

Clamp the rod holder onto one of your stanchions on the back of the boat, and attach a 2'-3' small line/string to the rod holder and the reel so it cannot fall overboard while you are underway. Once you're underway let 100'-150' of line out from the rod with your lure attached. You must set the "drag" of the reel so the fish can take some line out (the person who sells you the reel should be able to help set the drag), then put the "clicker" on so your reel can notify you if you have a "hookup." It is now a waiting game while you're cruising to your next destination. At this point some-

> By chance, the cruising sailboat or trawler happens to cruise at the best basic sppeds for trolling—6.5-8.5 knots—so why not give it a shot!

one must be the "watch" person to listen for the reel clicker if it goes off or clear weeds from the lure in case any become entangled while you're underway. Keep in mind that just like leaving or approaching a dock, the captain and crew must have a plan for the moment when you hook the fish so you can catch the fish. Things to think about: Whose turn is it to reel in the fish (maybe set 1/2 or 1 hour periods for each person to be "on duty" if everyone would like to try this? Who will keep steering the boat while you reel in the fish? Who will drop the sails? Or is the crew capable enough to tighten up and point the boat into the wind while "fighting" the fish? Who will start the motor on a sailboat during the "fight" to give you some additional steerage and maneuverability? Who can slow and maneuver the boat as the fish approaches the boat so you can "gaff" the fish? Who will deal with the fish once it is in the boat? Where will you store or filet the fish so you can keep it fresh?

Completing the Catch

There is an old fishing adage that more fish are lost next to the boat than any other way while trolling. The art of "gaffing" the fish or getting it into the boat some other way is critical to completing a catch while trolling. You probably will not be able to pick a large open water fish up by the line and the rod and hoist it into the boat. If you try to do so, it is very likely you will pull the hook out and the fish will swim away. The usual method to get the fish into the boat is to snag the fish with a gaff (a long pole with a large hook on the end of it to stick into the fish and then lift the fish into the boat). The second (less used) method is to try to drop a line with a loop over the tail of the fish while it is next to the boat, and lift the fish into the boat tail first (called a tail hook). When purchasing a gaff, please think about the style boat you have and the length of the gaff required to reach over the side and hook a fish while it is in the water next to the boat.

Good luck!

Abaco: The Year In Review - 2002

by Victor Patterson

Like the rest of the world, the shadow of 9/11 was over Abaco in 2002. In addition to the shocking impact of the loss of so many innocent lives, many in Abaco were concerned about the attack's impact on air travel and on tourism in Abaco. After a few months, people felt more confident about traveling. Some who might have ordinarily traveled to Europe or even further preferred to come to Abaco because it is close to the United States and is considered a very safe destination. After all, the biggest terrorist act on record in The Bahamas happened during an election when a supporter of one political party threw bananas at a supporter of the other party. The end result is that Abaco had a very healthy year for tourism, and many businesses reported higher grosses for 2002 than they did for 2001.

A general election was held in May 2002. Prime Minister Hubert Ingraham, the representative for North Abaco, had led the Free National Movement (FNM) government for 9½ years and had announced that he would step down. The FNM held a hotly contested election to choose a new leader and Tommy Turnquest, the Minister of Tourism, came out on top. The fallout from this event harmed the party. The Progressive Liberal Party (PLP) was led by Perry Christie, a former law partner of Mr. Ingraham. Given that they only held 4 seats out of 40, many people felt that they had an uphill fight to capture the government. In North Abaco, political newcomer Fritz Bootle challenged Mr. Ingraham. In South Abaco, incumbent Robert Sweeting of the FNM ran against Edison Key of the PLP. Mr. Sweeting had previously announced plans to retire but stepped up for the third time when the FNM's announced candidate decided not to run. Mr. Key was running for the seat for the seventh time. The FNM had generally been considered a center-right party while the PLP usually took a somewhat leftist position, but in the campaign all lines got blurred as the PLP took positions on tax policy that were further to the right than the FNM. The PLP won on the national level, surprising many observers by the size of their victory. They captured 29 seats, including 21 of the 22 in Nassau. Abaco bucked the national trend by re-electing both of the FNM members. Mr. Christie was named the new Prime Minister and Cynthia "Mother" Pratt became The Bahamas' first woman Deputy Prime Minister.

There was also a local government election in July of 2002. There seemed to be less interest on the part of the voters this time, probably because it came on the heels of the general election. Also, people now have more of an idea of the limits of what local government can accomplish. Turnout dipped below 50% in many districts—well below the general election numbers of 89%. In the critical Central District (comprised of Marsh Harbour, Dundas Town, Murphy Town and Spring City), Mike Malone was selected to be the Chief Councilor; a post that he had previously held from 1996 to 1999.

At long last, the port project in Marsh Harbour was started. The engineering firm of American Bridge was selected to construct the new facility at the site of the previous dock near the entrance to Marsh Harbour. This involves significant dredging, filling and the creation of several new roads and the widening of existing ones. Also, numerous buildings will be constructed on the reclaimed land (see photo on page 153). At the end of the day, Abaco should have a port that can not only accommodate the existing heavy traffic, but will be able to meet future needs too. Unfortunately, any upgrade for the Marsh Harbour International Airport remains strictly on paper, although the new terminal building has been designed and approved.

Another project that has not moved forward as of this point is a replacement for Golden Harvest, the island's largest grocery store. Nearly two years after it was destroyed by fire, the site remains vacant. Abaco Markets Ltd, the owners of the store,

expanded Sawyers Market and Solomon's Wholesale (two of their other locations) in an attempt to meet the demand. Also being upgraded is Price Rite, a competing grocery store. The once strong stock of Abaco Markets (which trades on the Bahamas' own stock exchange) has seen significant erosion over the last year and is now trading around its IPO price. The Chairman of its board, Mr. Reginald Sands, resigned to pursue other projects.

Hurricane Michelle brushed Abaco in late 2001. A category one storm on the Saffer-Simpson scale, it nevertheless caused significant damage in Nassau. In Abaco, other than tree damage, the most notable effect was that it blew down the island's only traffic light. The main junction of Marsh Harbour was turned into a 4-way stop while local government officials scrambled to replace the landmark. One was finally obtained, but a curious snag occurred when the Customs department demanded that import duty be paid on the light before they released it. This policy caused deep resentment by many who considered it unreasonable in the extreme and found it reminiscent of the situation following Hurricane Floyd when duty was also demanded on relief supplies. In any case, money was raised from the business community to pay for the duty and the light was replaced.

The softening of the US economy had an impact on the local real estate market. Prices continued to climb and property continued to sell, but fewer parcels changed hands in 2002. The retail market had an average year, as did the crawfishermen. The construction industry remained strong and both second homeowners and locals continued to build at a steady rate. Given the looming presence of the Free Trade of the Americas treaty that is scheduled to come into effect in 2005, the three main hardware firms of Standard Hardware, Abaco Hardware and Man-O-War Hardware merged into one company, although they will continue to maintain separate stores. The intention is to be able to fend off competition from Home Depot - like stores that may rush in if and when import duty is eliminated as a method of taxation. At the end of the year, Abaco was left with a solid, if not booming, economic picture.

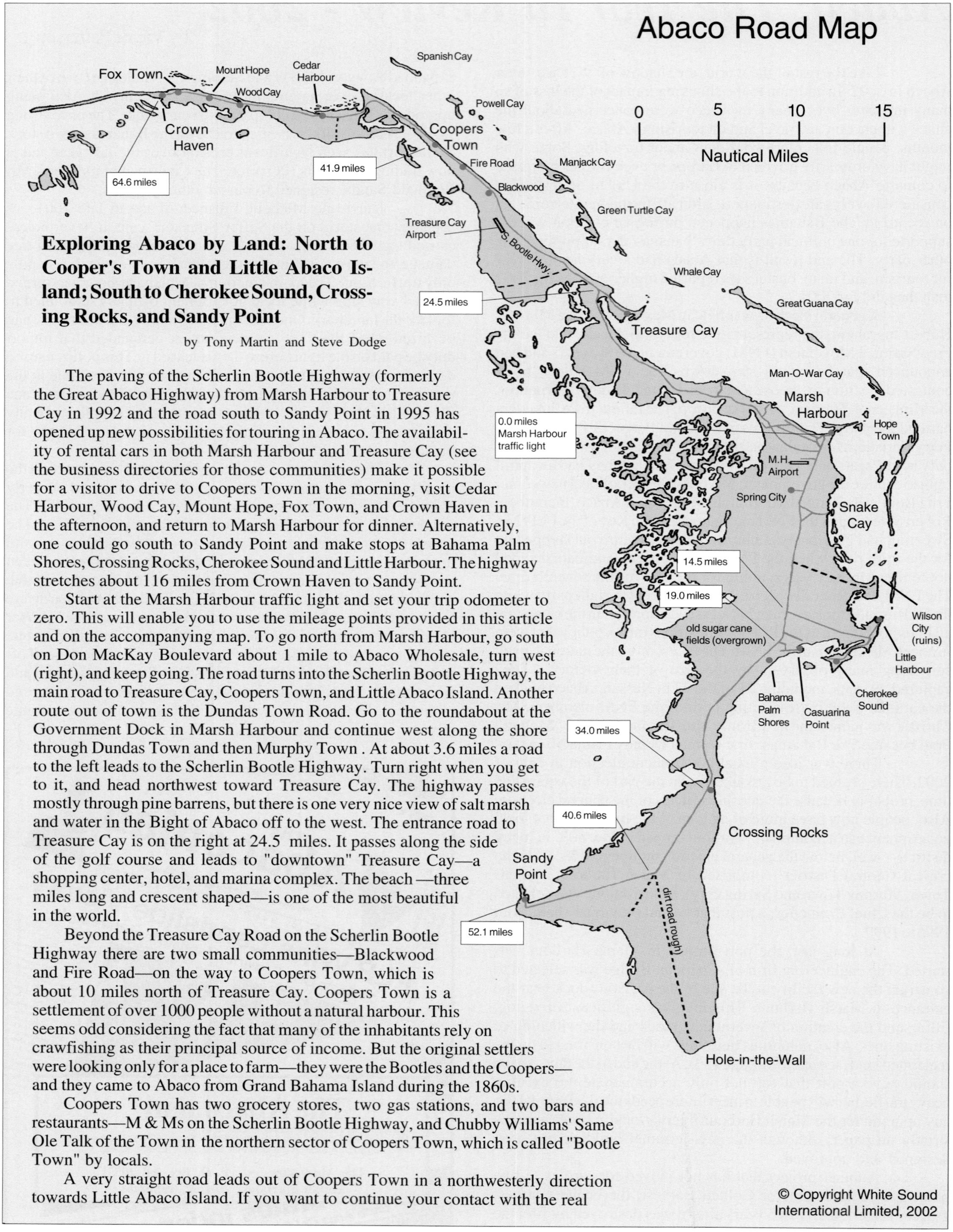
Abaco Road Map
0 5 10 15
Nautical Miles
Fox Town
Mount Hope
Cedar Harbour
Spanish Cay
Wood Cay
Powell Cay
Crown Haven
Coopers Town
64.6 miles
41.9 miles
Fire Road
Manjack Cay
Blackwood
Green Turtle Cay
Treasure Cay Airport
S. Bootle Hwy.
Whale Cay
24.5 miles
Great Guana Cay
Treasure Cay
Man-O-War Cay
Marsh Harbour
0.0 miles
Marsh Harbour traffic light
Hope Town
M.H. Airport
Spring City
Snake Cay
14.5 miles
19.0 miles
Wilson City (ruins)
old sugar cane fields (overgrown)
Little Harbour
Cherokee Sound
Bahama Palm Shores
Casuarina Point
34.0 miles
40.6 miles
Crossing Rocks
Sandy Point
dirt road (rough)
52.1 miles
Hole-in-the-Wall
© Copyright White Sound International Limited, 2002

Exploring Abaco by Land: North to Cooper's Town and Little Abaco Island; South to Cherokee Sound, Crossing Rocks, and Sandy Point

by Tony Martin and Steve Dodge

The paving of the Scherlin Bootle Highway (formerly the Great Abaco Highway) from Marsh Harbour to Treasure Cay in 1992 and the road south to Sandy Point in 1995 has opened up new possibilities for touring in Abaco. The availability of rental cars in both Marsh Harbour and Treasure Cay (see the business directories for those communities) make it possible for a visitor to drive to Coopers Town in the morning, visit Cedar Harbour, Wood Cay, Mount Hope, Fox Town, and Crown Haven in the afternoon, and return to Marsh Harbour for dinner. Alternatively, one could go south to Sandy Point and make stops at Bahama Palm Shores, Crossing Rocks, Cherokee Sound and Little Harbour. The highway stretches about 116 miles from Crown Haven to Sandy Point.

Start at the Marsh Harbour traffic light and set your trip odometer to zero. This will enable you to use the mileage points provided in this article and on the accompanying map. To go north from Marsh Harbour, go south on Don MacKay Boulevard about 1 mile to Abaco Wholesale, turn west (right), and keep going. The road turns into the Scherlin Bootle Highway, the main road to Treasure Cay, Coopers Town, and Little Abaco Island. Another route out of town is the Dundas Town Road. Go to the roundabout at the Government Dock in Marsh Harbour and continue west along the shore through Dundas Town and then Murphy Town . At about 3.6 miles a road to the left leads to the Scherlin Bootle Highway. Turn right when you get to it, and head northwest toward Treasure Cay. The highway passes mostly through pine barrens, but there is one very nice view of salt marsh and water in the Bight of Abaco off to the west. The entrance road to Treasure Cay is on the right at 24.5 miles. It passes along the side of the golf course and leads to "downtown" Treasure Cay—a shopping center, hotel, and marina complex. The beach —three miles long and crescent shaped—is one of the most beautiful in the world.

Beyond the Treasure Cay Road on the Scherlin Bootle Highway there are two small communities—Blackwood and Fire Road—on the way to Coopers Town, which is about 10 miles north of Treasure Cay. Coopers Town is a settlement of over 1000 people without a natural harbour. This seems odd considering the fact that many of the inhabitants rely on crawfishing as their principal source of income. But the original settlers were looking only for a place to farm—they were the Bootles and the Coopers—and they came to Abaco from Grand Bahama Island during the 1860s.

Coopers Town has two grocery stores, two gas stations, and two bars and restaurants—M & Ms on the Scherlin Bootle Highway, and Chubby Williams' Same Ole Talk of the Town in the northern sector of Coopers Town, which is called "Bootle Town" by locals.

A very straight road leads out of Coopers Town in a northwesterly direction towards Little Abaco Island. If you want to continue your contact with the real

Bahamas, drive on. You will be rewarded with quizzical but friendly faces and the experiences that being "off the beaten track" often provide.

The landscape provides no pine at this point, just coppice. Five miles from Coopers Town you cross a causeway (locally known as "The Bridge"). This signals the beginning of Little Abaco, formerly a separate island. It has its own distinct character and life style. Now

Looking north from the causeway connection Great and Little Abaco Islands. The Government reportedly has plans to replace the causeway with a bridge in order to resotre natural tidal flow to the Bight of Abaco.

you are heading generally west instead of northwest and pine begins to replace the coppice. There is a Lucayan Indian site and the ruins of an old sisal mill in this area. Both are off the paved road and should only be attempted with local knowledge and a truck with good road clearance.

Further along the road is a water tower which marks the edge of Cedar Harbour. The piles of conch shells, the fishing boats,

A newly dredged channel, breakwater and dock at Cedar Harbour, Little Abaco Island. Photo taken July 2002.

A typical scene of the Scherlin Bootle Highway passing through a pine forest. This photo was taken north of the Treasure Cay Airport.

and the mangroves afford good photo opportunities. Four and a half miles further on (59.2 miles from Marsh Harbour) lies Wood Cay , settled by a family from Fire Road at the beginning of the century who were trying to get away from the wild hogs that kept eating their crops. The Tangelo Hotel is located here; it has twelve moderate sized, though comfortable and reasonably priced rooms (about $60.00), and a restaurant and bar (phone 242 365-2222). One of the most reliable local mechanics, Charley Mills, has his gas station and garage a little further along at Chuck's Auto Service. Again, the pine gives way to smaller trees and less than two miles further west we approach the smallest of Little Abaco's five settlements—Mount Hope. This is the only settlement not directly accessible by boat and appears on few maps. It is worth stopping to sample the food at B. J.'s Restaurant.

Just a mile further along the highway is Fox Town, the largest and most scenic of Little Abaco's villages. Numerous small cays and rocks dot the harbour, and the Hawksbill Cays lie about a mile offshore. Fox Town has about 500 inhabitants, and its main winding street contains a wide variety of residences, some ultra modern with satellite dishes, others with wooden siding and little changed since the ancestors of the present inhabitants chose this site for its potential as a fishing community. Groceries and fuel are available at Fox Town Shell.

A mere half mile further on, we reach the end of the line—Crown Haven. It is 64.6 miles north of Marsh Harbour. Older members of this community once lived on Cave Cay, an isolated islet to the southwest, until a hurricane in the late thirties destroyed their homes. The authorities of the day provided land on the main island for them to start anew and Crown Haven was born. From here it is a short trip to get to Grand Bahama by boat, and local people often have closer connections with that island than the rest of Abaco. Passenger ferry service was recently initiated between Crown Haven and McLean's Town on Grand Bahama Island (see page 158).

To go south from Marsh Harbour to Sandy Point, begin by heading south on Don MacKay Boulevard from the traffic light. At the airport roundabout (about 3 miles) go straight. The road passes through pine forests. There are turnoffs to the left for Snake Cay (at about 6 miles), Cherokee Sound and Little Harbour (at 14.5 miles), Casuarina Point (19.0 miles), and Bahama Palm Shores, as well as other minor roads. Snake Cay is the old port for Owens-Illinois' lumber operation which was active during the 1960s; it is no longer in use. The road to Cherokee Sound was recently paved, but the side road from that to Little Harbour is still dirt, and it is rough. It is 11.5 miles to Cherokee Sound, which is picturesque and charming. The Cherokee Food Fair is well stocked with groceries, and also offers apartments for transients at about $65.00 per night. Pete's Pub and Gallery at Little Harbour offers food, drinks, bronze sculptures and other original art—all in a very casual, very friendly atmosphere. Casuarina Point is a small residential community comprised of the old executive housing built by Owens-Illinois. On the road to Casuarina Point is Different of Abaco, a rustic bonefishing resort with rooms, a bar, a restaurant, and a flock of flamingos imported from Inagua. Rooms are about $225. per night for a double.

About 3 miles further south (at about 22 miles from Marsh Harbour) is the turnoff to Bahama Palm Shores, a residential development with a beautiful ocean beach, some large palm trees, and some interesting homes. About 12 miles further south (34.0 miles from Marsh Harbour) is the road to Crossing Rocks, a small town located just off the Atlantic Ocean Beach. During 2000 the town was moved a little inland after the devastation of hurricane Floyd. There is a bar and restaurant—Trevor's Midway Motel— at the entrance road. The town is a short drive east on the road. It has a pretty beach with some off-lying rocks.

At 6.6 miles beyond the Crossing Rocks road (and 40.6 miles south of Marsh Harbour) the highway forks. The road to Hole-in-the-Wall goes southeast. It is 15 miles to the lighthouse and very rough; it should be attempted only in a truck with good road clearance. It passes through the Sandy Point Forest Preserve, which is administered by the Bahamas National Trust and is home to the endangered Abaco parrot.

The paved road to the southwest goes to Sandy Point, the only settlement on the west side of Great Abaco Island. It is 11.5 miles from the fork, and the road parallels a beautiful beach which is often used for community cookouts. Sandy Point is a small fishing village which has grocery stores, restaurants, and rooms for rent. Oeisha's Resort caters mostly to bonefishermen; rooms start at about $69.00 per night (phone 242 366-4139). Five miles northwest of Sandy Point (by water only) is Gorda Cay, recently developed by the Disney Corporation as a cruise ship stop they named Castaway Cay. The *Disney Magic* began regular visits to the island in July, 1998.

A Brief History of Abaco

by Steve Dodge
Griswold Distinguished Professor of History
Millikin University

The Spaniards called it Habacoa,* and they were not impressed. Although they were the first Europeans to explore Abaco and the Bahamas, they settled on larger islands further to the south such as Hispaniola and Cuba, then moved on to conquer large and wealthy Indian civilizations in Mexico and Peru. When the enslaved Indians of Cuba and Hispaniola died of smallpox and overwork, the Spaniards sailed to Habacoa and other Bahamian islands to recruit new Indian slaves. Thus, the Lucayan Indians, whom Columbus had described as gentle and kind, were victims of genocide and were gone before 1550. The sites of their numerous settlements have been discovered and various artifacts have been found, but none of the sites in Abaco have been fully excavated by archaeologists. The British eventually colonized Eleuthera Island and New Providence Island (Nassau) in the Bahamas, and claimed the entire archipelago as their colony, but no permanent settlements were made in Abaco for over 200 years after the departure of the Lucayans. The French made an attempt to establish a colony in Abaco in 1625. They called it Lucaya or Lucayonique, but it was not successful and no trace of the settlement has been found. The early French maps of Abaco are generally more accurate than others which have survived, but pirates undoubtedly knew the waters better than anyone else.

Abaco was well situated for piracy. The small cays offered excellent anchorages as well as good lookout points, and the combination of the shallow banks and the off-shore barrier reef discouraged pursuers. Few records exist concerning the haunts of pirates, but we do know that Vain the Great Pirate based himself at Green Turtle Cay in Abaco after fleeing Nassau when the first royal governor, Woodes Rogers, arrived in 1717. He was discovered by Benjamin Hornygold, a recently-converted pirate sent by Rogers, but Vain managed to escape from Green Turtle Cay and from the Bahamas. Other pirates, a few wreckers, and some transient fishermen may have made their residence at Abaco from time to time, but there were no permanent settlements by the 1770s when the British North American colonies declared their independence from Britain.

Not all the colonists supported the patriot cause during the American Revolution; from 10 to 20 percent of the population favored Great Britain. Their reasons were various. Some genuinely liked George III, some disliked the patriots, and some feared that democracy and republicanism would imperil their security or their property. These loyalists were treated badly by the patriots–their property was often confiscated and they were expelled from the villages in which they lived. Many moved to areas such as New York and Florida which were controlled by Britain during the war. When Britain conceded independence to the United States, many of the loyalists chose to move again rather than become citizens of the United States. Encouraged by exaggerated claims for the agricultural and commercial potential of Abaco, some of them became convinced that it would be a good place to build a new British Empire.

Over 600 persons left New York for Abaco in August, 1783. They settled at Carleton, named after Sir Guy Carleton, the British commanding officer in New York. The location of Carleton, unknown for many years, has recently been determined; it was near the north end of the Treasure Cay Beach. Before the loyalists had been at Carleton for three months, a minor dispute regarding each man's responsibility to work in the cooperative provisions store had esca-

lated into a revolution. Many of the town's residents supported a Committee of Safety which overthrew the authority of Captain John Stephens and placed him under arrest. When they received word that reinforcements were on the way from the British garrison at St. Augustine, they feared these troops would support Stephens, so two-thirds of the residents left Carleton, moved six leagues (18 miles) to the southeast, and founded Marsh's Harbour. Within the next five years some of the remaining settlers at Carleton moved on to other locations, and Carleton ceased to exist.

The dissident group at Marsh's Harbour was joined by additional refugees from New York, some of whom founded Maxwell, which was named for the Governor of the Bahamas and was adjacent to Marsh's Harbour. It was probably located on the southeastern shore, perhaps at Boat Harbour, which is now the site of the Great Abaco Beach Hotel and Boat Harbour Marina. Refugees from Florida came to Abaco also. A group settled in southern Abaco at Spencer's Bight (about 10 miles south of Marsh's Harbour) and a former member of the Carolina Rangers, Lt. Col. Brown, was granted a large parcel of land at Eight Mile Bay, about eight miles south of Spencer's Bight, where he intended to establish a plantation. Within a year or two he moved his slaves from Abaco to Caicos, where he had acquired another grant of crown land. As far as can be determined this was the only attempt by a loyalist to cultivate cotton on a large scale in Abaco.

Many of the loyalists were displeased with Abaco. They had come to Abaco to farm, but they found only small pockets of soil on the limestone island. Rainfall was plentiful, but there were long, dry periods when crops dried and burned up. Life was not as easy as the promotional literature said it would be. When the free provisions provided by the Crown were exhausted, many of the new migrants decided to leave the island. About 2000 had come to Abaco during the middle 1780s, but only 400 (200 whites and 200 blacks) were left in 1790. Those who had money or influence probably left Abaco. Those who stayed probably had no alternative.

The few hundred loyalists who remained in Abaco were joined by migrants from Harbour Island, Eleuthera, an old Bahamian settlement. Young men from Harbour Island were reportedly impressed with the beauty of the Abaco girls, and also with the large and unexploited fishing grounds of Abaco. They knew that survival in the Bahamas meant that one had to fish as well as farm, and new communities were established on the outer cays which were closer to the reef and the best fishing. New Plymouth was founded on Green Turtle Cay. It was the most important settlement in Abaco during most of the nineteenth century. Its men relied on farming, fishing, and wrecking–no one became wealthy, but they made a living. According to tradition, Wyannie Malone, a widow from South Carolina, was the founder of Hope Town on Elbow Cay. During the 1820s a single young couple settled on Man-O-War Cay; in 1977 230 of Man-O-War's population of 235 could trace their ancestry to Pappy Ben and Mammy Nellie. A small settlement was also established on Great Guana Cay.

The settlers who survived in Abaco learned to be self-sufficient. They had no choice in the matter; they lacked government mail service until 1867 when the House of Assembly provided a subsidy for a privately-owned vessel to make one round trip per month between Nassau and Abaco. Nassau, capital of the Bahamas, was no great metropolis–its population was only 10,000 in 1864–but it was Abaco's only link with the outside world. The Abaconians attempted to become involved in various export operations during the late nineteenth and the early twentieth centuries–pineapples, sisal, lumber, sponge–all provided a living for a large number of Abaconians for a period of time, but failed to move the economy much beyond the subsistence level. The problem was not that the

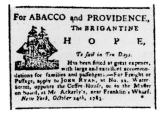

For ABACCO and PROVIDENCE,
The BRIGANTINE
H O P E,
To sail in Ten Days.

The first group of loyalists to leave New York for Abaco did so in September, 1783. This advertisement for the sailing of the *Hope*, which carried a second or third group of immigrants to Abaco, appeared in the *Royal Gazette* (New York) on October 24, 1783.

people did not work hard; the problem was that they lacked knowledge of foreign markets. They always seemed to be doing the right thing at the wrong time or in the wrong way. They shipped pineapples to the United States in bulk, and frequently lost a large portion of the crop to spoilage in the ships' holds. They shifted into sisal production just as the market for sisal was deteriorating.

One of the most reliable sources of income for Abaconians during the mid-nineteenth century was wrecking, but it declined in importance long before 1900. Wrecking did not necessarily mean luring a ship to its destruction. It meant salvaging the cargo and usable parts of ships that wandered onto the reef or the banks. Wreckers saved many sailors' lives. Because Abaco is situated adjacent to one of the busiest north-south shipping lanes in the Atlantic, a seemingly inexhaustible supply of ships were wrecked in Abaco during the 19th century. One of the best-known wrecks was that of the *U.S.S. Adirondack*, a brand new steam sloop which was the pride of the Union Navy in 1862. En route to Nassau to inform Union ships there to search for the infamous Confederate raider, the Alabama, the *Adirondack* struck the reef at Man-O-War Cay, where her remains can still be seen. Shortly after this wreck, the British Imperial Lighthouse Service contributed to the decline of wrecking by building lighthouses throughout the Bahamas. The lighthouse at Hope Town on Elbow Cay was completed in 1863, despite attempts

The *U.S.S. Ossipee*, shown here, was a sister ship to the *U.S.S. Adirondack*, the remains of which can still be seen on the reef near Man-O-War Cay. This photograph was provided courtesy of the Naval Historical Foundation, Collection of W. Beverly Mason, Jr.

by local residents to protect their livelihoods by sabotaging the construction project.

By 1900 Hope Town was the largest and most prosperous settlement in Abaco. It was the seat for a commissioner, and its population of almost 1200 lived by fishing, sponging, shipping and boat building. Abaco boats were admired for their design as well as their fine construction, and were known as the best in the Bahamas. Abaco dinghies, small open boats with a single sail, were sought by most Bahamian fishermen, and Abaco-built smacks (sloops with bowsprits) and schooners brought a premium in the marketplace. During World War I and the early 1920s, large lumber-carrying schooners of more than 200 tons were built at Hope Town and at Man-O-War Cay. There is only one boat carpenter left in Hope Town today -- Winer Malone builds Abaco dinghies in his shed near the harbour using only hand tools and providing the visitor with an accurate view of how boats were built in Abaco a century ago. Man-O-War Cay is the most active boat building center in Abaco today. Two boatyards there build outboard powerboats. Beginning in 1979 fiberglass as well as wood hulls were made. These Bahamian-built boats are typically heavier and stronger than their US-built counterparts; they are built to withstand many years of hard use in high seas. They are sought after by fishermen and others throughout the islands, so contemporary Abaco continues to export boats as it has done since the early nineteenth century.

The first glimpse of twentieth-century life style in Abaco was Wilson City, a company town located about 10 miles south of Marsh's Harbour. Founded in 1906, it was the marvel of its age, boasting modern conveniences such as electricity and an ice plant, both rarities in the Out Islands. It was built by the Bahamas Timber Company, which operated a saw mill and dock facilities at the site. Many residents of Hope Town and Marsh's Harbour moved to Wilson City where they found steady employment, but this operation was short-lived; the company closed the mill at Wilson City in 1916. Several years later, during the early 1920s, two developments

The mill at Wilson City. Photo from Gray Russell, former resident of Wilson City. Copied by Steve Dodge with assistance of Leo Savola.

provided Abaco with improved communication with the outside world. The installation of a radio-telephone station at Hope Town made instant communication with Nassau possible, and the diesel-powered Priscilla replaced the Albertine Adoue schooner which had been serving as the mail boat.

The improved transportation and communication had only a limited impact on the Abaconians. The depression of the early 1930s inhibited economic development, and the lives of most Abaconians were still very similar to those of their ancestors some 100 years before. Boat building and fishing, supplemented by small farming, were the principle economic activities, and most Abaconians lived at or near the subsistence level. Real change did not occur until after World War II, when the lumber industry was revived by Owens-Illinois Corporation and tourists from the United States, Canada, and Britain discovered Abaco.

Owens-Illinois had acquired the 100 year lease originally granted to the Bahamas Timber Company. In 1959 the company built the first roads which connected the several communities on Great Abaco, and the first motor vehicles were introduced. An airport was built at Marsh Harbour and port facilities were constructed at Snake Cay. The company cut the Caribbean Pine forest of Abaco and exported it for use as pulpwood. Marsh Harbour boomed–several banks and a small shopping center with a supermarket were constructed. When Owens-Illinois completed its pulpwood operation in Abaco during the late 1960s, the company decided to utilize its investments and labor force in Abaco by building a huge sugar plantation. Sugar was exported from Abaco in 1968, 1969 and 1970, but the company lost money and the operation, which is the largest farm in the Bahama Islands, was closed. The land was sold to the government of the Bahamas, and the government, after considering various schemes, including converting it into a ranch for raising cattle, has leased it to B. J. Harmon, a Florida company which will grow and export citrus. Tourism developed slowly after World War II when cruising yachtsmen and others discovered the islands. Some bought land at very reasonable prices and built vacation or retirement homes. Many of these people have become a permanent part of Abaconian society. Dr. George Gallup's family still maintains a vacation house he built in Hope Town during the 1950s, and Randolph Johnston, an artist from New England, settled at Little Harbour, Abaco, at about the same time. He built a beachside home and studio where he produced lost wax castings in bronze for gallery shows in New York and Paris. Small resorts and hotels were established to service tourists who preferred the quiet and measured pace of a vacation in Abaco to the more active life-style of Nassau and Freeport, which became major tourist destinations during the 1950s and 1960s. Abaco is still off the beaten tourist track and offers the visitor an opportunity to enjoy unspoiled waters, reefs, and cays, good swimming, snorkeling, sailing and beachcombing -- all in an atmosphere of clean air and friendly, honest people. Though an increasing number of tourists visit Abaco each year, the charm and warmth of its environment and its people have not changed.

In 1967 the Progressive Liberal Party (PLP), led by Lynden Pindling, gained a majority in the House of Assembly and formed a government. The party represented the black majority (85% of the population of the Bahamas is black), and Abaco, which is about 50% white, voted for the opposition. When the PLP decided to seek independence for the Bahamas in 1972, many of the residents of Abaco resisted it. They petitioned Queen Elizabeth II, and asked to be separated from the Bahamas so they could remain a British Crown Colony. Citing the loyalty of their ancestors to the Crown, they begged the Queen to reciprocate. Their petition was not granted, and though a small group contemplated the possibility of a revolution to separate Abaco from the Bahamas and make it independent, those plans received little support. Although many Abaconians eventually shifted their support to the PLP government of Lynden Pindling, Abaco remained a centre of opposition activity. Its representatives in the House of Assembly were usually members of the official opposition party, the Free National Movement, and were frequently involved in debates and disputes with government representatives. The Pindling government was defeated in the general election held on 19 August 1992, and Hubert Ingraham, FNM representative for Coopers Town, Abaco, became the new Prime Minister. The change of government was achieved democratically and peacefully. Ingraham brought a new burst of economic activity and long overdue reforms such as the implementation of local government. He was re-elected in 1997 for a second five-year term. In May 2002 the FNM lost a general election and Perry Christie, leader of the PLP, became Prime Minister. The Bahamas will celebrate the 30th anniversary of their independence on 10 July 2003. The nation has been successful in achieving significant economic growth and has developed a viable democratic political system. Bahamians are rightfully proud of their achievement.

*The name Habacoa is of Taino (Indian) origin. It meant Large Upper Outlier and was originally used to refer to the island now called Andros. The name first appeared on a Spanish map in 1500 when Juan de la Cosa used it to designate a large island in the northern Bahamas. The Taino name for Abaco was Lucayoneque, which means Peoples' Distant Waters Land. See Julian Granberry, "Lucayan Toponyms," *Journal of the Bahamas Historical Society* 13 1 (October, 1991), 3-12.

Steve Dodge, who is also the author of this *Cruising Guide to Abaco, Bahamas*, is Professor Emeritus of History at Millikin University in Decatur, Illinois. He has also written *Abaco: The History of an Out Island and its Cays* (1995).

Medical Tips
for Tropical Waters

Drs. Raymond Heimbecker
and Jane Garfield

Luckily for our visitors there are few serious health hazards in the Abacos. But there are some potential threats to normal well-being that could make a vacation less pleasant. The visitor who is aware of these may well be able to avoid them completely by taking the proper precautions. Preventive medicine is always the best therapy. This brief manual is designed to help people avoid medical problems while in Abaco, or to help them treat difficulties which may arise in a simple and effective manner.

The only routine immunization that visitors should have before coming to Abaco is Tetanus Toxoid. This must be renewed every ten years.

The most important tip for visitors is to bring enough of the medications that they are taking to last for their entire trip. The corollary to that is **never** to check important medications. Bags do get lost. Every few months we get frantic calls from people who have checked their medication in their luggage and are without it.

The most common problems that doctors in Abaco encounter are:
1. Ear infections, both acute and chronic
2. Fish poisonings due to ciguatera and/or spoilage
3. Skin reactions caused by UV exposure (sunburn),
   poison wood, Portuguese Man-O'War and other
   jelly fish, and Sea Lice.
4. Lacerations and Injuries

Only rarely do we see patients with acute heart or abdominal problems, strokes, major fractures or life threatening accidents. But when these emergencies occur there are physicians available in Marsh Harbour to provide immediate care and arrange for transfer to a hospital if need be. A number of air ambulance services will come to the Bahamas to pick up patients. The local physicians can call these when needed. The patient or the family must be able to provide a credit card which has the funds available to cover the two to six thousand dollar bill which will be incurred. If the medical situation is urgent but not life threatening, arrangements can often be made for one of the

Sun Protection ... whenever possible!

excellent pilots in the area who have their own planes to fly the patient out. In all but the most severe weather a patient can be in a hospital within two hours.

EAR PROBLEMS

Ear problems occur all too frequently. In most cases these involve the ear canal and are caused by a fungus. We advise those swimmers who are prone to these itchy, painful, sometimes discharging ear infections to treat them preventively by placing a few drops of white vinegar and clean water, half and half, in the ear canal. This solution should be used before and after each and every snorkeling trip or dive. This will go a long way toward preventing serious ear canal infections. Scuba divers can and do develop middle ear problems due to poor equalization. Even though diving in the Abacos is usually quite shallow, the routine SCUBA precautions are important. If the diver has any mild nasal congestion, the use of a decongestant before each dive would be helpful. No one with a cold should dive, and no one should continue a dive if equalization is difficult. Most important of all, a dive must be immediately aborted if the diver experiences pain, bleeding, or dizziness. Each year there are three to four perforated ear drums as a result of ignoring these basic precautions.

FISH POISONING

The second medical problem, and one that is not uncommon, is tropical fish poisoning or ciguatera. It is caused by a photosynthetic dinoflagellate (a microscopic free swimming organism). The flagellates live among the algae on coral reefs. Especially (but not only) when the reefs are stirred up, these organisms are eaten by small fish and enter the food chain. Larger reef fish eventually harbour the toxin which accumulates in the flesh of the fish. The unwary person who eats the ciguateric fish may become ill. The reef fish most commonly involved are the larger grouper, barracuda, and snappers. The free swimmers, that is, fish that do not feed on the reef, are not involved. The smaller reef feeders are usually less dangerous because both by weight and age they accumulate less poison.

There is no way to detect or neutralize the toxin in an affected fish, and no amount of cooking or freezing will detoxify an affected fish. All of the old wives tales of how to test fish meat for ciguatera are just myths and do not work. Obviously the best way to deal with ciguatera is to avoid it. The best way to do that is to ask local Abaconians what kind of fish to avoid before eating fish, and do not eat fish if you do not know what kind it is.

Occasionally someone may eat a "mystery" fish and toxic fish poisoning may follow. The first symptom is often numbness and tingling, especially around the mouth, lips, and tongue. This may be followed by nausea, vomiting, diarrhea, severe aches and pains, and generalized weakness. The poison is neurotoxic. A unique symptom is heat/cold reversal. Hot water or warm weather may feel cold and vice versa. Each person seems to react differently. Some will recover in a few weeks; some will be debilitated for many months. Although we haven't seen this in the Abacos, the person may become comatose and die. The most serious chronic effects are prolonged muscle weakness and the temperature inversion. Once a person has developed ciguatera, that person will remain hypersensitive for the rest of their lives.

Recently six people developed severe life threatening ciguatera poisoning. They were on boats cruising in the Berry Islands and they caught a 60 lb Amberjack. They cooked it and ate part of it for dinner. Almost immediately they all became ill with nausea and vomiting and diarrhea. Two of them became prostrate and were taken by air to the hospital in Nassau by the US Coast Guard. The other four, although quite sick, were able to pilot their boats to Nassau where they too required hospitalization. All of them survived, but the long term effects of the poisoning will persist for months and perhaps years. The temperature reversal phenomenon and the fatigue are particularly long lasting. The message is clear: **do not eat large reef feeding fish.**

There have been two recent breakthroughs in our knowledge of ciguatera. First, an easily used colorimetric test to determine whether or not a fish is ciguateric is now available. Second, we now have a treatment for the severely ill comatose patients. This is Mannitol, a solution that must be given intravenously. Unfortunately, it is of no use for the other symptoms of the poisoning. It is kept on hand in one of the local clinics in Abaco.

The other common fish poisoning is simply spoilage caused by inadequate refrigeration. The well known symptoms of nausea, vomiting and diarrhea are usually short lasting. The only treatment is oral fluid replacement. All the members of the mackerel family are extremely susceptible to this type of spoilage. It is extremely important especially in the summer to put fish on ice as soon as they are caught, and to cook them immediately after they come off the ice.

SKIN PROBLEMS

The most common problems doctors encounter in the Abacos involve the skin. Severe sun burn, poison wood, and stings from Portuguese Men O'War, other jelly fish, or sea lice can all cause skin inflammations that can make a person miserable.

Visitors from northern climates are often unaware that even in the winter the Abaco sun is strong and can produce severe burns. Proper clothing and modern barrier creams that cut down on both ultraviolet A and B exposure are vital. For swimmers and divers water resistant sunblock creams are a must. Severe burns will require fluid replacement and a trip to the clinic. Local aloe plants, when sliced length wise and applied directly to the burned area, will provide some relief.

Poison wood is a bush or a tree that has clusters of five shiny green leaves (see illustration). The bark is gray, but is mottled with black stains caused by sap, which seeps through the bark and then turns black. Walking through the thick bush, or clearing land, are the usual ways for the susceptible person to get a poisonwood rash. It is similar to, but far more intense than, poison ivy. Within three days

Poison Wood has clusters of five leaves and mottled gray, tan and black bark. It is more volatile than Poison Ivy. Drawing from Jack Patterson and George Stevenson, *Native Trees of the Bahamas*. Used with permission.

extreme itching and burning occur, and redness and blisters appear. Cortisone cream is far more helpful than calamine lotion, and cool showers are also useful. If the rash is severe, widespread, or around the eyes, a trip to the clinic is indicated. If the juice gets into the eyes it may cause loss of vision and even blindness.

The Portuguese Man O'War can cause a severe stinging burning rash that may be painful for several days. Be sure to warn your children who otherwise would be attracted by the bright and iridescent blue colours of the balloon shaped Man O'War as it drifts up on the beaches. These balloons are difficult to see while swimming and may cause severe chest and leg burning as you swim through the long tentacles. The red streaks should be gently cleaned with rubbing

The Portuguese Man O'War looks like a clear bluish balloon floating on the surface. Its tentacles can be over ten feet long.

alcohol to "turn off" the toxin. Meat Tenderizer is also useful for this purpose. Don't scrub with soap and water. If the stung person develops shortness of breath, backache or muscle pain he/she should be brought to the nearest clinic.

Fire coral and fire sponges may be encountered on the reefs. They can cause a painful rash. The most important rule is to wear gloves at all times and DON'T touch or pick up anything. Again, rubbing alcohol may help.

Sea anenomes are feared by many, but one of the authors (R.H.) has waded amongst them for many years without harm. Perhaps some people are more sensitive than others.

An itchy skin rash has become a problem for some summer visitors during recent years. It is popularly attributed to "sea lice," but no such animal actually exists. The rash is most likely caused by the larvae of the Thimble Jellyfish (Linuche Unguiculata). These almost invisible larvae are produced in large clusters called "blooms" by the adult jellyfish during the summer months. They may be carried by wind and currents into shore. When the larvae contact with people the larvae discharge stinging nematocysts which may persist for several days (for further information see *The Journal of the American Medical Association*, vol. 269, no. 13, April 7, 1993, p. 1669). Nothing is felt at the time; the rash develops several hours after contact. It is always most pronounced in the areas covered by swimwear, and small children are particularly vulnerable, often developing a severe rash accompanied by a fever, nausea, and vomiting. And this can happen even if the child has just been playing at the edge of the sea rather than actually swimming in the water. These severe cases should be seen by a phsysician. In general the rash subsides in 96 hours.

Avoid sea lice if possible; rely on local knowledge. Recently a number of Abaconians have applied meat tenderizer to susceptible areas before swimming and have avoided trouble altogether. Also, a fresh water shower after removing the bathing suit or trunks taken as soon as possible may wash away enough larvae so that a rash will not occur. If a rash does develop, cortisone cream will help the itchiness. A clinic visit is only necessary for severely affected patients. There is evidence that a previous bout with sea lice sensitizes the person, and that the next exposure may result in an instant stinging sensation while in the water.

SPINES AND BARBS, CUTS AND LACERATIONS

Sea urchin spines and sting ray barbs cause discomfort and pain. The sea urchin that is most likely to cause problems in Abaco is the one with short white spines. The unwary wader or swimmer may step on or touch one of these--the spines penetrate the skin and break off to become very painful. There are usually many imbedded spines that require individual removal. The old remedy of immediately applying lemon juice or other more easily available acid softens the spines but doesn't help extract them. An infection often sets in around the spines. Obviously, prevention is best--wear flippers and gloves--but also, beware that sea urchin spines can penetrate these, so watch where you walk and what you touch.

A much more painful problem is caused by sting ray barbs. Rays often bury themselves in the sand in shallow water. An unwary person walking quietly may surprise the ray by stepping on it. The ray then

Sea Urchins are frequently found in crevices with their toxin-laden black spines sticking out.

objects strenuously and struggles to free itself by flipping its barbed tail into the person's foot, ankle, or leg. The pain is immediate, intense, and unless treated, long-lasting. The local physicians inject local anesthetic into the area which provides pain relief. Also, meticulous cleaning and removal of any barb fragments is important. Prevention is best--look before you walk, and shuffle and splash some water around--enough to awaken and frighten a buried ray into finding another spot for napping.

Visitors often acquire coral cuts while swimming or exploring. The best treatment is immediate and frequent cleaning with soap and water. Antiseptic and antibiotic creams are useless and provide a wonderful culture medium for skin bacteria. Leave the cut open if possible, or bandage it loosely and change the bandage frequently.

More serious lacerations, especially those that are bleeding heavily, require immediate attention. STOP the bleeding by direct pressure. Don't bother with pressure points. Five minutes of uninterrupted pressure (time it) right over the bleeding area will stop 99% of all bleeding. Don't peek--just keep strong pressure on, and if possible elevate the bleeding area above the heart. Follow this with bulky dressing firmly applied with tape, but keep the pressure on as much as possible. If necessary the local doctors will close the wounds. If there is numbness or inability to move any injured part, come to the nearest physician as soon as possible.

For small lacerations there is an excellent bandage available. It can be acquired from a doctor or pharmacy at home and should be in everyone's first aid kit. These bandages are called SteriStrips and are produced by 3M. The most useful ones are one-quarter inch in width. Use these to close small lacerations closely and accurately.

FINDING MEDICAL HELP

It is not difficult to get medical assistance when necessary. The various inns, caretakers, and shop keepers have both VHF radios and telephones and can contact the doctors at any hour of the day or night. The boater with a VHF will be able to call on channel 16 for referral and/or immediate assistance. Remember a May Day call is only to be used when there is imminent danger of loss of life.

For routine care the local clinics are open at certain times, and can also open when emergencies occur. There are clinics in Hope Town, Man-O-War, and Marsh Harbour. These are staffed by physicians or nurses. Other doctors living in the area will and do provide invaluable aid when necessary. We hope you won't need this information and that with awareness of some of the avoidable hazards you will not encounter them, and that you will have a healthy and safe time in this wonderful area.

Drs. Heimbecker and Garfield have a wealth of experience treating medical problems in Abaco gained during the past twenty or thirty years. Both have done volunteer work and Dr. Garfield was the resident physician in both Hope Town and Man-O-War Cay for several years.

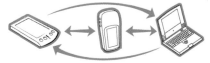

Marsh Harbour Classified Business Directory

EMERGENCY SERVICES
Ambulance and Trauma One, 367-2911
Marsh Harbour Police, 367-2560
Marsh Harbour Fire, 367-2000

AIRLINES AND CHARTERS
Abaco Air Ltd, Airport, AB-20492, 367-2266, 367-2205, fax 367-3256
Air Florida
Air Sunshine, Airport, AB-22154, 367-2800, fax 367-2800,
American Eagle, Airport, AB-20259, 367-2231
Bahamasair, Airport, AB-20488, 367-2095, fax 367-2039
Cherokee Air Ltd, Bay Street, AB-20485, 367-2089, fax 367-2530
Continental Connection, Airport, 367-3415
Island Express, Airport, 367-3597
Majors Air Services Ltd, Airport, 367-4826
US Air, Express, Airport, AB-20259, 367-2231
Vintage Props & Jets, Airport, 367-4852,
Zig Zag, Airways, Airport Road, AB-20422, 367-2889

AIRPLANE SERVICE AND FUEL
Abaco Flight Services Ltd, Airport, AB-20492, 367-2205, fax 367-3256
Abaco Petroleum Co Ltd, School Lane, AB-20899 , 367-3953, fax 367-3954
Zig Zag Airways, Airport Road, AB-20422, 367-2889

APPLIANCES
Abaco Hardware Ltd, Don MacKay Blvd, AB-20577, 367-2170, fax 367-2928
Abaco Stereo, Don MacKay Blvd, AB-20577, 367-2265, fax 367-3043
Corner Value, Queen Elizabeth Dr, AB-20490, 367-2250, fax 367-3810
Lowe's Pharmacy, Lowe's Shopping Ctr, AB-20503, 367-2667, fax 367-3130
Marco , Don MacKay Blvd, AB-20521, 367-3186, fax 367-3469
Standard Hardware, Queen Elizabeth Dr, AB-20498, 367-2811, fax 367-2645
Western Auto , Don MacKay Blvd, AB-20507, 367-2300, fax 367-2391

ARCHITECTS
AB Architects, Queen Elizabeth Dr, AB-20676, 367-4355
Cooper's Architect Services, Memorial Plaza, 367-2810
Key's Architectural Design, Dove Plaza , 367-4143
Ryan's Architect Consultant, Stratton Drive, AB-20579, 367-2001, fax 367-3001
Timothy Neil, RIBA , Marsh Harbour, AB-20006, 367-2076

ATTORNEYS
Alexiou Knowles & Co, Stratton Drive, AB-20409, 367-2010, fax 367-2394
E. P. Toothe & Assoc., AB-20088, 367-3368, fax 367-3923
Callenders & Co., Dove Plaza, AB-20415, 367-2991, fax 367-3013
Frederik Gottlieb, Sands Corner, AB-20405, 367-3120, fax 367-3118

AUTOMOBILE PARTS, SERVICE AND REPAIRS
Abaco Starters, SC Bootle Highway, AB-20347, 367-4970
AID, Don MacKay Blvd, AB-20407, 367-2077, fax 367-3296
Bodie's Engine Repair, 367-2108
Davis Auto Repairs, Forest Drive, 367-3311
General's Auto, Forest Drive, 367-2411
Getafix, Airport Road, 367-3166
K & S Auto Service, Don MacKay Blvd, AB-20520, 367-2655
Lou's Video, Bay Street, 367-2043
Marsh Harbour Auto Parts, Don MacKay Blvd, AB-20446, 367-2111
Marsh Harbour Service St, AB-20438, 367-2840
Pinder's Marine and Auto , Bay Street, 367-2274
Pinder's Auto Body & Paint, Marsh Harbour, 367-3121
Quality Star Auto Centre, Don McKay Blvd, 367-2979, fax 367-2977
Rainbow Paint and Body, Marsh Harbour, AB-20523, 367-4900, fax 367-3462
Shell Dundas Town, Dundas Town, AB-20726, 367-3883, fax 367-3882
TNT Service Station, SC Bootle Highway, AB-20437, 367-4970

Western Auto Parts Centre, Don MacKay Blvd, 367-4227

AUTOMOBILE RENTALS & SALES
A & A Auto Sales, Don MacKay Blvd, AB-20484, 367-2022
A & A Car Rentals, AB-20463, 367-2148
A & P Auto Rentals, Don MacKay Blvd, AB-20520, 367-2655, fax 367-2464
Covenant Car Rentals, Murphy Town, AB-20652, 367-4007
D's Minivan Rentals, AB-20655, 367-3980
Dolphin Auto Rentals, Queen Elizabeth Drive, AB-20060, 367-4406, fax 367-3365
Flamingo Car Rentals, SC Bootle Highway, AB-20325, 367-4787
Reliable Car Rental, Abaco Towns, AB-20089, 367-4234
Rental Wheels, East Bay Street, 367-4643
SeaStar Car Rentals, Nathan Key Drive, AB-20531, 367-4887
Veronica's Car Rentals, AB-20463, 367-2725
Wilmac Rent-a-Car, Airport, AB-20347, 367-4313
Z & C Auto Sales, Dove Plaza, 367-4143

BAKERIES
Island Bakery , B & V Plaza, AB-20479, 367-2129
Java Coffee Shop, East Bay Street, 367-5523

BANKS
Bank of Nova Scotia, Abaco Shopping Ctr, AB-20567, 367-2142, fax 367-2565
Barclay's Bank International, Traffic Light, AB-20401, 367-2152, fax 367-2659
CIBC Bahamas Ltd, , Don MacKay Blvd, AB-20402, 367-2166, fax 367-2156
Commonwealth Bank, Traffic Light, AB-20582, 367-2370, fax 367-2372
Royal Bank of Canada, Don MacKay Blvd, AB-20417, 367-2420, fax 367-2547

BARS/TAVERNS
Ambassador Motel, Dundas Town, , AB-20484, 367-2022, fax 367-2133
Angler's Pub, Boat Harbour, AB-20511, 367-2158
Bistro, Conch Inn, East Bay Street, 367-4444
Bustick Bay Resort, SC Bootle Highway
Corner Restaurant & Bar, Christie St DT, AB-20112, 367-4346
Emerald's, Airport, 367-4973
Jib Room, Marsh Harbour, AB-20518, 367-2700
The Lazy Parrot, SC Bootle Highway,367-5331
Mangoes, East Bay Street, AB-20529, 367-2366
The Ranch, Don MacKay Blvd, AB-20446, 367-2733
Sapodilly's, East Bay Street, AB-20058, 367-3498
Sea Shells, Don McKay Blvd., 367-4460
Sid's Pub, Spring City, 367-7333
Snappas, Harbor View Marina, 367-2278
Surf Side Club, Dundas Town, 367-2762
Wally's , East Bay Street, AB-20455, 367-2074

BEAUTY SALONS/BARBERS
Creations Barber Shop, Don Mackay Blvd, 367-4850,
Essence Beauty Shop, Queen Elizabeth Dr, 367-2386
Glamour Rama, Dundas Town, 367-3966,
Hair Affair, Dove Plaza, 367-2378
Island Image, Dundas Town, AB-20112, 367-3507
Laine's Kuts & Kurls, Memorial Plaza, 367-3623
Rosalyn's Beauty Salon, Dundas Town, 367-2030
Snazzie's Beauty Salon, Pole Line Road, AB-20557, 367-4781

BEVERAGES
Island Delight, Harbour, AB-20585, 367-3384, fax 367-3298
Sawyer's Soft Drinks, Stratton Drive, AB-20410, 367-2797

BICYCLE RENTAL
Rental Wheels, East Bay Street, AB-20871, 367-4643

BOAT ENGINE REPAIR
Hartwell Russell, Caribbean Constr, AB-20403, 367-2502
Pinder's Marine and Auto , Bay Street, 367-2274

BOAT RENTALS
Blue Wave Boat Rentals, East Bay Street, 367-3910, fax 367-3911
Concept Rentals, Conch Inn, 367-5570
D & E Boat Rentals, Harbour View Marina , 367-2182
Florida Yacht Charters, Boat Harbour, AB-20511, 367-4853, fax 367-4854

LaySue Rentals, Bay Street, AB-20685, 367-4414, fax 367-4356
Moorings Yacht Charter, Conch Inn Complex, 367-4000, fax 367-4004
Pier One Boat Rentals, Marsh Harbour Marina, AB-21008, 367-3587, cell 359-6982
Rainbow Rentals, Bay Street, AB-20070, 367-4602, fax 367-4601,
Rich's Rentals, Harbour, AB-20419, 367-2742, fax 367-2682
Sea Horse Rentals, Boat Harbour Marina, 367-2513, fax 367-2516

BOAT STORAGE
Abaco Outboard Engines Ltd, Dundas Town, AB-20430, 367-2452, fax 367-2354
Marsh Harbour Boat Yard Storage and Lift, 367-5205
OutBoard Shop, Pelican Shores, AB-20419, 367-2703
Rich's Rentals, Harbour, AB-20419, 367-2742, fax 367-2682

BOOKS
Abaco Treasures, Don Mackay Blvd, AB-20523, 367-3460, fax 367-3462
Beacon's Book House, Abaco Shopping Centre,367-5363
Bellvue Office Depot, Don MacKay Blvd, AB-20186, 367-2701, fax 367-3654
Tropical Treasures, East Bay Street, AB-20556, 367-4822

BUILDERS/ CONTRACTORS
Al Key , AB-20261, 367-2293
P. G. Archer, AB-20484, 367-2113
Bahamas Building Systems, 367-2848, fax 367-2708
Bahamas Hot Mix, Queen Elizabeth Drive, 367-2337, fax 367-2354
Caribbean Construction Ltd, Don MacKay Blvd, AB-20403, 367-2502
JFA Construction, 359-6994
Nixon Brothers Builders, Dundas Town, AB-20252, 367-2605
Pinder's Construction, AB-20061, 367-2063
Scandi Homes, Key Club Drive, AB-20277, 367-3241,
Bill Swain & Sons, B & L Plaza, AB-20546, 367-2120,
Williams Construction, Dundas Town, AB-20527, 367-4472,

BUILDING SUPPLIES
Abaco Glass Co, Don MacKay Blvd, AB-20507, 367-2442
Abaco Hardware, Don MacKay Blvd, AB-20488, 367-2927, fax 367-2928
Rock & Fill Ltd, Don MacKay Blvd, AB-20207, 367-3650, fax 367-2988
Standard Hardware, Queen Elizabeth Dr, AB-20498, 367-2660, fax 367-2645

CARPENTERS/CABINET MAKERS
Donald Russell, 367-2436
Stewart Sands, 367-2328
Tim Duggan, 367-2631

CHILD CARE, PRE-SCHOOL AND KINDERGARTEN
Agape, MH Gospel Chapel, AB-20426, 367-4777
Early Learning Academy, Murphy Town, 367-3307
Grace Baptist, Forest Drive, AB-20048, 367-2926
New Direction, Dundas Town
Shjanea - Bethany Gospel, Murphy Town, 367-3608
Ms Stoodley, Government Sub, AB-20165, 367-2436

CHURCHES
AB Apostilic, Crockett Drive, 367-2082
Aldersgate Methodist, Don McKay Blvd, AB-20443, 367-2009, 367-2566,
1st Assembly of God, Stratton Drive, AB-20560, 367-2130
Bethany Gospel Chapel, Murphy Town, 367-4472
Bible Truth Hall, Pelican Shores, AB-20472, 367-2579
Calvary Baptist Church, Stratton Drive Area, 367-2105
Church of Christ, Don MacKay Blvd, 367-3381
Church of God, (MRF Bible), Dundas Town, 367-2740
Church of God of Prophecy, Dundas Town, 367-2071
Church of God of Prophecy, Forest Drive
Church of the Latter Rain, Dundas Town, 367-4557
Creole Gospel Chapel, Crockett Drive, 367-3784

Faith Chapel, Queen Elizabeth Dr, 367-2508
Friendship Tabernacle, Dundas Town, 367-4238
Grace Baptist Church, Forest Drive, AB-20048, 367-2926
Kingdom Hall (JW), Forest Drive
M. H. Gospel Chapel, Don MacKay Blvd, AB-20426, 367-2204
MRF Bible Movement, Dundas Town, 367-2605
New Vision Ministries, Abaco Shopping Ctr, AB-20183, 367-3242, fax 367-3474
Seventh Day Adventist, Queen Elizabeth Dr, 367-2948
Soul Saving Ministries, Forest Drive, 367-4497
St Andrews Methodist, Dundas Town, 367-2007
St Francis De Sales (RC), Don MacKay Blvd, 367-2714
St John the Baptist Anglican, Don MacKay Blvd, AB-20543, 367-2518
Trumpet Assemblies of God, Forest Drive, 367-2914
Zion Baptist, Murphy Town, 367-3563

CIGARS & CIGARETTES
Solomons Abaco Ltd, Fire Break Road, AB-20563, 367-2602, fax 367-2731

CINEMA
RND, Airport Roundabout, 367-4382

CLOTHING
Adam & Eve, Flamingo Place, 367-5792
Alexis Fashion, Queen Elizabeth Dr, AB-20484, 367-2241
Corner Value, Queen Elizabeth Dr, AB-20490, 367-2250
Gashea's Handbags & Accs, Hudson Building, 367-2828
His & Her Jeans, Abaco Shopping Ctr, AB-20539, 367-2011
Iggy Biggy, East Bay Street, AB-20121, 367-3596
Kara's Fashions, Don MacKay Bld, AB-20546, 367-2195
Lowe's Pharmacy, Lowe's Shopping Ctr, AB-20503, 367-2667, fax 367-3130
Mangoes Boutique, East Bay Street, AB-20529, 367-2366
Mr Mister, Airport Roundabout, AB-20657, 367-4308
Sand Dollar Shop, East Bay Street, AB-20473, 367-4405
Seventeen Shop, Airport Roundabout, AB-20317, 367-4117
Sports World, 367-4693
Step-N-Style, Hudson Building, AB-20720, 367-4041
Victor's, Don MacKay Blvd, AB-20388, 367-3853
Vyrona's Health & Variety, Queen Elizabeth Dr, AB-20597, 367-3002
Wally's Boutique, East Bay Street, AB-20455, 367-2074

COMPUTER SALES AND SERVICE
Abacom Computer Service, D & S Shopping Ctr, AB-20078, 367-3475, fax 367-3771
Computer Creations, Don MacKay Blvd, 367-2004
Davco Computer Systems, Don Mackay Blvd, AB-20860, 367-3683, fax 367-3257
(See also INTERNET SERVICES)

CUSTOMS AGENTS, BROKERS
Arawak Agency, Bay Street, AB-20485, 367-2089, fax 367-2530
Frederick's Agency, Queen Elizabeth Dr, AB-20468, 367-2333, fax 367-3136
Trinity Customs Brokers, Hudson Building, AB-20253, 367-4297

DELIVERY, COURIER SERVICES
FedEx, DHL, at Travel Spot, Memorial Plaza, AB-20528, 367-2817, fax 367-3018
Frederick's Agency (UPS), Queen Elizabeth Dr, AB-20468, 367-2333, fax 367-3136
GWS Worldwide Exp, Abaco Shopping Ctr, AB-20552, 367-2722, fax 367-3207

DENTISTS
Agape Dental Clinic, Rear Memorial Plaza, AB-20676, 367-4355
Diamante Dental, Queen Elizabeth Dr, AB-20579, 367-4968
Greater Abaco Dental Clinic, Don MacKay Blvd, AB-20288, 367-4070

DIVING
Dive Abaco, Conch Inn Marina and Boat Harbour, AB-20555, 367-2787, fax 367-4779

Marsh Harbour Classified Business Directory (cont.)

DRUG STORES, PHARMACIES

Chemist Shoppe, D & S Shopping Ctr, AB-20459, 367-3106
(See also Supermarkets)

ELECTRICIANS, ELECTRICAL SUPPLIES

Edwards Electric, Queen Elizabeth Dr, AB-20590, 367-2314
Ellis Stuart, Bay & Maxwell, AB-20053, 367-3790
Key's Electric, Dove Plaza, AB-20458, 367-2640

ELECTRONICS, REPAIRS AND SALES

Abaco Stereo, Don MacKay Blvd, AB-20577, 367-2265, fax 367-3043
Avtech, Don MacKay Blvd, 367-4262, fax 367-4262
Doug's Place, D & S Shopping Ctr, AB-20310, 367-2672
Electronics Service Centre, Queen Elizabeth Dr, AB-20421, 367-2830
Marsh Harbour Electronics, Memorial Plaza, AB-20265, 367-2894
Merlin Electronics, Marsh Harbour Marina, 367-2163, fax 367-3388, VHF 16
Sight & Sound Electronics, Abaco Shopping Ctr, AB-20183, 367-3242, fax 367-3474
Super Beeper, 367-4345
Western Auto, Don MacKay Blvd, AB-20507, 367-2300, fax 367-2391

EXTERMINATORS

The Bug Reaper, Marsh Harbour, AB-20919, 367-4202
The Exterminators, Marsh Harbour, AB-20185, 367-3021

FARMS

Abaco Big Bird Farm, Abaco Highway, AB-20435, 367-4540, fax 367-7004
Bahama Palm, Abaco Highway
Bahama Star, SC Bootle Highway
Bahama Neem, Abaco Highway, 367-4117
Harmon Farms, Abaco Highway
Porkies Farms, Abaco Highway, AB-20378, 367-7030, fax 367-7033
Rocky Farms, Cherokee Road

FERRIES

Albury's Ferry Service, The Crossing, 367-3147, 365-6010, fax 365-6487

FISH, RETAIL & WHOLESALE

Long's Landing Seafoods, Bay & William, 367-3079
MH Exporters & Importers, Harbour, AB-20585, 367-2697, fax 367-3937
Star Lite Sea Food, Dundas Town, 367-2384

FISHING GUIDES

Crestwell Archer, Conch Inn Marina, 367-2775
Fish Abaco (Ira Russell), 367-3419
Pinder, Chris & Buddy , Marsh Harbour, AB-20303, 367-2234
Jay Sawyer, Marsh Harbour, 367-2089
Terrance Davis, Dundas Town, AB-20227, 367-4464

FISHING TACKLE

Abaco Hardware, Don MacKay Blvd, AB-20488, 367-2927, fax 367-2928
B & D Marine, Traffic Light, AB-20490, 367-2622, fax 367-2395
National Marine, Don MacKay Blvd, AB-20535, 367-2326, fax 367-2326
Standard Hardware, Queen Elizabeth Dr, AB-20498, 367-2660, fax 367-2645
Triple J Marine, Bay Street, AB-20512, 367-2163, fax 367-3388

FITNESS CENTRES, GYMS

Abaco Fitness, Memorial Plaza, 367-5939

FUEL, AUTOMOBILE

K & S Auto Service, Don MacKay Blvd, AB-20520, 367-2655
Marsh Harbour Auto Parts, Don MacKay Blvd, AB-20446, 367-2111
Quality Star Auto Centre, Don MacKay Blvd, 367-2979, fax 367-3519
Shell (MH)Service Station , Don MacKay Blvd, AB-20438, 367-2840
Shell (DT) Service Station, Royal Plaza DT, 367-3883
TNT Service Station, SC Bootle Highway, AB-20347, 367-4970

FUEL, BOAT

Boat Harbour Marina, Boat Harbour, AB-20511, 367-2736, fax 367-2979

Conch Inn Marina, East Bay Street, AB-20434, 367-4000, fax 367-4004
Harbour View Marina, East Bay Street, AB-20457, 367-2175
Marsh Harbour Marina, Pelican Shores, AB-20518, 367-2700, fax 367-2033
Port of Call, Bay Street, AB-20777, 367-2287, fax 367-4885

FURNITURE

Good As New
Lowe's Pharmacy, Lowe's Shopping Ctr, AB-20503, 367-2667, fax 367-3130
Bella's, Don MacKay Blvd. 769-2230
Western Auto, Don MacKay Blvd, AB-20507, 367-2300, fax 367-2391

GIFT SHOPS

Abaco Gold, East Bay Street, AB-20473, 367-4405, fax 367-4404
Abaco Treasures, Don MacKay Blvd, AB-20523, 367-3460, fax 367-3462
Brass & Leather Shop, Abaco Shopping Ctr, AB-20382, 367-3643
Far East Traders, East Bay Street
Galleria, East Bay Street, 367-4881
Iggy Biggy, East Bay Street, AB-20121, 367-3596
Java Coffee Shop, East Bay Street, 367-5523
John Bull, East Bay Street, AB-20529, 367-2473, fax 367-2954
Solomon's Mines, East Bay Street, AB-20563, 367-3191, fax 367-3041
Sunset Souvenirs, East Bay Street, AB-20404, 367-2658
T Shirt Shop, East Bay Street, 367-4881
Tropical Treasures & Treats, East Bay Street, AB-20556, 367-4822

GROCERY STORES AND WHOLESALE OUTLETS

Abaco Wholesale Ltd, Don MacKay Blvd, AB-20499, 367-2020, fax 367-2242
Fruits & Vegetables Sales, Don MacKay Blvd, 367-4337
Golden Harvest, Queen Elizabeth Dr, AB-20578, 367-2310, fax 367-2322(under construction)
Lightbourne's Discount Ctr, Queen Elizabeth Dr, 367-2651
M&R Grocery, Crockett Drive,365-6010
Price Right, Stratton Drive, 367-7283
Sea Shore Meats and Sea Food, Dundas,367-5149
Solomons Abaco Ltd, Fire Break Road, AB-20563, 367-2601/2, fax 367-2731

GROCERY CONVENIENCE STORES (EXTENDED HOURS)

A & A Food Store, Crockett Drive, 367-4521
Abaco Saver's Mart, Don MacKay Blvd
Bahamas Family Market,Traffic Light,AB-20423, 367-3714
Brown Bay Food Store, Dundas Town
Cash & Carry, Murphy Town
Central Convenience Store, Forest Drive, 367-4290
Concept Convenience Store, Conch Inn Plaza, 367-5570
Mannie's Convenience St, Murphy Town
Muriel's Food Store, Murphy Town
Roderick's Convenience St, Crockett Drive, 367-3237
Shell Shop, Royal Plaza DT, AB-20726, 367-3883, fax 367-3882

HARDWARE AND PAINT

Abaco Hardware, Don MacKay Blvd, AB-20488, 367-2927, fax 367-2928
AID, Don MacKay Blvd, AB-20407, 367-2077, fax 367-3296
B & D Marine, Traffic Light, AB-20461, 367-2622, fax 367-2395
Brand Parts, Queen Elizabeth Dr, AB-20306, 367-4185
Standard Hardware, Queen Elizabeth Dr, AB-20498, 367-2660, fax 367-2645
Western Auto Parts, Don MacKay Blvd, AB-20507, 367-4227

HOTELS, RESORTS, MOTELS AND GUEST HOUSES

Abaco Beach Hotel & Resort, Boat Harbour, AB-20511, 367-2158, fax 367-2819
Ambassador Motel, Crockett Drive, AB-20484, 367-2022, fax 367-2113
Conch Inn Resort, East Bay Street, AB-20434, 367-2800, fax 367-4004
D's Guest House, Crockett Drive, 367-3980
Island Breezes Motel, East Bay Street, AB-20453, 367-3776, fax 367-4179
Lofty Fig Villas, East Bay Street, AB-20437, 367-2681

MH Airport Motel, Don MacKay Blvd, AB-20513, 367-4402, fax 367-4401
Pelican Beach Villas, Pelican Shores, AB-20304, 367-3600

HOUSE/APARTMENT RENTALS

Abaco Real Estate, Stratton Drive, AB-20404, 367-2719, fax 367-2359
Abaco Towns-by-the-Sea, East Bay Street, AB-20486, 367-2227, fax 367-3927
Bahamas Realty, East Bay Street, AB-20856, 367-3262, fax 367-3260

ICE

Abaco CholCE, Don MacKay Blvd, AB-20757, 367-4842, fax 367-4841
Abaco Ice, East Bay Street, AB-20585, 367-3384, fax 367-3298
Boat Harbour Marina, Boat Harbour, AB-20511, 367-2736, fax 367-2979
Conch Inn Marina, East Bay Street, AB-20434, 367-2800
Golden Harvest, Queen Elizabeth Dr, AB-20578, 367-2310
Harbour View Marina, East Bay Street, AB-20457, 367-2175
Marsh Harbour Marina, Pelican Shores, AB-20518, 367-2700, fax 367-2033
Standard Hardware,Queen Elizabeth Drive, 367-2660
Port of Call, Bay Street, AB-20777, 367-2287, fax 367-4885
(Also at all Liquor Stores)

INSURANCE

Abaco Insurance Agency, Stratton Drive, AB-20404, 367-2549, fax 367-3075
Family Guardian, B & L Plaza, AB-20901, 367-3264, fax 367-3265
Imperial Life of Canada, Flamingo Plaza, AB-20471, 367-3432, fax 367-3299
Insurance Management Ltd, Queen Elizabeth Dr, AB-20660, 367-4204, fax 367-4206
J.S. Johnson Ltd, Dove Plaza, AB-20521, 367-2688, fax 367-3083
Nassau Underwriters Agency, Queen Elizabeth Dr, AB-20471, 367-2222, fax 367-2888
Star Insurance, Hudson Building, 367-3418, fax 367-4086

INTERNET SERVICES

Out Island Inter.Net, Queen Elizabeth Dr, AB-20991, 367-3006

INTERIOR DESIGN

Commercial Interior Design, Traffic Light, AB-20737, 367-2031

JANITORIAL SERVICES

C & P Janitorial, Little Orchard, AB-20460, 367-2814

JEWELLERY

Abaco Gold, East Bay Street, AB-20473, 367-4405, fax 367-4404
Abaco Treasures, Don MacKay Blvd, AB-20523, 367-3460, fax 367-3462
Galleria, East Bay Street, 367-4881
John Bull, East Bay Street, AB-20084, 367-2473, fax 367-2954
Little Switzerland, East Bay Street, AB-20563, 367-3191, fax 367-3048
Simcoe Jewellers, Memorial Plaza

LAUNDRIES, CLEANERS AND LAUNDROMATS

Classic Coin Wash, Stratton Drive, AB-20453, 367-2750
Express Dry Cleaner, Forest Drive, 367-4012
Harbour View Marina, East Bay Street, AB-20457, 367-2175
Triple J Marine, Bay Street, AB-20285, 367-2163, fax 367-3388
Viola's Laundrymat, Johnson St DT

LIQUOR STORES

A & K Liquor Store, Queen Elizabeth Dr, AB-20565, 367-2179
Archer Brothers, Crockett Drive, AB-20484, 367-2022
Bristol Cellars,Queen Elizabeth Drive,367-2180
Burns House #1, Don MacKay Blvd, AB-20444, 367-2135, fax 367-2151
Burns House #3, Queen Elizabeth Dr, AB-20444, 367-2172
Valacq Liquors, Don McKay, Airport Rd.,367-4460

MARINAS

Abaco Yacht Haven, East Bay St., AB-20242, 367-3079
Boat Harbour Marina, Boat Harbour, AB-20511, 367-2819
Conch Inn Marina, East Bay Street, AB-20469, 367-4000, fax 367-4004

Harbour View Marina, East Bay Street, AB-20457, 367-2182
Marsh Harbour Marina, Pelican Shores, 367-2700, fax 367-2033
Port of Call, Bay Street, AB-20777, 367-2287, fax 367-4885

MARINE STORES

Abaco Hardware, Don MacKay Blvd, AB-20488, 367-2827, fax 367-2928
B & D Marine, Traffic Light, AB-20490, 367-2622, fax 367-2395
Marine Store, next to Marsh Harbour Boat Yard
National Marine, Don MacKay Blvd, AB-20535, 367-2326, fax 367-2326
Standard Hardware, Queen Elizabeth Dr, AB-20498, 367-2660, fax 367-2645

NEWS, MAGAZINES

Abaco Journal, Forest Drive, AB-20642, 367-2580, fax 367-2580
Abaconian, Abaco Shopping Ctr, AB-20551, 367-2677, fax 367-2677
what's hap'nen Abaco, Abaco Shopping Ctr, 367-3202, fax 367-3202
What's On (Abaco), Memorial Plaza, AB-20921, 367-4065, fax 367-4066,

NURSERIES, FLORISTS

Buds & Blooms, Memorial Plaza, AB-20438, 367-2837, fax 367-4887
Gardener's Eden, Don MacKay Blvd, AB-20472, 367-2260, fax 367-3379
Pine Woods Nursery, Don MacKay Blvd, AB-20422, 367-2674, fax 367-4755
Tropical Farm Nursery, Rear Abaco Whsle, 367-2783

OFFICE SUPPLIES & STATIONERY

Bellevue Business Depot, Don MacKay Blvd, AB-20823, 367-3915, fax 367-3914

OPTICAL

Abaco Optical Services, Lowe's Shopping Ctr, AB-20091, 367-3546

OUTBOARD MOTOR SALES AND SERVICE

Abaco Outboard (Yamaha), Dundas Town, AB-20430, 367-2452, fax 367-2354
B & D Marine (Suzuki), Traffic Light, AB-20490, 367-2622
Master Marine (Honda), Bay St., AB-20229, 367-4760, fax 367-4765
National Marine (Mercury), Don MacKay Blvd, AB-20535, 367-2326
Outboard Shop (Evinrude), Pelican Shores, AB-20098, 367-2703

PAINTING

Midway Painting Contractors, Government Sub, AB-20622, 367-3849

PARTY SUPPLIES

Party Time, Queen Elizabeth Dr, AB-20025, 367-2785

PETROLEUM DISTRIBUTORS AND DEALERS

Abaco Petroleum Co Ltd, Don MacKay Blvd., AB-20899, 367-2951, fax 367-3271
Shell Bahamas Ltd, Murphy Town, AB-20508, 367-2253, fax 367-4188
Tropical Petroleum Distr, Murphy Town, AB-20247, 367-4929

PETS & PET SUPPLIES

Caribbean Veterinary Centre,Don MacKay Blvd.,367-3551
Community Animal Hospital, Don MacKay Blvd, 367-3647
Pets are People Too, Queen Elizabeth Drive
Pine Woods Nursery, Don MacKay Blvd, AB-20095, 367-2674, fax 367-2223

PHOTO DEVELOPMENT & SUPPLIES

Snap Shop, D & S Shopping Ctr, AB-20459, 367-3020

PHYSICIANS, CLINICS

Abaco Family Medicine, Lowe's Shopping Ctr, 367-2295
Abaco Medical Clinic, School Lane, 367-4240
MH Government Clinic, Don MacKay Blvd, 367-2510

PLUMBERS

Clifford Henfield, Dundas Town
Pinders Plumbing, Key Club Road, 367-2598
Twins Plumbing, Dundas Town, 367-3456
Whymns Plumbing Co, Dundas Town, 367-4759

PRINTING

Abaco Custom Signs, Stratton Drive, AB-20404, 367-3081, fax 367-3075

Marsh Harbour Classified Business Directory (cont.)

Abaco Print Shop, Abaco Shopping Ctr, AB-20551, 367-2677

PROPANE GAS

Abaco Gas Co, Corner Value Store, AB-20490, 367-2250, fax 367-3810

RADIO STATIONS AND BROADCAST COMPANIES

Radio Abaco, Dundas Town, 367-2935, fax 367-4242
ZNS, Loyalist Centre, 367-4044, fax 367-4025 100 Jamz

REAL ESTATE SALES

Abaco Real Estate Agency, Stratton Drive, AB-20404, 367-2719, fax 367-2359
Abaco Realtors, Marsh Harbour, AB-20496, 367-7248, fax 367-7248
Bahamas Realty, East Bay Street, AB-20856, 367-3262, fax 367-3260
Coldwell Banker, Queen Elizabeth Drive, 367-2992
Damianos, East Bay, 367-5046
H G Christie Ltd, AB-20777, 367-4608, fax 367-4885
Sea Grape Realty, Queen Elizabeth Dr, AB-20123, 367-2749, fax 367-2748

REFRIGERATION SALES & REPAIRS

Arctic Breeze, Don MacKay Blvd, AB-20559, 367-2458
K & W Refrigeration, Off Don MacKay, AB-20454, 367-4949, fax 367-4949
Marco Air Conditioning, Don MacKay Blvd, AB-20192, 367-3186, fax 367-3469

RESTAURANTS, TAKE AWAYS AND SNACKS

Abaco Snacks, Don MacKay Blvd
Airport Restaurant, Airport, 367-4973
Ambassador Inn, Crockett Drive, AB-20484, 367-2022, fax 367-2113
Angler's Restaurant, Boat Harbour Marina , AB-20511, 367-2158
Arnold's Poinciana T-A, Dundas Town, 367-2517
Bay View Restaurant, Dundas Town, AB-20029, 367-3738 (take-away only)
Bistro , East Bay Street, AB-20280, 367-4444

C & G's Snacks and Bakery, behind Memorial Plaza
Candie's Snack Place, Airport, AB-20453, 367-2493
Cool Spot Restaurant, Dundas Town, 367-3626
Corner Restaurant, Christie St DT, AB-20112, 367-4346
Dis We Style Take Out, Crockett Drive, 367-4244
Katie's, Memorial Plaza, AB-20853, 367-4657, 367-4346
Golden Grouper, Dove Plaza, AB-20557, 367-2301
Jamie's Place, East Bay Street, 367-2880
Java Coffee Shop, East Bay Street, 367-5523
Jib Room, Pelican Shores, AB-20518, 367-2700
Julie's Snack Shop, Dundas Town
KFC, Abaco Shopping Ctr, 367-2615, fax 367-2953
L & T Take Away, Dundas Town
La Bahia Take Away, Crockett Drive, 367-2886
Le Castaways, Bay Street, AB-20147, 367-4938
Mackerels, Dundas Town, 367-5932
Mangoes, East Bay Street, AB-20529, 367-2366, fax 367-3336
Mavis Country Kitchen, Don MacKay Blvd, 367-2002
Mother Merle's Fishnet, Dundas Town, AB-20476, 367-2770 (take-away only)
Patrece Snack & Bakery, Forest Drive, AB-20015, 367-4676
Pop's Place, 367-3796
Sapodilly's, East Bay Street, 367-3498
Sharkee's Island Pizza, East Bay Street, AB-20613, 367-3535
Sea Shells, DonMcKay Blvd, 367-4460
Snack Shack, East Bay Street, 367-4005
Snappas, Harborview Marina, 367-2278
Subway, B & V Plaza, 367-2798
Veronica's Take-Away, Murphy Town, 367-3380
Wally's , East Bay Street, AB-20455, 367-2074, fax 367-3073

SAILBOAT CHARTERS

Florida Yacht Charters, Boat Harbour, AB-20511, 367-4853, fax 367-4854
Moorings, Conch Inn Marina, AB-20469, 367-4000, fax 367-4004

SCHOOLS

Abaco Academy, Queen Elizabeth Dr, AB-20533, 367-3484
Abaco Central Secondary, Forest Drive, AB-20425, 367-2334, fax 367-3997

Agape Christian, Gospel Chapel Road, AB-20210, 367-4777, fax 367-3020
Central Abaco Primary, Forest Drive, 367-2718
Forest Heights Academy, Don MacKay Blvd, AB-20096, 367-3539
Long Bay School, Forest Drive, AB-20377, 367-2436
St Francis de Sales, Don MacKay Blvd, 367-4399
Wesley College, Don MacKay Blvd, AB-20443, 367-2009, fax 367-2566

SECURITY SYSTEMS & SERVICES

Abaco Alarm Systems, AB-20757, 367-4841

SEPTIC TANK/SANITATION

Abaco Sanitation Service, Don MacKay Blvd, 367-4422
Lou's Tank Service, East Bay Street, 367-2043

SHIPPING COMPANIES

Marsh Harbour Shipping Co, Queen Elizabeth Dr, AB-20498, 367-3341, fax 367-2645
United Abaco Shipping Co, Traffic Light, AB-20737, 367-2091, fax 367-2235

SHOES

Abaco Shoe Gallery, D &S Plaza
Brass & Leather Shop, Abaco Shopping Ctr, AB-20382, 367-3643
Shoe Place, Dove Plaza, 367-2424
Spooner's, Queen Elizabeth Dr, AB-20466, 367-2017

SIGNS, ETC

Abaco Custom Signs, 367-3081

STORAGE

Abaco Spaces, Don MacKay Blvd, 367-2414
Tropical Self Storage, Key Club Road, 365-6407, fax 365-6407

STRAWWORK

Darville's Straw Industry, behind Memorial Plaza, 367-2649
Sunset Straw & Souvenir, East Bay Street, AB-20404, 367-2658

SUNDRIES AND NOTIONS

Abaco Price Slashers, Dove Plaza, 367-4432
Classic Beauty Supplies, Loyalist Centre, 367-4221
Evergreen Beauty Supplies, Queen Elizabeth Dr, 367-4856
Nix & Naxs, Abaco Shopping Ctr, AB-20194, 367-3085

SURVEYORS

Lucayan Surveying Co, East Bay Street, AB-20460, 367-2749, fax 367-2748
Riviere & Associates, Don Mackay Blvd, AB-20188, 367-4585, fax 367-3091

TILES

Light Impressions, Abaco Shopping Ctr, AB-20183, 367-3242, fax 367-3474
Standard Hardware, 367-2660

TOURS

Abaco Outback, Harbour View Marina, 367-5358
Bahamas Naturalist Expds, 367-4505

TRAVEL AGENCIES

A & W Travel, Abaco Shopping Ctr, AB-20521, 367-2806, fax 367-3219
Travel Spot, Memorial Plaza, AB-20504, 367-2817, fax 367-3018
Trinity Travel & Tour, Hudson Building, 367-2606, fax 367-2607

TRUCKING

Abaco Trucking, AB-20207, 367-3650, fax 367-2988
Albury's Trucking, Key Club Road, AB-20068, 367-2976, fax 367-3930
E & D Trucking, AB-20597, 367-2480
Jerry's Trucking, Dundas Town, 367-2457

UPHOLSTERY

Abaco Awning & Marine Up, Hudson Building, 367-4846
AC Upholstery, Dundas Town, AB-20463, 367-2292
David Williams

WASTE DISPOSAL

E & D Waste Service, Crockett Drive, AB-20064, 367-2784

WATER, BOTTLED

Abaco Water Systems Ltd, AB-20135, 367-3344
Chelsea's Choice, Don MacKay Blvd, AB-20757, 367-4842, fax 367-4841

WELDING

Abaco Marine Props, Don MacKay Blvd, 367-4276, fax 367-4259
CJ's Welding, AB-20540, 367-4011, fax 367-4018
Hartwell Russell, Caribbean Constr, AB-20403, 367-2502

Green Turtle Cay Classified Business Directory

ADMINISTRATOR

Administrator's Office, 365-4211

ART GALLERY

Alton Lowe Gallery, 365-4264
Alton Lowe Museum, 365-4094
Memorial Sculpture Garden
Ocean Blue Gallery, Plymouth Rock Bar & Restaurant, 365-4234

BAKERY

McIntosh Restaurant & Bakery, 365-4625
Wreckin' Tree Bakery and Take Away, 365-4228

BANK

Barclay's Bank, 365-4144

BARS / TAVERNS

Blue Bee Bar, 365-4181
Bluff House Club and Marina, 365-4247
Green Turtle Club, 365-4271
New Plymouth Inn, 365-4161
Pineapples Bar and Grill, Other Sh. Club, 365-4226
Plymouth Rock Restaurant & Bar, 365-4234
Rooster's Rest Pub & Restaurant, 365-4066
Sundowner Restaurant & Bar, 365-4060
Wreckin' Tree Bakery and Take Away, 365-4228

BEAUTY SALONS / BARBERS

Hubert's Cut & Curls, 365-4100
Sharon's Salon, 365-4131

BICYCLE RENTALS

Brendal's Bike Rental, 365-4411
Curtis Bike Rental, 365-4128
D & P Bike Rental, 365-4655

BOAT BUILDING / REPAIR

Abaco Yacht Services, 365-4033/365-4216

BOAT RENTALS

Dames Boat Rentals, Bluff House, White Sound, 365-4247
Donny's Rentals, Black Sound, 365-4119

Reef Boat Rentals
Robert's Hardware and Marine, 365-4122

BOAT SALES

Dolphin Marine, White Sound, 365-4262
Robert's Hardware and Marine, 365-4122

BOAT STORAGE

Abaco Yacht Services Ltd., 365-4033/365-4216
Bluff House Club & Marina, 365-4247
Donny's Rentals, Black Sound, 365-4119
Green Turtle Club, 365-4271
Other Shore Club & Marina, 365-4195
Robert's Hardware and Marine, 365-4122

BOOKS

Curry's Food Store, 365-4171
Golden Reef, 365-4511
Lowe's Grocery Store, 365-4243
Loyalist Rose Shoppe, 365-4037
Shell Hut, 365-4188
Sid's Food Store, 365-4055

BUILDERS / CONTRACTORS

Alphonso McIntosh, 365-4030
Jonathan Curry
Lonnie Lowe, 365-4135
Maxwell McIntosh
Michael Levarity, 365-4228
Reggie Sawyer, 365-4268
Wayne Reckley, 365-4203

CHURCHES

Church of God, 365-4505
Gospel Chapel (Plymouth Brethren), 365-4198
Methodist, 365-4293
St. Peter's Anglican

CLINIC

Government Clinic, 365-4028
Green Turtle Dental Clinic, 365-4548

CLOTHING

Bluff House Club & Marina, 365-4247

Brendal's Dive Shop, 365-4411
Green Turtle Club Boutique, 365-4271
Golden Reef, 365-4511
Lowe's Grocery Store, 365-4243
Loyalist Rose Shoppe, 365-4037
Shell Hut, 365-4188
Sid's Food Store, 365-4055
Tropic Topic 365-4210

CUSTOMS

Customs Office, 365-4077

DIVING

Brendal's Dive Shop, 365-4411 / 800 780-9941
Green Turtle Club, 365-4271

FERRY

Green Turtle Ferry, 365-4151

FISH - RETAIL AND WHOLESALE

Abaco Seafoods, 365-4011/365-4012/365-4054
B & M Seafoods, 365-4387/365-4595
Curtis Seafood, 365-4128

FISHING GUIDES / CHARTERS

Eddie Bodie, 365-4069, 357-6784
Lincoln Jones, 365-4223
Joe Sawyer, 365-4173
Rickie Sawyer, 365-4261

FISHING TACKLE

Roberts' Hardware and Marine, 365-4122

FLOWERS

Native Creations, 365-4206

FUEL

Bluff House Club & Marina, 365-4247
Green Turtle Club Marina, 365-4271
Other Shore Club & Marina, 365-4195

GIFT SHOPS

Golden Reef, 365-4511
Loyalist Rose Shop, 365-4037
Native Creations, 365-4206

Ocean Blue Gallery, Plymouth Rock Bar & Restaurant, 365-4234
Shell Hut, 365-4188
Tropic Topic 365-4210

GOLF CART RENTALS

Bay Street Golf Cart Rental, Bluff House, 365-4070
D & P Golf Carts, Green Turtle Club, 365-4655
Island Property Management Rentals, 365-4465
New Plymouth Rentals, 365-4161
Sea Side Rentals, 365-4120
Shell Hut Rentals, 365-4188
T & A Rentals, 365-4259

GROCERY STORES

Curry's Food Store, 365-4171
Lowe's Grocery Store, 365-4243
Sid's Food Store, 365-4055
Roberta Food Store, 365-4284

HARDWARE

New Plymouth Hardware, 365-4305
Roberts' Hardware and Marine, 365-4122

HOTELS / RESORTS

Bluff House Club & Marina, 365-4247
Green Turtle Club, 365-4271
New Plymouth Inn, 365-4161

HOUSE / APT. RENTALS

E. A. Roberts Cottages, 365-4274
Linton's Beach Cottages, 365-4003
Martha Lowe, 365-4055
Other Shore Club & Marina, 365-4195
Golden Reef Apartments, 365-4221, 365-4511
Susan Roberts, 365-4105
Walter Sands, 365-4178

HOUSEHOLD GOODS

Curry's Food Store, 365-4171
Lowe's Grocery Store, 365-4243
Sid's Food Store, 365-4055
Roberta Food Store, 365-4284
Tropic Topic, 365-4284

Green Turtle Cay Classified Business Directory (cont.)

ICE
Abaco Yacht Services Ltd. 365-4033/365-4216
Bluff House Club & Marina, 365-4247
B & M Seafoods, 365-4387
Curry & Sons Liquor Store, 365-4155
Curry's Food Store, 365-4171
Green Turtle Club, 365-4271
Lowe's Grocery Store, 365-4243
Other Shore Club & Marina, 365-4195
Roberts' Hardware and Marine, 365-4122
Sid's Food Store, 365-4055

JEWELRY
Golden Reef, 365-4511
Native Creations, 365-4206
Shell Hut, 365-4188
Sid's Food Store, 365-4055

LAUNDRY
Abaco Yacht Services Ltd., 365-4033/365-4216
Bluff House Club and Marina, 365-4247
Green Turtle Club, 365-4271

LIQUOR STORES
Curry & Sons Liquor Store, 365-4155
Plymouth Rock Restaurant & Bar, 365-4234

MARINAS
Abaco Yacht Services Ltd., 365-4033/365-4216
Black Sound Marina, 365-45311
Bluff House Club & Marina, 365-4247
Green Turtle Club and Marina, 365-4271
Other Shore Club & Marina, 365-4195

MARINE STORES
Dolphin Marine, White Sound, 365-4262/VHF 16
Green Turtle Club, 365-4271
Roberts' Hardware and Marine, 365-4122

MUSEUM
Albert Lowe Museum, 365-4094

OUTBOARD MOTOR SALES / SERVICE
Abaco Yacht Services Ltd. (Yamaha), 365-4033/365-4216
Dolphin Marine (OMC), White Sound, 365-4262/VHF 16
Roberts' Hardware and Marine (OMC), 365-4122

PHOTOGRAPHIC SUPPLIES
Golden Reef, 365-4511
Also see Grocery Stores

POLICE DEPARTMENT
Police Department, 365-4450

POST OFFICE
Post Office, 365-4242

POWER COMPANY
Bahamas Electricity Corporation (BEC), 365-4087/365-4088

PROPANE
Lowe's Food Store, 365 4243
New Plymouth Hardware, 365-4305
Sid's Food Store, 365-4055

REAL ESTATE SALES
Lowe's Real Estate, 365-4054

RESTAURANTS
Blue Bee Bar, 365-4181
Bluff House Club & Marina, 365-4247
Green Turtle Club, 365-4271
Laura's Kitchen, 365-4287
McIntosh Restaurant and Bakery, 365-4625
New Plymouth Inn, 365-4161
Pineapples at The Other Shore Club, 365-4226
Plymouth Rock Restaurant & Bar, 365-4234
Rooster's Rest Pub & Restaurant, 365-4066
Sea Side Snacks, 365-4209
Sundowner, 365-4060
Wreckin' Tree Bakery and Take Away, 365-4228

SHIPPING
Moonraker Enterprises, 365-4305 / FAX 365-4372

TELEPHONE
Batelco, 365-4113/365-4114/365-4115

TRAVEL AGENCY
A & W Travel, 365-4238

VIDEO RENTALS
Roberts' Hardware and Marine, 365-4122
Shell Hut, 365-4188

Treasure Cay Classified Business Directory

Treasure Cay Community Church (Non-Denominational), 365-8318

AIRLINES AND CHARTERS
Airways International
Bahamasair, 365-8600
Gulfstream International, 359-6801
Island Express, 367-3597
Twin Air, 333-2444
US Air, 365-8686

ARCHITECT
Hartman Cooper Jr, 365-0137

AUTOMOBILE PARTS AND SERVICE
Andy's Auto, 365-8659

AUTOMOBILE RENTAL
Alison's Car Rental, 365-8193
Cornish Car Rentals, 365-8623
Jensen Edgecombe, VHF-16
Triple J Car Rental, 365-8761

BAKERIES
Florence's Café

BANKS
Royal Bank of Canada (Tues & Thurs), 365-8119

BARS, TAVERNS
Island Boil, 365-8849
Spinnaker, 365-8469
Tipsy Seagull
Touch of Class
Traveller's Nest, (Airport)

BICYCLE RENTALS
Wendell's Bike Rentals

BOAT RENTALS
C & C Rentals, 365-8582
J.I.C. Rentals, 365-8465

BOAT STORAGE
C & C Rentals, 365-8582
Treasure Cay Marina, 365-8578

CHURCHES
Full Gospel Assembly, 365-8097
Sts Mary and Andrew (RC), 367-2714
St Simon's by the Sea (Anglican), 365-8422
Unity Baptist Church, 365-8371

CLOTHING
Delly's Variety Store
Lowe's Food Store, 365-8663
Obsession, 365-8391

CRUISES, GUIDED TOURS, DIVING
Claude Burrows
C & C Boat Rentals, 365-8582
J.I.C. Boat Rentals, 365-8465
Treasure Cay Marina, 365-8535

DENTISTS
Howard R. Spencer, 365-8625

DIVING
Treasure Divers, 365-8465

DRUGS AND NOTIONS
G & M Variety Store
Mini Mart, 365-8350

ELECTRONICS, APPLIANCES, ETC
GIF Home Centre, 365-8200, 365-8226

FERRY AND TOURS
Abaco Adventures, 365-8749, 340-6832 (pager)

GIFT SHOPS
Abaco Ceramics, 365-8489
Treasure Cay Marina Store, 365-8441
Triple J Car Rental and Gift Shop, 365-8761

GOLF CART RENTALS
Chris Carts, 365-8053
Resort Cart Rentals, 365-8465

GROCERY STORES/ SUPERMARKETS
Friendly Food Mart
Lowe's Food Store, 365-8663
Mini Mart, 365-8350
G & M Variety Store

HAIRDRESSING
Ruby Love

HARDWARE AND PAINT
Lynco Paints, 365-8653
McKelly's Hardware, 365-8653

HOUSE/ APARTMENT RENTALS
Banyan Beach Condos, 324-0748
Brigantine Bay Villas, 365-8033
Island Dreams, 365-8507, 365-8508,
Ocean Villas, 365-8200, 365-8226
Silver Sands, 365-8039
Treasure Cay Real Estate, 365-8538
William Hertz Ltd, 365-8061, 365-8061

INSURANCE
Abaco Insurance Agency, 365-8650
J.S. Johnson

LIQUOR STORES
Burns House, 365-8082
Spanky's Liquor Store, 365-8385

NURSERIES
Carrollville Nursery, 365-8674
Great Abaco Nursery

PHYSICIANS
Dr Ron Wilson, 365-8288, 365-8287

PLUMBERS
JR Hodgkins, 365-8657
Arthur Roberts, 365-8487

PROPERTY MANAGEMENT
GIF Property Manage, 365-8200, 365-8200
Island Dreams, 365-8777, 365-8508
Treasure Keys , 365-8472, 365-8472

REAL ESTATE SALES
GIF Realty & Property, 365-8200, 365-8226
William Hertz Ltd, 365-8061, 365-8061

REFRIGERATION
Abaco Air Conditioning

RESTAURANTS
Airport Restaurant & Bar, 365-8438
Island Boil, 365-8849
Macy's Café
Spinnaker, 365-8469
Tipsy Seagull
Touch of Class

SECURITY
Sawyer Security Systems, 365-8198

Man-O-War Classified Business Directory

BAKERIES
Albury's Bakery, 365-6031
Lola's Bakery, 365-6073

BANKS
Canadian Imperial Bank of Commerce, 365-6098
Royal Bank 365-6323

BEAUTY SALONS / BARBERS
Bahama Waves 365-6310

BOAT BUILDERS
Albury Brothers, 365-6086
Edwin's Boat Yard, 365-6007 / 365-6006

BOAT RENTALS
Conch Pearl Rentals, 365-6059
Waterways, 365-6143

BOAT STORAGE
Albury Brothers, 365-6086
Edwin's Boat Yard, 365-6007 / 365-6006
Man-O-War Marina, 365-6008

BOOKS
Joe's Studio, 365-6082
Man-O-War Marina Dive Shop, 365-6013
Mary's Corner Store, 365-6178

BUILDERS/CONTRACTORS
Bill Albury, 365-6009
Neville Albury, 365-6063
Warren Albury, 365-6057
Wallace McDonald, 365-6048
Quality Construction, Rowan Sands, 365-6061

BUILDING SUPPLIES
Man-O-War Hardware and Building Supply Ltd., 365-6011

CARPENTERS/CABINET MAKERS
Emerson Albury, 365-6034
Joe Albury, 365-6082

CHURCHES
Brethren Church, 365-6048
Church Of God parsonage, 365-6088
New Life Bible Church

CLINIC
Community Clinic, 365-6081

CLOTHING
Albury's Sail Shop, 365-6014
Belle-Ena, 365-6077
Island Treasures, 365-6072
Joe's Studio, 365-6082
Man-O-War Marina Dive Shop, 365-6013
Mary's Corner Store, 365-6178

DIVING
Man-O-War Marina Dive Shop, 365-6013

ELECTRICIANS & ELECTRICAL SUPPLIES
Man-O-War Hardware and Building Supply Ltd., 365-6011
Roberts Electrical, 365-6020

FERRY
Albury's Ferry Service, 365-6010

FISH - RETAIL
Sweeting's Fish Dock, N of MOW Marina / S of Edwin's BY #2

FISHING GUIDES/CHARTERS
David Albury, 365-6059

FISHING TACKLE
Man-O-War Hardware and Building Supply Ltd., 365-601
Waterways

FUEL
Man-O-War Marina, 365-6008

GIFT SHOPS
Albury's Sail Shop, 365-6014
Island Treasures, 365-6072
Joe's Studio, 365-6082
Man-O-War Marina Dive Shop, 365-6013
Mary's Corner Store, 365-6178

GROCERY STORES
Albury's Harbour Store, 365-6004
Man-O-War Grocery Store, 365-6016

HARDWARE
Man-O_War Hardware and Building Supply Ltd., 365-6011

HOTELS/RESORTS
Schooner's Landing Resort 365-6072

HOUSE / APARTMENT RENTALS
Bill and Sherry Albury, 365-6009 / FAX 365-6126
David Albury, 365-6059
Denise McDonald, 365-6048
Gary Sawyer, 365-6072

Man-O-War Cay (cont.)

Joann Sands, 365-6093
Joe's Studio, 365-6082
Man-O-War Marina, 365-6008
Molly Sawyer, 365-6022
Sweeting's Cottages, 365-6056

HOUSEHOLD GOODS
Belle-Ena, 365-6077
Man-O-War Hardware and Building Supply Ltd., 365-6011

ICE
Man-O-War Grocery, 365-6016
Man-O-War Marina, 365-6008

INSURANCE
Gary Sawyer, 365-6072

JEWELRY
Belle-Ena, 365-6077
Island Treasures, 365-6072
Joe's Studio, 365-6082

LAUNDRY
Man-O-War Marina, 365-6008

MARINAS
Man-O-War Marina, 365-6008

MARINE STORES
Edwin's Boat Yard, 365-6007 / 365-6006
Man-O-War Marina Dive Shop, 365-6013
Man-O-War Hardware and Building Supply Ltd., 365-6011

OUTBOARD MOTOR SALES & SERVICE
Albury Brothers, 365-6086
Man-O-War Marina, 365-6008

PHOTOGRAPHY SUPPLIES
Island Treasures, 365-6072
Joe's Studio, 365-6082
Man-O-War Marina Dive Shop, 365-6013

PLUMBERS & PLUMBING SUPPLIES
Man-O-War Hardware and Building Supply Ltd., 365-6011
Roberts Electrical, 365-6020

PROPANE
Man-O-War LP Gas, 365-6138

REAL ESTATE SALES
Man-O-War Real Estate, 365-6178

Michael Albury, 365-6329

REFRIGERATION REPAIR
Man-O-War Marina, 365-6008

RESTAURANTS
Man-O-War Pavilion Restaurant, 365-6185
Hibiscus Cafe, 365-6380
Island Treats, 3656501

SAIL MAKER
Jay Manni, Edwin's Boat Yard, 365-6171

SHIPPING COMPANIES
Abacays, 365-6247

TELEPHONE COMPANY
Batelco, 365-6001 / 365-6002 / 365-6002

Hope Town Classified Business Directory

ARCHITECT
Timothy Neill, 366-3110

ARTISTS / ART GALLERIES
Abaco Inn, White Sound, 366-0133
Ebb Tide, Back Street, 366-0088
Iggy Biggy, Bay Street, 366-0354
Sea Spray Marina, White Sound, 366-0065

BAKED GOODS
Harbour View Grocery (bread), Bay Street, 366-0033
Vernon's Grocery, Back Street, 366-0037

BANK
Canadian Imperial Bank of Commerce, Fig Tree Lane, 366-0296

BARS/TAVERNS
Abaco Inn, White Sound, 366-0133
Cap'n Jack's, Bay Street, 366-0247
Club Soleil, Hope Town Marina, 366-0003
Garbonzo Reef Bar, Sea Spray Marina, White Sound, 366-0569
Harbour's Edge, 366-0087 / 366-0292
Hope Town Harbour Lodge, 366-0095, fax 366-0286
On Da Beach, Turtle Hill, 366-0557
Rudy's Place, Centerline Rd., 366-0062

BEAUTY SALON/BARBER
The Choppiing Block, Russel's Lane, 366-0052

BICYCLE RENTALS
Abaco Inn, White Sound, 366-0133
Harbour's Edge, 366-0087 / 366-0292

BOAT BUILDING AND REPAIR
Winer Malone (wood only), Back Street

BOAT RENTALS AND CHARTERS
Abaco Bahamas Charters, Back Creek (large sail-boats only)
Abaco Inn, White Sound, 366-0133
Cat's Paw Boat Rentals, 366-0380
Classic Marine, located at Sea Spray Marina, 366-0065
Island Marine, Parrot Cay, 366-0282
Sea Horse Marine, Back Creek, 367-2513
Sea Spray Resort and Marina, White Sound, 366-0065

BOAT STORAGE
Hope Town Marina (wet), 366-0003
Lighthouse Marina (wet/dry), 366-0154

BOOKS
Abaco Inn, White Sound, 366-0133
Ebb Tide, Back Street, 366-0088
El Mercado, Back Street, 366-0053
Hope Town Harbour Lodge, 366-0095, fax 366-0286
Kemp's Souvenir Center, Back Street, 366-0423
Lighthouse Marina, 366-0154
Sea Spray Marina, White Sound, 366-0065
Vernon's Grocery, Back Street, 366-0037

BUILDERS / CONTRACTORS
Andrew Russell
Damien Cole
Mark Malone (True Cuts)
Greg Russell
Ronnie Sands, 366-0657

BUILDING MATERIALS
Abaco Rock, 366-0228

Imports Unlimited, White Sound, 366-0136

CARPENTRY / BUILDING REPAIR
Bill Fuller (cabinetry), White Sound, 366-0116
Inside/Outside (Marty Cash), 366-0122
Donnie Maura, 366-0042

CHURCHES
Assembly of God, Cemetery Road
Lighthouse Ministries, White Sound
St. Francis de Sales (Roman Catholic) Marsh Harbour
St. James Methodist, Back Street

CLINIC
Hope Town Clinic, 366-0108

CLOTHING
Abaco Inn, White Sound, 366-0133
Ebb Tide, Back Street, 366-0088
El Mercado, Back Street, 366-0053
Fantasy Boutique, Bay Street, 366-0537
Iggy Biggy, Bay Street, 366-0354
Kemp's Souvenir Center, Back Street, 366-0423
Sea Spray Marina, White Sound, 366-0065

DIVING
Froggies, Queen's Highway, 366-0431
Snapper Charter (George Smith), Abaco Inn, 366-0133; cell-357-6558

ELECTRICIANS
Jamie Bethel, 366-0395

ENGINE REPAIR
Tom Cat Enterprises, White Sound, 366-0135

FERRY
Albury's Ferry Service, 365-6010

FISH - RETAIL
Alan Albury, Russell's Road, 366-0050

FISHING GUIDES / CHARTERS
Will Key, Day's Catch, Back Street, 366-0059
Maitland Lowe (bonefishing), 366-0461
Robert Lowe, Nigh Crk, 366-0266, VHF 16 *Sea Gull*
Truman Major, Hurricane Hole, 366-0101

FISHING TACKLE
Lighthouse Marina, 366-0154

FLORAL DESIGN
Bonnie Hall, Back Street, 366-0058

FUEL - AUTOMOBILE
Sea Spray Marina, White Sound, 366-0065

FUEL - BOAT (GAS AND DIESEL)
Lighthouse Marina, 366-0154
Sea Spray Marina, White Sound, 366-0065

GIFT SHOPS
Abaco Inn, White Sound, 366-0133
Ebb Tide, Back Street, 366-0088
El Mercado, Back Street, 366-0053
Fantasy Boutique, Bay Street, 366-0537
Iggy Biggy, Bay Street, 366-0354
Kemp's Souvenir Center, Back Street, 366-0423
Sea Spray Marina, White Sound, 366-0065

GOLF CART RENTAL
Hope Town Cart Rentals, 366-0064
Island Cart Rentals, 366-0448
T & N Cart Rentals, 366-0069

GROCERY STORES
Harbour View Grocery, Bay Street, 366-0033
LVA Convenience Store, White Sound Road, 366-0056
Sweetomg's Grocery, White Sound Road, 366-0391
Vernon's Grocery, Back Street, 366-0037

HARDWARE
Imports Unlimited, Centerline Road, White Sound, 366-0136
Lighthouse Marina, 366-0154

HOTELS / RESORTS
Abaco Inn, White Sound, 366-0133
Club Soleil Resort, 366-0003
Hope Town Harbour Lodge, 366-0095, fax 366-0286
Hope Town Hideaways, Fax/Phone 366-0224
Sea Spray Marina, White Sound, 366-0065
Turtle Hill Resort, Queen's Highway, voice/fax 366-0557

HOUSE / APT. RENTALS
Elbow Cay Properties, Bay Street, 366-0569
Hope Town Hideaways, Fax/Phone 366-0224
Hope Town Villas, 366-0030, fax 366-0377
Lighthouse Rentals, 366-0154
Malone Estates, Back Street, 366-0100 / 366-0060 / fax 366-0157
Parrot Cay Cottages, Parrot Cay, 366-0282, fax 366-0281
Sea Spray Marina, White Sound, 366-0065
Tanny Key Rentals, 366-0140

HOUSEHOLD GOODS
Imports Unlimited, Centerline Road, White Sound, 366-0136

ICE
Harbour's Edge, 366-0087 / 366-0292
Harbour View Grocery, Bay Street, 366-0033
Hope Town Marina, 366-0003
Lighthouse Marina, 366-0154
LVA Convenience Store, White Sound Road, 366-0056
Sea Spray Marina, White Sound, 366-0065
Vernon's Grocery, Back Street, 366-0037

INSURANCE
Hope Town Hideaways, Fax/Phone 366-0224

JEWELRY
Abaco Inn, White Sound, 366-0133
Ebb Tide, Back Street, 366-0088
El Mercado, Back Street, 366-0053
Fantasy Boutique, Bay Street, 366-0537
Iggy Biggy, Bay Street, 366-0354
Kemp's Souvenir Center, Back Street, 366-0423
Sea Spray Marina, White Sound, 366-0065

JUSTICE OF THE PEACE
Vernon Malone, Vernon's Grocery Store, 366-0037

LAUNDRY
Lighthouse Marina, 366-0154
Suds Ahoy Laundry and Laundromat, Back Street

LIQUOR STORES
Lighthouse Liquors, Back Street, 366-0567
A & E Liquors, White Sound, 366-0625

MARINAS
Hope Town Hideaways, Fax/Phone 366-0224
Hope Town Marina, 366-0003

Lighthouse Marina, 366-0154
Sea Spray Marina, White Sound, 366-0065

MARINE STORE
Lighthouse Marina, 366-0154

MARRIAGE OFFICER
Vernon Malone, Vernon's Grocery Store, 366-0037

NOTARY SERVICES
Vernon Malone, Vernon's Grocery Store, 366-0037

OUTBOARD MOTOR SALES / SERVICE
Island Marine (Evinrude), Parrot Cay, 366-0282
Lighthouse Marina (Yamaha), 366-0154
Sea Horse Marine (Johnson), Back Creek, 366-0023

PAINTING
Island Colours Painting Co. (Tim Albury), 366-0290

PROPANE
Willard Bethel, 366-0033 / 366-0086

PROPERY MANAGEMENT
Elbow Cay Properties, Bay Street, 366-0569
Hope Town Hideaways, Fax/Phone 366-0224
Inside Outside, 366-0122
Island Colours, 366-0290
Lighthouse Rentals, 366-0154
Malone Estates, Back Street, 366-0100 / 366-0060 / fax 366-0157

REAL ESTATE SALES
Hope Town Hideaways, Chris Thompson, Fax/Phone 366-0224
Lighthouse Rentals and Property Sales, Craig Knowles, Lighthouse Marina, 366-0154

RESTAURANTS
Abaco Inn, White Sound, 366-0133
Boat House, Sea Spray Marina, White Sound, 366-0065
Cap'n Jack's, Bay Street, 366-0247
Club Soleil, 366-0003
Cracker P's, Lubbers Quarters Cay
Harbour's Edge, 366-0087 / 366-0292
Hope Town Harbour Lodge, 366-0095, fax 366-0286
Muchies Take Away, 366-0423
Rudy's Place, Centerline Rd., 366-0062

SAILBOAT CHARTERS
Abaco Bahamas Charters, Back Creek (large sail-boats only) 800-626-5690

SERVICE CLUBS
Hope Town Association, contact Tony Bennet, 366-0339
Friends of the Environment, contact Island Marine, 366-0280
Hope Town Fire and Rescue, 366-0500, 366-0087 (Harbour's Edge), 366-0037/58 (Vernon's Grocery/ Vernone Malone)

SHIPPING COMPANIES
Abacays, Carib Freight, 365-6247
Bullet Proof (Tommy Albury), 366-0166

TELEPHONE COMPANY
Batelco, Back Street, 366-0000

TELEPHONE CARDS
Vernon's Grocery, Back Street, 366-0037

Abaco Government Offices

AGRICULTURE AND FISHERIES
Marsh Harbour, 367-2240

AUDITORS GENERAL
Marsh Harbour, 367-3688

BAHAMASAIR
Marsh Harbour, 367-2095, 367-2039

BAHAMAS ELECTRICITY CORPORATION
Marsh Harbour, 367-2740, Emergency Service, 367-2727, Fax 367-2183
Coopers Town, 365-0033
Fox Town, 365-2151
Green Turtle Cay, 365-4087, 365-4088
Moores Island, 366-6300
Sandy Point, 366-4397

BAHAMAS TELECOMMUNICATIONS CORP.
Marsh Harbour, 367-2200, 367-3399, Fax 367-2994
Cedar Harbour, 365-0290
Cherokee Sound, 366-2000, Fax 366-2250
Coopers Town, 365-0044, Fax 365-0294
Crossing Rocks, 366-2198, Fax 366-2199
Fox Town, 365-2000, Fax 365-2290
Great Guana Cay, 365-5000, Fax 365-5098
Green Turtle Cay, 365-4113, Fax 365-4390
Hope Town, 366-0000, Fax 366-0366
Man-O-War Cay, 365-6001, Fax 365-6266
Moores Island, 366-6015, Fax 366-6079
Sandy Point, 366-4000, Fax 366-4390
Treasure Cay, 365-8000, Fax 365-8490

BROADCASTING CORPORATION
Marsh Harbour, 367-4044, 367-4895, Fax 367-4025

CUSTOMS
Marsh Harbour, 367-2524, 367-2522, Airport, 367-2026
Green Turtle Cay, 365-4077

FINANCE AND PLANNING DEPARTMENT
Marsh Harbour, 367-3700

HEALTH CLINICS
Marsh Harbour, 367-2510, 367-2586, 367-2867, 367-4480
Coopers Town, 365-0019, 365-0300
Green Turtle Cay, 365-4028
Hope Town, 366-0108
Moores Island, 366-6105
Sandy Point, 366-4010

IMMIGRATION
Marsh Harbour, 367-2675, 367-2536

ISLAND ADMINISTRATOR
Marsh Harbour, 367-2343, 367-2344
Deputy, Coopers Town, 365-0000
Deputy, Sandy Point, 366-4001

LABOUR DEPARTMENT
Marsh Harbour, 367-2133

LANDS AND SURVEYS DEPARTMENT
Marsh Harbour, 367-2013

LOCAL GOVERNMENT
Northern Disrict Council, 365-0401
Central District Council, 367-4957/8, Fax 367-4984
Southern District Council, 366-4001

NATIONAL INSURANCE BOARD
Coopers Town, 365-0225, 365-0055, Fax 365-0245
Dundas Town, 367-2550, 367-2639, Fax 367-2970

POLICE DEPARTMENT
Marsh Harbour, 367-2560, 367-2594, Airport, 367-3500
Coopers Town, 365-0002
Crown Haven, 365-2111
Green Turtle Cay, 365-4450
Moores Island, 366-6100
Sandy Point, 366-4044
Treasure Cay, 365-8048

POST OFFICES
Marsh Harbour, 367-2571
Coopers Town, 365-0000
Green Turtle Cay, 365-4242
Hope Town, 366-0098
Man-O-War Cay, 365-6108
Sandy Point, 366-4001

ROAD TRAFFIC DEPARTMENT
Marsh Harbour, 367-2121
Coopers Town, 365-0198

SCHOOLS
District Supervisor, 367-2342
Abaco Central Primary (Dundas Town), 367-2718, (Marsh Harbour), 367-2757
Abaco Central Secondary (Murphy Town), 367-2334, Fax 367-3997
Amy Roberts School (Green Turtle Cay), 365-4108
Hope Town, 366-0177
James A. Pinder School (Sandy Point), 366-4015
Man-O-War Cay, 365-6049
Moores Island, 366-6012
SC Bootle Secondary (Coopers Town), 365-0065

SOCIAL SERVICES DEPARTMENT
Marsh Harbour, 367-2246
Coopers Town, 365-0055

TOURIST OFFICE
Marsh Harbour, 367-3067, Fax 367-3068

WATER AND SEWERAGE CORPORATION
Marsh Harbour, 367-2995, 367-3974, Fax 367-2993

WORKS
Marsh Harbour, 367-2540

YOUTH, SPORTS & CULTURE
Dundas Town, 367-2220

Wyannie Malone Historical Museum

See our exhibits of artifacts of Hope Town's heritage located in the museum building just north of the Post Office and the Clinic.

Memberships Available

Mailing Address:
Wyannie Malone Historical Museum
Hope Town, Abaco, Bahamas

Internet Web Sites with General Information about Abaco:

www.wspress.com The White Sound Press site. Includes a bulletin board with information for cruisers.
www.oii.net/ Abaco Bahamas' home page with info about Abaco and the community. Hosts the Abaco Community Bulletin Board, which was a major source of information regarding Floyd and relief efforts.
www.go-abacos.com This site includes *The Abaconian*.
www.batelnet.bs/ Bahamas Internet provider
www.abacolife.com *Abaco Life*, an island magazine
oii.net/Journal/ *Abaco Journal* on the Web
www.interknowledge.com/bahamas/ The Official home page of the Bahamas M. of Tourism

The new port facility in Marsh Harbour was under construction during summer, 2002. The old government pier and customs house can be seen at the left (east) side of the new and much larger pier area in this photo. Completion is expected around the end of 2002 or beginning of 2003. For a chart showing the new pier and the dredged commerical channel leading to it, see page 76.

Construction of a new public dock at Cooperstown was almost complete during summer, 2002. The old dock was destroyed by hurricane Floyd on 14 September 1999.

Tide Table - December 2002

Marsh Harbour • Abaco • Bahamas

Times given are for Marsh Harbour, but tides throughout Abaco vary by only a few minutes. Heights are in reference to Mean Low Water (MLW). Times are in Eastern Standard Time for December 2002.

Date	Time	Ht.	Time	Ht.	Time	Ht.	Time	Ht.
1 Su	515am	H 3.1	1134am	L -0.1	536pm	H 2.6	1136pm	L -0.3
2 M	609am	H 3.2	1231pm	L -0.3	631pm	H 2.6		
3 Tu	1227am	L -0.4	701am	H 3.4	125pm	L -0.4	723pm	H 2.6
● 4 W	117am	L -0.5	752am	H 3.4	216pm	L -0.4	814pm	H 2.6
5 Th	207am	L -0.5	842am	H 3.3	306pm	L -0.3	903pm	H 2.5
6 F	256am	L -0.4	931am	H 3.2	356pm	L -0.2	953pm	H 2.4
7 Sa	346am	L -0.3	1020am	H 3.0	445pm	L -0.1	1044pm	H 2.3
8 Su	437am	L -0.1	1109am	H 2.8	535pm	L 0.0	1136pm	H 2.2
9 M	529am	L 0.1	1158am	H 2.6	624pm	L 0.1		
10 Tu	1230am	H 2.2	625am	L 0.3	1249pm	H 2.4	713pm	L 0.2
◖ 11 W	126am	H 2.2	725am	L 0.4	142pm	H 2.3	803pm	L 0.3
12 Th	223am	H 2.2	826am	L 0.5	235pm	H 2.2	851pm	L 0.3
13 F	318am	H 2.2	926am	L 0.5	328pm	H 2.1	937pm	L 0.2
14 Sa	409am	H 2.3	1022am	L 0.4	419pm	H 2.1	1022pm	L 0.2
15 Su	456am	H 2.5	1113am	L 0.4	507pm	H 2.1	1105pm	L 0.2
16 M	540am	H 2.6	1200pm	L 0.3	552pm	H 2.1	1147pm	L 0.1
17 Tu	622am	H 2.7	1244pm	L 0.2	636pm	H 2.2		
18 W	1228am	L 0.0	702am	H 2.8	126pm	L 0.1	718pm	H 2.2
○ 19 Th	109am	L 0.0	741am	H 2.9	207pm	L 0.1	800pm	H 2.2
20 F	149am	L 0.0	821am	H 2.9	248pm	L 0.0	841pm	H 2.2
21 Sa	231am	L -0.1	901am	H 2.9	330pm	L 0.0	924pm	H 2.2
22 Su	314am	L -0.1	944am	H 2.9	412pm	L 0.0	1009pm	H 2.2
23 M	401am	L 0.0	1028am	H 2.8	456pm	L -0.1	1058pm	H 2.2
24 Tu	452am	L 0.0	1117am	H 2.7	543pm	L -0.1	1151pm	H 2.3
25 W	550am	L 0.0	1209pm	H 2.6	633pm	L -0.1		
26 Th	1248am	H 2.3	653am	L 0.1	107pm	H 2.4	726pm	L -0.1
◗ 27 F	150am	H 2.4	802am	L 0.1	209pm	H 2.3	823pm	L -0.2
28 Sa	253am	H 2.6	911am	L 0.0	313pm	H 2.2	920pm	L -0.3
29 Su	356am	H 2.7	1019am	L -0.1	417pm	H 2.2	1018pm	L -0.3
30 M	457am	H 2.8	1121am	L -0.2	517pm	H 2.2	1115pm	L -0.4
31 Tu	554am	H 2.9	1219pm	L -0.3	614pm	H 2.2		

● New Moon ◖ First Quarter ○ Full Moon ◗ Last Quarter

Tide Tables - 2003
Marsh Harbour • Abaco • Bahamas

Times given are for Marsh Harbour, but tides throughout Abaco vary by only a few minutes.
Heights are in reference to Mean Low Water (MLW). Times are in Eastern Standard Time from 1 January to 5 April,
Eastern Daylight Time from 6 April to 25 October, and Eastern Standard Time from 26 October to 31 December

January

Date	Time	Ht.	Time	Ht.	Time	Ht.	Time	Ht.
1 W	1206am	L -0.4	645am	H 3.0	104pm	L -0.3	703pm	H 2.3
2 Th	1259am	L -0.4	737am	H 3.1	155pm	L -0.3	754pm	H 2.3
3 F	150am	L -0.4	826am	H 3.0	242pm	L -0.3	842pm	H 2.3
4 Sa	239am	L -0.4	913am	H 2.9	328pm	L -0.2	929pm	H 2.3
5 Su	327am	L -0.3	959am	H 2.8	412pm	L -0.2	1015pm	H 2.2
6 M	414am	L -0.1	1043am	H 2.6	454pm	L -0.1	1100pm	H 2.2
7 Tu	502am	L 0.0	1126am	H 2.4	536pm	L 0.0	1146pm	H 2.2
8 W	552am	L 0.2	1210pm	H 2.2	618pm	L 0.1		
9 Th	1234am	H 2.1	644am	L 0.3	1256pm	H 2.0	702pm	L 0.1
10 F	125am	H 2.1	740am	L 0.4	145pm	H 1.9	749pm	L 0.2
11 Sa	218am	H 2.1	839am	L 0.4	238pm	H 1.8	838pm	L 0.2
12 Su	313am	H 2.2	938am	L 0.4	333pm	H 1.8	929pm	L 0.2
13 M	407am	H 2.2	1034am	L 0.3	427pm	H 1.8	1020pm	L 0.1
14 Tu	459am	H 2.3	1126am	L 0.2	518pm	H 1.8	1110pm	L 0.0
15 W	548am	H 2.5	1214pm	L 0.1	607pm	H 1.9	1158pm	L -0.1
16 Th	634am	H 2.6	1259pm	L 0.0	653pm	H 2.0		
17 F	1244am	L -0.2	718am	H 2.7	142pm	L -0.1	737pm	H 2.1
18 Sa	129am	L -0.2	801am	H 2.8	223pm	L -0.2	821pm	H 2.2
19 Su	215am	L -0.3	844am	H 2.8	305pm	L -0.3	905pm	H 2.3
20 M	301am	L -0.3	927am	H 2.8	346pm	L -0.3	950pm	H 2.4
21 Tu	350am	L -0.3	1012am	H 2.8	429pm	L -0.3	1038pm	H 2.5
22 W	441am	L -0.3	1059am	H 2.6	513pm	L -0.3	1129pm	H 2.5
23 Th	536am	L -0.2	1148am	H 2.5	601pm	L -0.3		
24 F	1224am	H 2.6	636am	L -0.1	1243pm	H 2.3	653pm	L -0.2
25 Sa	123am	H 2.6	740am	L 0.0	143pm	H 2.2	750pm	L -0.2
26 Su	227am	H 2.6	849am	L 0.1	248pm	H 2.0	851pm	L -0.2
27 M	334am	H 2.7	957am	L 0.0	354pm	H 2.0	955pm	L -0.2
28 Tu	439am	H 2.7	1101am	L 0.0	459pm	H 2.0	1057pm	L -0.2
29 W	541am	H 2.8	1159am	L -0.1	558pm	H 2.1	1155pm	L -0.3
30 Th	636am	H 2.8	1251pm	L -0.1	652pm	H 2.2		
31 F	1249am	L -0.3	726am	H 2.9	139pm	L -0.2	740pm	H 2.3

February

Date	Time	Ht.	Time	Ht.	Time	Ht.	Time	Ht.
1 Sa	138am	L -0.3	812am	H 2.9	222pm	L -0.2	825pm	H 2.3
2 Su	225am	L -0.3	854am	H 2.8	302pm	L -0.2	907pm	H 2.4
3 M	309am	L -0.2	934am	H 2.7	340pm	L -0.2	947pm	H 2.4
4 Tu	351am	L -0.1	1012am	H 2.5	417pm	L -0.1	1026pm	H 2.4
5 W	433am	L 0.0	1049am	H 2.4	453pm	L 0.0	1105pm	H 2.3
6 Th	516am	L 0.1	1126am	H 2.2	530pm	L 0.0	1146pm	H 2.3
7 F	601am	L 0.3	1206pm	H 2.1	609pm	L 0.1		
8 Sa	1230am	H 2.2	650am	L 0.4	1249pm	H 1.9	653pm	L 0.2
9 Su	119am	H 2.2	745am	L 0.5	139pm	H 1.8	742pm	L 0.3
10 M	215am	H 2.2	846am	L 0.5	237pm	H 1.8	837pm	L 0.3
11 Tu	316am	H 2.2	948am	L 0.5	338pm	H 1.8	936pm	L 0.2
12 W	418am	H 2.3	1048am	L 0.4	439pm	H 1.8	1034pm	L 0.2
13 Th	515am	H 2.5	1141am	L 0.2	534pm	H 2.0	1129pm	L 0.0
14 F	606am	H 2.6	1229pm	L 0.1	625pm	H 2.1		
15 Sa	1221am	L -0.1	654am	H 2.8	113pm	L -0.1	713pm	H 2.3
16 Su	110am	L -0.3	740am	H 2.9	156pm	L -0.2	759pm	H 2.5
17 M	159am	L -0.4	824am	H 3.0	237pm	L -0.3	845pm	H 2.7
18 Tu	248am	L -0.4	908am	H 2.9	319pm	L -0.4	931pm	H 2.8
19 W	337am	L -0.4	954am	H 2.9	402pm	L -0.4	1019pm	H 2.9
20 Th	429am	L -0.3	1040am	H 2.7	447pm	L -0.4	1109pm	H 2.9
21 F	523am	L -0.2	1130am	H 2.5	536pm	L -0.3		
22 Sa	1203am	H 2.9	621am	L -0.1	1224pm	H 2.3	629pm	L -0.2
23 Su	103am	H 2.8	724am	L 0.1	124pm	H 2.2	728pm	L 0.0
24 M	209am	H 2.7	833am	L 0.2	231pm	H 2.1	834pm	L 0.0
25 Tu	320am	H 2.6	942am	L 0.2	341pm	H 2.0	942pm	L 0.1
26 W	429am	H 2.7	1047am	L 0.2	448pm	H 2.1	1048pm	L 0.0
27 Th	531am	H 2.7	1144am	L 0.1	547pm	H 2.2	1146pm	L 0.0
28 F	624am	H 2.8	1233pm	L 0.0	638pm	H 2.3		

March

Date	Time	Ht.	Time	Ht.	Time	Ht.	Time	Ht.
1 Sa	1239am	L -0.1	711am	H 2.8	116pm	L 0.0	724pm	H 2.4
2 Su	125am	L -0.1	753am	H 2.8	156pm	L -0.1	804pm	H 2.5
3 M	208am	L -0.1	831am	H 2.7	232pm	L -0.1	842pm	H 2.6
4 Tu	249am	L -0.1	907am	H 2.7	306pm	L -0.1	918pm	H 2.6
5 W	327am	L 0.0	941am	H 2.6	340pm	L 0.0	953pm	H 2.6
6 Th	405am	L 0.1	1015am	H 2.4	413pm	L 0.1	1028pm	H 2.6
7 F	443am	L 0.2	1049am	H 2.3	447pm	L 0.2	1104pm	H 2.5
8 Sa	523am	L 0.3	1125am	H 2.2	524pm	L 0.2	1144pm	H 2.4
9 Su	607am	L 0.4	1205pm	H 2.0	605pm	L 0.3		
10 M	1230am	H 2.4	658am	L 0.6	1252pm	H 2.0	654pm	L 0.4
11 Tu	124am	H 2.3	758am	L 0.6	149pm	H 1.9	751pm	L 0.4
12 W	227am	H 2.3	903am	L 0.6	254pm	H 1.9	855pm	L 0.4
13 Th	335am	H 2.4	1006am	L 0.5	400pm	H 2.0	1000pm	L 0.3
14 F	438am	H 2.5	1102am	L 0.4	501pm	H 2.2	1101pm	L 0.1
15 Sa	534am	H 2.7	1152am	L 0.2	555pm	H 2.4	1158pm	L 0.0
16 Su	625am	H 2.9	1239pm	L 0.0	646pm	H 2.7		
17 M	1251am	L -0.2	714am	H 3.0	123pm	L -0.2	734pm	H 2.9
18 Tu	142am	L -0.4	801am	H 3.0	207pm	L -0.3	822pm	H 3.1
19 W	232am	L -0.4	847am	H 3.0	250pm	L -0.4	909pm	H 3.3
20 Th	323am	L -0.4	934am	H 2.9	336pm	L -0.4	958pm	H 3.3
21 F	415am	L -0.3	1022am	H 2.8	423pm	L -0.3	1050pm	H 3.2
22 Sa	509am	L -0.2	1113am	H 2.6	513pm	L -0.2	1145pm	H 3.1
23 Su	606am	L 0.0	1208pm	H 2.4	609pm	L 0.0		
24 M	1246am	H 2.9	708am	L 0.2	109pm	H 2.3	712pm	L 0.2
25 Tu	153am	H 2.8	815am	L 0.3	218pm	H 2.2	820pm	L 0.3
26 W	305am	H 2.7	923am	L 0.4	328pm	H 2.2	931pm	L 0.3
27 Th	413am	H 2.6	1025am	L 0.4	434pm	H 2.3	1036pm	L 0.2
28 F	513am	H 2.7	1119am	L 0.3	530pm	H 2.4	1134pm	L 0.2
29 Sa	604am	H 2.7	1205pm	L 0.2	618pm	H 2.5		
30 Su	1223am	L 0.1	648am	H 2.7	1246pm	L 0.1	700pm	H 2.6
31 M	108am	L 0.1	727am	H 2.7	123pm	L 0.1	738pm	H 2.7

April

Date	Time	Ht.	Time	Ht.	Time	Ht.	Time	Ht.
1 Tu	148am	L 0.0	804am	H 2.7	157pm	L 0.1	814pm	H 2.8
2 W	226am	L 0.0	838am	H 2.6	231pm	L 0.1	848pm	H 2.8
3 Th	303am	L 0.1	911am	H 2.5	304pm	L 0.1	921pm	H 2.8
4 F	339am	L 0.2	944am	H 2.4	337pm	L 0.2	955pm	H 2.8
5 Sa	416am	L 0.3	1018am	H 2.3	411pm	L 0.3	1030pm	H 2.7
6 Su	554am	L 0.4	1153am	H 2.2	548pm	L 0.4		
7 M	1209am	H 2.6	636am	L 0.5	1233pm	H 2.2	629pm	L 0.4
8 Tu	1254am	H 2.5	725am	L 0.6	120pm	H 2.1	718pm	L 0.5
9 W	147am	H 2.5	821am	L 0.6	216pm	H 2.1	816pm	L 0.5
10 Th	248am	H 2.5	922am	L 0.6	320pm	H 2.1	922pm	L 0.4
11 F	355am	H 2.5	1024am	L 0.5	426pm	H 2.2	1030pm	L 0.4
12 Sa	500am	H 2.6	1120am	L 0.3	528pm	H 2.5	1135pm	L 0.2
13 Su	559am	H 2.7	1212pm	L 0.2	625pm	H 2.7		
14 M	1235am	L 0.0	654am	H 2.8	101pm	L 0.0	718pm	H 3.0
15 Tu	130am	L -0.2	746am	H 2.9	149pm	L -0.2	809pm	H 3.3
16 W	224am	L -0.3	835am	H 3.0	235pm	L -0.3	858pm	H 3.4
17 Th	316am	L -0.4	925am	H 2.9	323pm	L -0.3	948pm	H 3.5
18 F	407am	L -0.4	1014am	H 2.9	411pm	L -0.3	1039pm	H 3.5
19 Sa	500am	L -0.3	1104am	H 2.7	501pm	L -0.2	1132pm	H 3.3
20 Su	554am	L -0.1	1157am	H 2.6	555pm	L -0.1		
21 M	1229am	H 3.1	651am	L 0.1	1253pm	H 2.5	653pm	L 0.1
22 Tu	129am	H 2.9	751am	L 0.3	155pm	H 2.3	756pm	L 0.3
23 W	235am	H 2.8	853am	L 0.4	302pm	H 2.3	905pm	L 0.4
24 Th	342am	H 2.6	955am	L 0.4	409pm	H 2.3	1014pm	L 0.4
25 F	447am	H 2.6	1053am	L 0.4	510pm	H 2.4	1117pm	L 0.4
26 Sa	543am	H 2.5	1143am	L 0.4	603pm	H 2.5		
27 Su	1212am	L 0.3	633am	H 2.5	1228pm	L 0.3	649pm	H 2.6
28 M	101am	L 0.2	716am	H 2.5	108pm	L 0.2	730pm	H 2.8
29 Tu	144am	L 0.2	756am	H 2.5	145pm	L 0.2	808pm	H 2.9
30 W	225am	L 0.2	833am	H 2.5	221pm	L 0.2	844pm	H 2.9

● New Moon ◀ First Quarter ○ Full Moon ▶ Last Quarter

Tide Tables - 2003
Marsh Harbour • Abaco • Bahamas

Times given are for Marsh Harbour, but tides throughout Abaco vary by only a few minutes.
Heights are in reference to Mean Low Water (MLW). Times are in Eastern Standard Time from 1 January to 5 April,
Eastern Daylight Time from 6 April to 25 October, and Eastern Standard Time from 26 October to 31 December

May

Date	Time	Ht.	Time	Ht.	Time	Ht.	Time	Ht.
● 1 Th	303am	L 0.1	908am	H 2.5	257pm	L 0.2	918pm	H 2.9
2 F	340am	L 0.2	943am	H 2.4	331pm	L 0.2	953pm	H 2.9
3 Sa	416am	L 0.2	1018am	H 2.4	407pm	L 0.3	1028pm	H 2.8
4 Su	454am	L 0.3	1053am	H 2.3	443pm	L 0.3	1105pm	H 2.8
5 M	532am	L 0.4	1130am	H 2.2	521pm	L 0.4	1144pm	H 2.7
6 Tu	614am	L 0.4	1211pm	H 2.2	604pm	L 0.4		
7 W	1229am	H 2.6	701am	L 0.5	1258pm	H 2.2	654pm	L 0.5
8 Th	120am	H 2.6	752am	L 0.5	153pm	H 2.2	752pm	L 0.5
◐ 9 F	218am	H 2.6	848am	L 0.4	254pm	H 2.3	858pm	L 0.4
10 Sa	321am	H 2.5	944am	L 0.4	357pm	H 2.5	1006pm	L 0.3
11 Su	424am	H 2.6	1040am	L 0.2	458pm	H 2.7	1111pm	L 0.2
12 M	525am	H 2.6	1133am	L 0.1	556pm	H 3.0		
13 Tu	1213am	L 0.0	623am	H 2.7	1225pm	L -0.1	651pm	H 3.2
14 W	110am	L -0.2	718am	H 2.7	116pm	L -0.2	745pm	H 3.4
15 Th	206am	L -0.3	811am	H 2.8	207pm	L -0.3	837pm	H 3.5
○ 16 F	259am	L -0.3	903am	H 2.8	258pm	L -0.3	930pm	H 3.5
17 Sa	352am	L -0.3	955am	H 2.7	350pm	L -0.3	1023pm	H 3.4
18 Su	444am	L -0.2	1047am	H 2.6	443pm	L -0.2	1116pm	H 3.3
19 M	538am	L -0.1	1141am	H 2.5	538pm	L 0.0		
20 Tu	1212am	H 3.1	632am	L 0.1	1237pm	H 2.5	636pm	L 0.1
21 W	110am	H 2.9	728am	L 0.2	136pm	H 2.4	738pm	L 0.3
22 Th	210am	H 2.7	823am	L 0.3	238pm	H 2.4	842pm	L 0.4
◐ 23 F	310am	H 2.5	918am	L 0.3	338pm	H 2.4	947pm	L 0.4
24 Sa	408am	H 2.4	1010am	L 0.4	435pm	H 2.4	1047pm	L 0.4
25 Su	503am	H 2.3	1058am	L 0.3	527pm	H 2.5	1142pm	L 0.4
26 M	552am	H 2.3	1143am	L 0.3	613pm	H 2.6		
27 Tu	1231am	L 0.3	638am	H 2.3	1225pm	L 0.3	655pm	H 2.7
28 W	116am	L 0.3	720am	H 2.3	106pm	L 0.2	735pm	H 2.8
29 Th	158am	L 0.2	800am	H 2.3	145pm	L 0.2	814pm	H 2.8
30 F	238am	L 0.2	838am	H 2.3	224pm	L 0.2	852pm	H 2.9
● 31 Sa	317am	L 0.2	916am	H 2.3	303pm	L 0.2	929pm	H 2.9

June

Date	Time	Ht.	Time	Ht.	Time	Ht.	Time	Ht.
1 Su	355am	L 0.2	954am	H 2.3	341pm	L 0.2	1007pm	H 2.8
2 M	434am	L 0.2	1032am	H 2.2	420pm	L 0.3	1045pm	H 2.8
3 Tu	514am	L 0.2	1112am	H 2.2	501pm	L 0.3	1126pm	H 2.8
4 W	555am	L 0.3	1154am	H 2.2	547pm	L 0.3		
5 Th	1210am	H 2.7	639am	L 0.3	1242pm	H 2.3	638pm	L 0.3
6 F	1259am	H 2.6	726am	L 0.3	134pm	H 2.4	736pm	L 0.3
◐ 7 Sa	153am	H 2.6	816am	L 0.2	232pm	H 2.5	839pm	L 0.3
8 Su	252am	H 2.5	909am	L 0.1	331pm	H 2.7	945pm	L 0.2
9 M	353am	H 2.5	1003am	L 0.1	432pm	H 2.9	1050pm	L 0.1
10 Tu	455am	H 2.5	1059am	L 0.0	531pm	H 3.1	1153pm	L 0.0
11 W	555am	H 2.5	1154am	L -0.1	629pm	H 3.2		
12 Th	1252am	L -0.1	654am	H 2.5	1250pm	L -0.2	725pm	H 3.4
13 F	149am	L -0.2	750am	H 2.5	144pm	L -0.3	820pm	H 3.4
○ 14 Sa	243am	L -0.2	844am	H 2.6	239pm	L -0.3	914pm	H 3.4
15 Su	336am	L -0.2	938am	H 2.6	333pm	L -0.2	1007pm	H 3.3
16 M	427am	L -0.2	1030am	H 2.6	427pm	L -0.1	1100pm	H 3.2
17 Tu	518am	L -0.1	1123am	H 2.5	521pm	L 0.0	1152pm	H 3.0
18 W	608am	L 0.0	1216pm	H 2.5	616pm	L 0.1		
19 Th	1244am	H 2.8	657am	L 0.1	110pm	H 2.4	713pm	L 0.3
20 F	136am	H 2.6	745am	L 0.2	204pm	H 2.4	811pm	L 0.4
◐ 21 Sa	229am	H 2.4	833am	L 0.3	258pm	H 2.4	911pm	L 0.5
22 Su	321am	H 2.2	921am	L 0.3	351pm	H 2.5	1009pm	L 0.5
23 M	414am	H 2.2	1008am	L 0.4	442pm	H 2.5	1104pm	L 0.5
24 Tu	505am	H 2.1	1055am	L 0.3	531pm	H 2.6	1156pm	L 0.4
25 W	554am	H 2.1	1142am	L 0.3	618pm	H 2.6		
26 Th	1244am	L 0.4	641am	H 2.1	1227pm	L 0.3	703pm	H 2.7
27 F	129am	L 0.3	726am	H 2.2	112pm	L 0.3	745pm	H 2.8
28 Sa	211am	L 0.3	809am	H 2.2	155pm	L 0.2	827pm	H 2.8
● 29 Su	253am	L 0.2	850am	H 2.2	237pm	L 0.2	907pm	H 2.9
30 M	333am	L 0.2	931am	H 2.3	319pm	L 0.2	947pm	H 2.9

July

Date	Time	Ht.	Time	Ht.	Time	Ht.	Time	Ht.
1 Tu	413am	L 0.1	1012am	H 2.3	401pm	L 0.2	1027pm	H 2.9
2 W	452am	L 0.1	1053am	H 2.4	446pm	L 0.2	1109pm	H 2.8
3 Th	533am	L 0.1	1137am	H 2.4	533pm	L 0.2	1153pm	H 2.8
4 F	614am	L 0.1	1224pm	H 2.5	625pm	L 0.2		
5 Sa	1240am	H 2.7	659am	L 0.1	115pm	H 2.6	721pm	L 0.2
6 Su	131am	H 2.6	746am	L 0.1	210pm	H 2.7	823pm	L 0.3
◐ 7 M	228am	H 2.5	838am	L 0.0	308pm	H 2.8	927pm	L 0.2
8 Tu	328am	H 2.4	934am	L 0.0	410pm	H 3.0	1033pm	L 0.2
9 W	431am	H 2.3	1032am	L 0.0	512pm	H 3.1	1137pm	L 0.1
10 Th	534am	H 2.3	1132am	L -0.1	613pm	H 3.2		
11 F	1238am	L 0.0	636am	H 2.4	1231pm	L -0.1	712pm	H 3.3
12 Sa	135am	L 0.0	734am	H 2.5	129pm	L -0.1	808pm	H 3.3
○ 13 Su	228am	L -0.1	829am	H 2.5	225pm	L -0.2	901pm	H 3.3
14 M	319am	L -0.1	921am	H 2.6	318pm	L -0.1	951pm	H 3.2
15 Tu	407am	L -0.1	1012am	H 2.6	410pm	L -0.1	1040pm	H 3.1
16 W	452am	L 0.0	1100am	H 2.6	501pm	L 0.0	1126pm	H 2.9
17 Th	536am	L 0.0	1148am	H 2.6	551pm	L 0.2		
18 F	1212am	H 2.7	619am	L 0.1	1235pm	H 2.6	642pm	L 0.3
19 Sa	1257am	H 2.5	701am	L 0.2	122pm	H 2.5	734pm	L 0.5
20 Su	143am	H 2.3	744am	L 0.3	210pm	H 2.5	828pm	L 0.6
◐ 21 M	230am	H 2.2	829am	L 0.4	301pm	H 2.5	924pm	L 0.6
22 Tu	321am	H 2.1	917am	L 0.4	353pm	H 2.5	1021pm	L 0.6
23 W	415am	H 2.0	1007am	L 0.5	447pm	H 2.6	1116pm	L 0.6
24 Th	510am	H 2.0	1059am	L 0.5	540pm	H 2.6		
25 F	1209am	L 0.6	602am	H 2.1	1151am	L 0.4	630pm	H 2.7
26 Sa	1257am	L 0.5	652am	H 2.2	1240pm	L 0.4	717pm	H 2.8
27 Su	143am	L 0.4	739am	H 2.3	128pm	L 0.3	801pm	H 2.9
28 M	225am	L 0.3	823am	H 2.4	213pm	L 0.2	844pm	H 3.0
● 29 Tu	306am	L 0.2	906am	H 2.5	258pm	L 0.2	925pm	H 3.0
30 W	346am	L 0.1	949am	H 2.6	344pm	L 0.1	1006pm	H 3.0
31 Th	425am	L 0.0	1032am	H 2.7	430pm	L 0.1	1049pm	H 3.0

August

Date	Time	Ht.	Time	Ht.	Time	Ht.	Time	Ht.
1 F	505am	L 0.0	1116am	H 2.8	519pm	L 0.1	1133pm	H 2.9
2 Sa	546am	L 0.0	1203pm	H 2.9	611pm	L 0.2		
3 Su	1220am	H 2.8	631am	L 0.0	1254pm	H 3.0	707pm	L 0.2
4 M	111am	H 2.6	719am	L 0.1	149pm	H 3.0	808pm	L 0.3
◐ 5 Tu	207am	H 2.5	813am	L 0.1	249pm	H 3.0	913pm	L 0.3
6 W	309am	H 2.4	912am	L 0.2	354pm	H 3.1	1020pm	L 0.3
7 Th	415am	H 2.3	1015am	L 0.2	459pm	H 3.1	1125pm	L 0.3
8 F	522am	H 2.4	1119am	L 0.1	603pm	H 3.2		
9 Sa	1226am	L 0.2	625am	H 2.4	1221pm	L 0.1	702pm	H 3.2
10 Su	121am	L 0.2	722am	H 2.5	119pm	L 0.0	756pm	H 3.2
11 M	211am	L 0.1	815am	H 2.6	213pm	L 0.0	846pm	H 3.2
○ 12 Tu	257am	L 0.1	904am	H 2.7	304pm	L 0.0	932pm	H 3.2
13 W	340am	L 0.0	949am	H 2.8	351pm	L 0.1	1015pm	H 3.1
14 Th	421am	L 0.1	1032am	H 2.8	437pm	L 0.2	1056pm	H 2.9
15 F	459am	L 0.2	1114am	H 2.8	522pm	L 0.3	1136pm	H 2.7
16 Sa	537am	L 0.2	1155am	H 2.8	607pm	L 0.4		
17 Su	1215am	H 2.6	615am	L 0.3	1236pm	H 2.7	654pm	L 0.6
18 M	1256am	H 2.4	655am	L 0.5	120pm	H 2.7	743pm	L 0.7
19 Tu	140am	H 2.3	738am	L 0.5	209pm	H 2.6	837pm	L 0.8
◐ 20 W	230am	H 2.1	827am	L 0.6	303pm	H 2.6	935pm	L 0.8
21 Th	326am	H 2.1	921am	L 0.7	401pm	H 2.6	1035pm	L 0.8
22 F	426am	H 2.1	1019am	L 0.6	501pm	H 2.6	1132pm	L 0.7
23 Sa	524am	H 2.2	1116am	L 0.6	556pm	H 2.8		
24 Su	1223am	L 0.6	619am	H 2.3	1211pm	L 0.5	646pm	H 2.9
25 M	109am	L 0.5	708am	H 2.5	102pm	L 0.4	732pm	H 3.0
26 Tu	152am	L 0.3	754am	H 2.6	150pm	L 0.2	816pm	H 3.1
● 27 W	233am	L 0.2	839am	H 2.8	238pm	L 0.1	859pm	H 3.2
28 Th	313am	L 0.1	922am	H 3.0	325pm	L 0.1	942pm	H 3.2
29 F	353am	L 0.0	1007am	H 3.1	413pm	L 0.1	1026pm	H 3.1
30 Sa	434am	L 0.0	1053am	H 3.2	503pm	L 0.1	1112pm	H 3.0
31 Su	518am	L 0.0	1141am	H 3.3	556pm	L 0.2		

● New Moon ◐ First Quarter ○ Full Moon ◑ Last Quarter

Tide Tables - 2003
Marsh Harbour • Abaco • Bahamas

Times given are for Marsh Harbour, but tides throughout Abaco vary by only a few minutes.
Heights are in reference to Mean Low Water (MLW). Times are in Eastern Standard Time from 1 January to 5 April,
Eastern Daylight Time from 6 April to 25 October, and Eastern Standard Time from 26 October to 31 December

September

Date	Time	Ht.	Time	Ht.	Time	Ht.	Time	Ht.
1 M	1200am	H 2.8	604am	L 0.1	1233pm	H 3.3	653pm	L 0.3
2 Tu	1253am	H 2.7	656am	L 0.2	131pm	H 3.2	754pm	L 0.4
3 W	152am	H 2.5	753am	L 0.3	234pm	H 3.1	900pm	L 0.5
4 Th	257am	H 2.4	858am	L 0.4	343pm	H 3.1	1008pm	L 0.5
5 F	407am	H 2.4	1006am	L 0.4	451pm	H 3.1	1113pm	L 0.5
6 Sa	515am	H 2.5	1113am	L 0.4	555pm	H 3.1		
7 Su	1212am	L 0.4	617am	H 2.6	1215pm	L 0.3	652pm	H 3.2
8 M	103am	L 0.3	711am	H 2.7	111pm	L 0.2	742pm	H 3.2
9 Tu	149am	L 0.2	759am	H 2.9	201pm	L 0.2	827pm	H 3.2
10 W	231am	L 0.2	843am	H 3.0	247pm	L 0.2	908pm	H 3.1
11 Th	309am	L 0.2	923am	H 3.0	331pm	L 0.2	946pm	H 3.0
12 F	345am	L 0.2	1001am	H 3.0	412pm	L 0.3	1023pm	H 2.9
13 Sa	421am	L 0.3	1038am	H 3.0	452pm	L 0.4	1059pm	H 2.7
14 Su	455am	L 0.4	1115am	H 3.0	533pm	L 0.5	1135pm	H 2.6
15 M	531am	L 0.5	1153am	H 2.9	615pm	L 0.7		
16 Tu	1213am	H 2.4	609am	L 0.6	1234pm	H 2.8	701pm	L 0.8
17 W	1255am	H 2.3	652am	L 0.7	121pm	H 2.7	753pm	L 0.9
18 Th	144am	H 2.2	741am	L 0.8	215pm	H 2.6	852pm	L 0.9
19 F	241am	H 2.2	838am	L 0.8	316pm	H 2.6	953pm	L 0.9
20 Sa	345am	H 2.2	941am	L 0.8	419pm	H 2.7	1052pm	L 0.8
21 Su	448am	H 2.3	1043am	L 0.7	518pm	H 2.8	1144pm	L 0.7
22 M	545am	H 2.5	1142am	L 0.6	611pm	H 2.9		
23 Tu	1231am	L 0.5	636am	H 2.7	1236pm	L 0.4	700pm	H 3.1
24 W	114am	L 0.3	724am	H 2.9	127pm	L 0.2	746pm	H 3.1
25 Th	156am	L 0.1	810am	H 3.2	217pm	L 0.1	832pm	H 3.2
26 F	238am	L 0.0	855am	H 3.4	306pm	L 0.0	917pm	H 3.2
27 Sa	321am	L -0.1	942am	H 3.5	356pm	L 0.0	1003pm	H 3.1
28 Su	405am	L -0.1	1030am	H 3.6	447pm	L 0.0	1051pm	H 3.0
29 M	451am	L 0.0	1120am	H 3.5	541pm	L 0.1	1142pm	H 2.8
30 Tu	541am	L 0.1	1215pm	H 3.4	638pm	L 0.3		

October

Date	Time	Ht.	Time	Ht.	Time	Ht.	Time	Ht.
1 W	1237am	H 2.7	637am	L 0.2	115pm	H 3.3	741pm	L 0.4
2 Th	139am	H 2.5	739am	L 0.4	221pm	H 3.1	847pm	L 0.5
3 F	248am	H 2.4	848am	L 0.5	332pm	H 3.0	954pm	L 0.6
4 Sa	359am	H 2.5	959am	L 0.5	440pm	H 3.0	1056pm	L 0.5
5 Su	506am	H 2.6	1106am	L 0.5	541pm	H 3.0	1151pm	L 0.4
6 M	605am	H 2.7	1206pm	L 0.4	634pm	H 3.0		
7 Tu	1239am	L 0.4	655am	H 2.8	1259pm	L 0.3	721pm	H 3.0
8 W	121am	L 0.2	739am	H 3.0	146pm	L 0.3	802pm	H 3.0
9 Th	159am	L 0.2	818am	H 3.1	228pm	L 0.3	841pm	H 2.9
10 F	235am	L 0.2	855am	H 3.1	308pm	L 0.3	917pm	H 2.8
11 Sa	310am	L 0.3	931am	H 3.1	347pm	L 0.3	952pm	H 2.7
12 Su	344am	L 0.3	1005am	H 3.1	425pm	L 0.4	1026pm	H 2.6
13 M	418am	L 0.4	1041am	H 3.0	503pm	L 0.5	1101pm	H 2.5
14 Tu	454am	L 0.5	1117am	H 2.9	543pm	L 0.6	1138pm	H 2.4
15 W	531am	L 0.6	1157am	H 2.8	627pm	L 0.7		
16 Th	1219am	H 2.3	613am	L 0.7	1242pm	H 2.7	716pm	L 0.8
17 F	107am	H 2.2	702am	L 0.7	134pm	H 2.6	812pm	L 0.8
18 Sa	204am	H 2.2	800am	L 0.8	233pm	H 2.6	911pm	L 0.8
19 Su	308am	H 2.2	905am	L 0.8	336pm	H 2.6	1008pm	L 0.7
20 M	411am	H 2.3	1011am	L 0.7	437pm	H 2.7	1101pm	L 0.5
21 Tu	510am	H 2.6	1113am	L 0.5	534pm	H 2.8	1149pm	L 0.3
22 W	603am	H 2.8	1210pm	L 0.3	626pm	H 2.9		
23 Th	1235am	L 0.1	654am	H 3.1	104pm	L 0.1	716pm	H 3.0
24 F	120am	L 0.0	742am	H 3.4	156pm	L 0.0	804pm	H 3.0
25 Sa	206am	L -0.1	830am	H 3.5	247pm	L -0.1	853pm	H 3.0
26 Su	152am	L -0.2	819am	H 3.6	239pm	L -0.2	841pm	H 2.9
27 M	239am	L -0.2	910am	H 3.6	331pm	L -0.1	932pm	H 2.8
28 Tu	329am	L -0.1	1003am	H 3.5	425pm	L 0.0	1025pm	H 2.7
29 W	423am	L 0.0	1059am	H 3.4	523pm	L 0.2	1122pm	H 2.6
30 Th	521am	L 0.2	1200pm	H 3.2	624pm	L 0.3		
31 F	1226am	H 2.5	625am	L 0.3	105pm	H 3.0	728pm	L 0.4

November

Date	Time	Ht.	Time	Ht.	Time	Ht.	Time	Ht.
1 Sa	134am	H 2.4	735am	L 0.4	213pm	H 2.8	831pm	L 0.4
2 Su	244am	H 2.4	846am	L 0.5	318pm	H 2.8	929pm	L 0.4
3 M	348am	H 2.5	952am	L 0.4	417pm	H 2.7	1021pm	L 0.3
4 Tu	443am	H 2.7	1050am	L 0.4	508pm	H 2.7	1106pm	L 0.3
5 W	531am	H 2.8	1141am	L 0.3	553pm	H 2.7	1147pm	L 0.2
6 Th	613am	H 2.9	1226pm	L 0.3	634pm	H 2.6		
7 F	1225am	L 0.2	652am	H 3.0	107pm	L 0.2	712pm	H 2.6
8 Sa	102am	L 0.2	728am	H 3.0	146pm	L 0.2	748pm	H 2.5
9 Su	137am	L 0.2	803am	H 3.0	223pm	L 0.2	823pm	H 2.5
10 M	213am	L 0.2	838am	H 3.0	301pm	L 0.3	858pm	H 2.4
11 Tu	248am	L 0.3	914am	H 2.9	339pm	L 0.4	934pm	H 2.3
12 W	324am	L 0.3	950am	H 2.8	418pm	L 0.4	1011pm	H 2.2
13 Th	402am	L 0.4	1029am	H 2.7	500pm	L 0.5	1053pm	H 2.1
14 F	444am	L 0.5	1112am	H 2.6	546pm	L 0.6	1140pm	H 2.1
15 Sa	533am	L 0.5	1201pm	H 2.6	636pm	L 0.6		
16 Su	1234am	H 2.1	629am	L 0.6	1256pm	H 2.5	729pm	L 0.5
17 M	134am	H 2.2	733am	L 0.5	156pm	H 2.5	823pm	L 0.4
18 Tu	235am	H 2.3	840am	L 0.5	257pm	H 2.5	916pm	L 0.3
19 W	335am	H 2.6	945am	L 0.3	356pm	H 2.5	1008pm	L 0.1
20 Th	431am	H 2.8	1046am	L 0.1	453pm	H 2.6	1058pm	L -0.1
21 F	525am	H 3.1	1143am	L -0.1	547pm	H 2.7	1148pm	L -0.2
22 Sa	618am	H 3.3	1237pm	L -0.2	639pm	H 2.7		
23 Su	1238am	L -0.4	709am	H 3.5	130pm	L -0.3	731pm	H 2.7
24 M	128am	L -0.4	801am	H 3.5	223pm	L -0.3	823pm	H 2.7
25 Tu	219am	L -0.4	854am	H 3.5	316pm	L -0.3	915pm	H 2.6
26 W	312am	L -0.3	948am	H 3.4	410pm	L -0.2	1009pm	H 2.5
27 Th	407am	L -0.2	1044am	H 3.2	505pm	L -0.1	1107pm	H 2.4
28 F	506am	L 0.0	1142am	H 3.0	602pm	L 0.1		
29 Sa	1208am	H 2.3	608am	L 0.1	1242pm	H 2.7	659pm	L 0.1
30 Su	112am	H 2.3	714am	L 0.3	144pm	H 2.6	756pm	L 0.2

December

Date	Time	Ht.	Time	Ht.	Time	Ht.	Time	Ht.
1 M	216am	H 2.3	822am	L 0.3	244pm	H 2.4	850pm	L 0.2
2 Tu	317am	H 2.4	926am	L 0.3	341pm	H 2.3	941pm	L 0.2
3 W	412am	H 2.5	1024am	L 0.3	433pm	H 2.3	1027pm	L 0.2
4 Th	500am	H 2.6	1115am	L 0.3	520pm	H 2.2	1110pm	L 0.1
5 F	544am	H 2.7	1201pm	L 0.2	603pm	H 2.2	1151pm	L 0.1
6 Sa	624am	H 2.7	1243pm	L 0.2	643pm	H 2.2		
7 Su	1231am	L 0.0	703am	H 2.8	123pm	L 0.1	721pm	H 2.2
8 M	109am	L 0.0	741am	H 2.8	202pm	L 0.1	759pm	H 2.2
9 Tu	147am	L 0.0	817am	H 2.8	241pm	L 0.1	836pm	H 2.2
10 W	225am	L 0.1	854am	H 2.7	319pm	L 0.1	913pm	H 2.1
11 Th	303am	L 0.1	931am	H 2.7	357pm	L 0.2	952pm	H 2.1
12 F	342am	L 0.1	1009am	H 2.6	437pm	L 0.2	1032pm	H 2.1
13 Sa	424am	L 0.2	1050am	H 2.5	518pm	L 0.2	1117pm	H 2.1
14 Su	512am	L 0.2	1134am	H 2.5	602pm	L 0.2		
15 M	1207am	H 2.1	606am	L 0.3	1224pm	H 2.4	650pm	L 0.1
16 Tu	102am	H 2.2	707am	L 0.3	120pm	H 2.3	741pm	L 0.1
17 W	201am	H 2.4	812am	L 0.2	220pm	H 2.3	834pm	L 0.0
18 Th	302am	H 2.6	919am	L 0.1	322pm	H 2.2	930pm	L -0.1
19 F	402am	H 2.8	1023am	L 0.0	423pm	H 2.3	1026pm	L -0.3
20 Sa	501am	H 3.0	1123am	L -0.2	522pm	H 2.3	1121pm	L -0.4
21 Su	558am	H 3.1	1221pm	L -0.3	619pm	H 2.4		
22 M	1216am	L -0.5	654am	H 3.3	116pm	L -0.4	714pm	H 2.4
23 Tu	111am	L -0.5	748am	H 3.3	209pm	L -0.4	807pm	H 2.4
24 W	205am	L -0.5	841am	H 3.3	300pm	L -0.4	900pm	H 2.4
25 Th	259am	L -0.5	934am	H 3.1	351pm	L -0.4	954pm	H 2.4
26 F	353am	L -0.4	1026am	H 3.0	442pm	L -0.3	1047pm	H 2.4
27 Sa	448am	L -0.2	1118am	H 2.7	532pm	L -0.2	1142pm	H 2.3
28 Su	545am	L 0.0	1211pm	H 2.5	622pm	L -0.1		
29 M	1238am	H 2.3	645am	L 0.1	104pm	H 2.4	712pm	L 0.0
30 Tu	135am	H 2.2	746am	L 0.2	159pm	H 2.1	802pm	L 0.1
31 W	233am	H 2.2	848am	L 0.3	255pm	H 2.0	852pm	L 0.1

● New Moon   ◖ First Quarter   ○ Full Moon   ◗ Last Quarter

Index - Selected Abaco Place Names

Alec Cays 37
Allans-Pensacola Cay 37, 38
Ambergris Cay 42
Angelfish Point 37

Bahama Palm Shores 119, 136
Baker's Bay 52, 56,62
Barracuda Rocks 22
Bell Channel 17, 20
Big Cay 76
Big Hog Cay 37
Big Mangrove 119
Bight of Old Robinson 116, 120
Bimini 12
Black Pt. 52, 58
Black Sound 46
Boat Harbour 52, 53, 74, 94
Boilers, The 116, 119, 120
Bonefish Cay 42
Bridges Cay 116, 117, 120

Carleton Pt. 52, 58
Carters Cays 13, 22, 31, 32
Carters Cays Bank 32
Casuarina Point 119, 120, 136
Cedar Harbour 37, 136
Center of the World Rock 37
Channel Cay 53, 114, 115
Channel Rock 52, 56
Cherokee Point 120
Cherokee Sound 13, 119, 120, 136
Chub Rocks 52, 56
Cistern Cay 52
Coopers Town 42
Cornish Cay 53, 114, 115
Cornwall Point 119
Crab Cay 37, 42, 44
Cross Harbour 119
Cross Harbour Point 119
Crossing Bay 62
Crossing Rocks 119, 136
Crown Haven 32, 136

Delia'a Cay 62
Dont Rock 52, 56
Double Breasted Bars 22
Double Breasted Cays 22, 26
Dover Sound 20
Duck Cay 120

Eagle Rock 98, 99
Eight Mile Bay 119
Eight Mile Rock Bay 119
Elbow Cay 13, 53, 74, 98, 99, 106, 110
Elephant Rock 24, 26

Fanny Bay 76
Felix Cay 26
Fish Cays (north) 32, 34
Fish Cays (south) 52, 56, 62
Foots Cay 52, 62
Fowl Cay 126
Fox Town 32, 35, 136
Freeport 12, 17

Garden Cay 68, 74
Gaulding Cay 114, 115, 126
Gilpin Bay 119
Goat Cay 40
Goole Cay 116, 117, 120
Gorda Cay 13
Grand Bahama Island 13, 17, 18, 20
Grand Cays 13, 22, 26
Grand Lucayan Waterway 17, 20
Great Abaco Island 13, 37, 42, 43, 52, 56, 74, 110, 116, 117, 119, 120,136
Great Guana Cay 13, 52, 56, 62, 63, 136
Great Isaac 12
Great Sale Cay 13, 17, 22
Green Turtle Cay 13, 42, 46, 47, 52, 136
Grouper Rocks 32
Guinea Schooner Bay 119
Guineaman's Cay 38
Gully Cay 31
Gumelemi Cay 56, 62

Hawksbill Cays 32, 35, 37
High Bank Bay 119
High Cay 42, 43
Hog Cays 37
Hole-in-the-Wall 13, 119, 136
Hope Town 53, 74, 94, 98, 136
Hope Town Point 98

Indian Cay Channel 18

Johnny's Cay 53, 68, 74, 126

Leisure Lee 56
Little Abaco Island 13, 17, 32, 37
Little Ambergris Cay 42
Little Harbour 13, 53, 116, 117,119, 120, 136
Little Sale Cay 13, 22
Loggerhead Bars 56
Loggerhead Channel 52, 56, 62
Lubbers Quarters Bank 74, 110
Lubbers Quarters 53, 94, 98, 110
Lynyard Cay 13, 53, 114, 115, 116, 119, 120

Man-O-War Cay 13, 52, 68, 69, 74, 136
Mangrove Cay 12, 17
Manjack Cay 13, 42, 44, 136
Marsh Harbour 13, 52, 53, 74, 76-78,82,84,86, 94, 136
Mastic Point 119
Matt Lowe's Cay 52, 53, 68, 74
Memory Rock 12, 17
Moraine Cay 32, 36, 37
Mores Island 13

New Plymouth 46
New Spoil Bank Cay 62
Noname Cay 46, 52, 56
North Bar Channel 53, 114, 115
North Man-O-War Channel 13, 68, 94

Ocean Point 120
Old Kerrs 119

Parrot Cays 53, 74, 98, 110
Pawpaw Cays 32
Pelican Cays 46, 52, 53, 114, 115
Pelican Point 53, 116
Pelican Rock 22
Point Set Rock 53, 68, 74
Porgie Rock 53, 74, 110
Powell Cay 13, 42, 43, 136

Rhoda Rocks 22, 29
Rocky Point 119
Romers Cays 22

Sale Cay Rocks 13, 22
Sand Bank Point 56, 58
Sand Cay 28

Sandy Cay (Abaco/Grand Cays) 26
Sandy Cay (Abaco/MOW) 68, 77
Sandy Cay (Abaco/NBar) 53, 114, 115, 126
Sandy Cay (Grand Bahama) 12, 18
Sandy Point 13, 119, 136
Sanka Shoal 52, 53, 74
Sarah Wood Bars 119
Scotland Cay 52, 62
Seal Cay 24, 26
Snake Cay 53, 115, 136
Soldier Cay 43
South Man-O-War Channel, 68, 74
South West Point 13, 119
Spanish Cay 13, 37, 40, 42
Squances Cay 37, 40, 42
Strangers Cay 13, 22, 29
Sugar Loaf Cay 74

Tahiti Beach 98, 110
Tea Table Cay 24
Thomas Bay 119
Tilloo Bank 53, 114, 115
Tilloo Cay 13, 53, 110, 114, 115
Tilloo Cut 94, 98, 110
Tom Brown's Cay 24, 26
Tom Curry's Point 116, 117, 120
Treasure Cay 13, 52, 58, 136
Triangle Rocks 13, 22
Two Rocks 52, 56

Umbrella Cay 37, 38

Veteran Rock 32

Walker's Cay 13, 22, 24, 25, 124
Water Cay 52, 56
West End 12, 18
West End Point 32
West End Rocks 22, 32
Whale Cay 13, 52, 56, 136
Whale Cay Channel 52, 56
White Sand Ridge 12
White Sound (Elbow Cay) 53, 98, 106, 110
White Sound (GTC) 46
Winding Bay 120
Witch Point 53, 94, 110
Wood Cay 12, 17, 18, 136

Index to Advertisers in The Cruising Guide to Abaco: 2003

A & P Auto Rental, 90
Abaco Adventures, , 158
Abaco Bahama Charters, 101
Abaco Beach Resort, 95
Abaco Ceramics, 60
Abaco Hardware, 92
Abaco Inn, 107
Abaco Insurance, 93
Abaco Life,
Abaco Marine Prop., 73
Abaco Markets, 138
Abaco Outback,81
Abaco Outboard Engines,73
Abaco Pathfinders, 133
Abaco Real Estate, 75
Abaco Treasures, 83
Abaco Vacation Res., Inc., 51
Abaco Water,61
Abaco Yacht Services, 73
Abaconian, 135
AID, 83
Albury's Ferry, 160
Albury's Trucking, 88
Ancor Marine Grade Products, 66
Applied Micro-Video,141
Arawak Agency, 90
Atlantic Cat, 16

B & D Marine, 91
Bahama Beach Club, 61
Bahamas Air-Sea Rescue Assoc., 27,37
Bahamas Lighthouse Preservation,
Bahamas Realty, 97
Banyan Beach Club, 60
Barefoot Man, 113
Bistro Restaurant,84
Black Sound Marina, 51
Blue Water Grill, 65
Bluff House Marina and Resort, 49
Boat Harbour Marina, 95
Boeshield T-9, 145
Boy Scouts, 8
Bradford Marine, 16
Breeze Booster, 50
Brendal's Dive Center, 48
Brigantine Bay Villas, 60
Brown Tips Boat Services,81
Brownie's Third Lung,105

Cannonsport Marina, 16
Cap'n Jack's, 103
Cat's Paw Boat Rentals,99

Casa Blanca House Rental,109
Chemist Shoppe, 89
Cherokee Air, 93
Club Soleil Resort, 102
Coldwell Banker, 92
Conch Inn Motel and Marina,79
Continental Connection, 39
Cooperstown Shell,43
Cracker P's Restaurant, 112
Curry's Food Store, 50

Damianos Realty, 88
Daytona Marina and Boat Works, 23
Dive Abaco, 93
Dolphin Marine, 86

e-Marine,34
Edwin's Boat Yard, 71
Ekali Estates,101

Florida Coastal Airlines, 104
Florida Yacht Charters, 96
Four Winds Cottages, 54
Fox Town Shell, 35
Frederick's Agency, 88
Friends of the Environment, 112
Froggies Out Island Adventures, 102
Fugawi,145

Garmin,3
Glendenning, 40
Golden Reef, 50
Great Abaco Club, 97
Green Turtle Club, 50
Green Turtle Ferry, 159
Green Turtle Marine Const., 45
Guana Beach Resort, 66
Guana Harbour Grocery, 64
Guana Seaside Village, 66
Gulfstream/Continental, 39
GWS Express,90

Harbour's Edge Restaurant, 100
Harbour View Haven, 64
Harbour View Marina, 81
H G Christie LTD Real Estate, back cover
Honda/Master Marine, 88
Hope Town Guide, 103
Hope Town Harbour Lodge, 104
Hope Town Hideaways, 103
Hope Town Marina, 103
Hope Town Villas, 103
HydroBubble Anchor,27

Insurance Management, 90
Iggy Biggy Boutique, 85
Island Bay Motel, 26
Island Cart Rentals,101
Island Marine, 102
Island Style Gift Shop,60

Java, 84

Lands End Oil, 144
Laysue Rentals, 73
Leisure Locker,118
Lighthouse Marina, 100
Lighthouse Preservation Soc.,
Lighthouse Rentals, 100
Long's Landing,85
Lowe's Food Store,51
Lubbers Quarters Association,111

Mackerel's Restaurant,77
Man-O-War Grocery, 70
Man-O-War Hardware, 71
Man-O-War Marina, 71
Man-O-War Marina Dive Shop, 70
Man-O-War Pavilion Restaurant, 72
Mangoes Restaurant and Marina, 80
Maptech, 9
Marine Max,30
Marsh Harbour Boatyards, 83
Marsh Harbour Marina, 87
Marsh Harbour Shipping, 159
Master Marine/Honda, 83
Merlin's Electronics, 87
Monarch Moor Whips, 144
Montague Bicycles, 137
Moorings,79

Native Creations, 51
Navigator PC, 21
Nipper's Bar and Grill, 65

Oceanfrontier Hideaway, 64
Old Bahama Bay, 19
Outboard Shop, 86

Pete's Pub and Gallery, 117
Pier One Boat Rentals, 93
Pineapples Bar & Grill,47
Port of Call Marina, 89
Prozac, the Ferry, 158

Radio Abaco,

Rainbow Rentals, 80
Reef Relief, 153
Rental Wheels, 85
Rich's Rentals, 85
Roberts Hardware & Marine, 50,86
Rosie's Place, 26

Sail Abaco, 87
Sail Shop, 70
Sailfish Marina, 11
Salt-Away,145
Sea Horse Marine, 97
Sea Horse Boat Rentals, 97
Sea Grape Realty, 112
Sea Images,113
Sea Shells Restaurant,91
Sea Shore Villas, 64
Sea Spray Resort & Marina, 108
Sea Star Auto Rental, 91
Sea Tow, 72
Sharkee's Pizza, 92
Sid's Food Store, 48
SlideMoor,113
Snap Shop, 89
Spanish Cay, 41
Standard Hardware, 92
Sunset Souvenirs, 91
Sweeting's Grocery, 109

Tide Watches,109
Treasure Cay Hotel and Resort, 59
Treasure Divers,61
Triple J Car Rental and Gift Shop,60
Turtle Hill Resort, 101
Twin Vee, 160

UPS,88

Vernon's Grocery, 100
Vetus Den Ouden Inc., 36
Vintage Props and Jets, 55

Walker's Cay Club and Marina, 25
William H. Albury,25
William Brewer Liquors,93
Westview Cottage, 104
White Sound Press, 138, inside back cover
WoodyWax,33
Wrecking Tree, 45
Wyannie Malone Historical Museum, 103

Yamaha,73

Ferry and Ship Routes to, from and Within Abaco, Bahamas

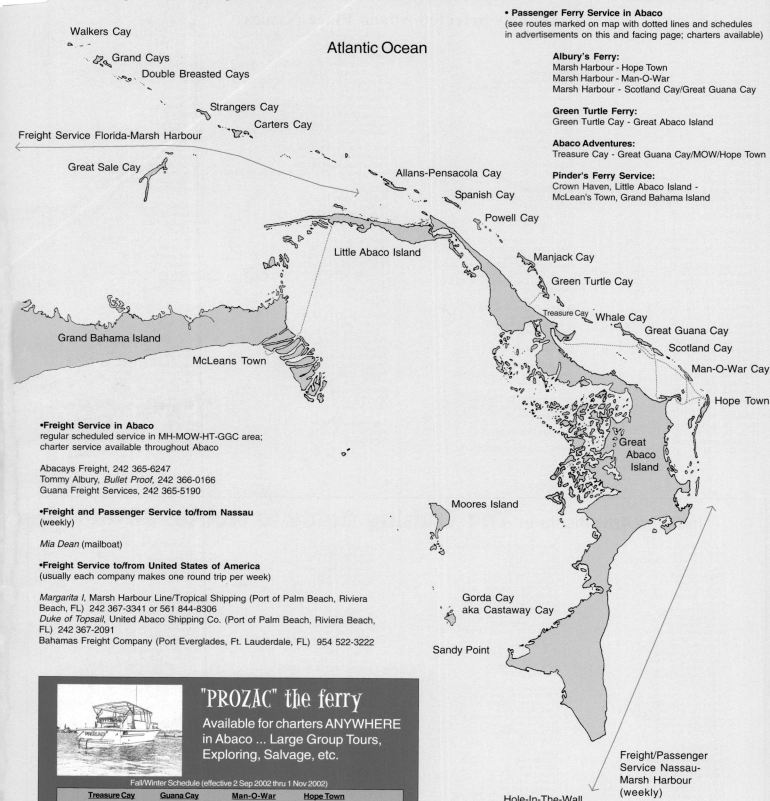

Atlantic Ocean

Walkers Cay
Grand Cays
Double Breasted Cays
Strangers Cay
Carters Cay

Freight Service Florida-Marsh Harbour

Great Sale Cay

Allans-Pensacola Cay
Spanish Cay
Powell Cay

Little Abaco Island

Manjack Cay
Green Turtle Cay
Treasure Cay
Whale Cay
Great Guana Cay
Scotland Cay
Man-O-War Cay

Grand Bahama Island

McLeans Town

Hope Town

Great Abaco Island

Moores Island

Gorda Cay
aka Castaway Cay

Sandy Point

Hole-In-The-Wall

Freight/Passenger Service Nassau-Marsh Harbour (weekly)

• Passenger Ferry Service in Abaco
(see routes marked on map with dotted lines and schedules in advertisements on this and facing page; charters available)

Albury's Ferry:
Marsh Harbour - Hope Town
Marsh Harbour - Man-O-War
Marsh Harbour - Scotland Cay/Great Guana Cay

Green Turtle Ferry:
Green Turtle Cay - Great Abaco Island

Abaco Adventures:
Treasure Cay - Great Guana Cay/MOW/Hope Town

Pinder's Ferry Service:
Crown Haven, Little Abaco Island -
McLean's Town, Grand Bahama Island

•Freight Service in Abaco
regular scheduled service in MH-MOW-HT-GGC area; charter service available throughout Abaco

Abacays Freight, 242 365-6247
Tommy Albury, *Bullet Proof*, 242 366-0166
Guana Freight Services, 242 365-5190

•Freight and Passenger Service to/from Nassau
(weekly)

Mia Dean (mailboat)

•Freight Service to/from United States of America
(usually each company makes one round trip per week)

Margarita I, Marsh Harbour Line/Tropical Shipping (Port of Palm Beach, Riviera Beach, FL) 242 367-3341 or 561 844-8306
Duke of Topsail, United Abaco Shipping Co. (Port of Palm Beach, Riviera Beach, FL) 242 367-2091
Bahamas Freight Company (Port Everglades, Ft. Lauderdale, FL) 954 522-3222

© Copyright White Sound Press, 2002

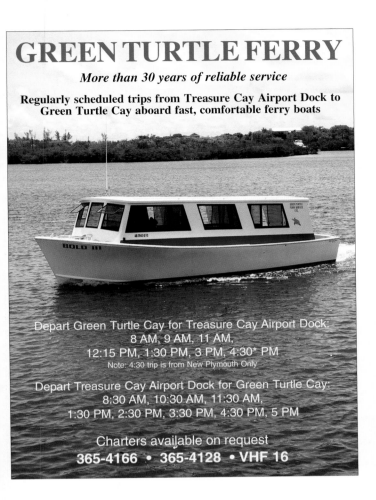
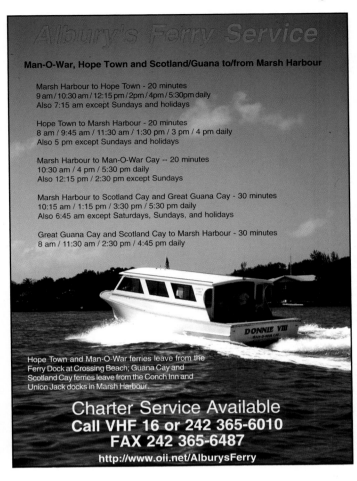